CW01303975

40 Cult Movies

From *Alice, Sweet Alice* to *Zombies of Mora Tau*

Jon Towlson

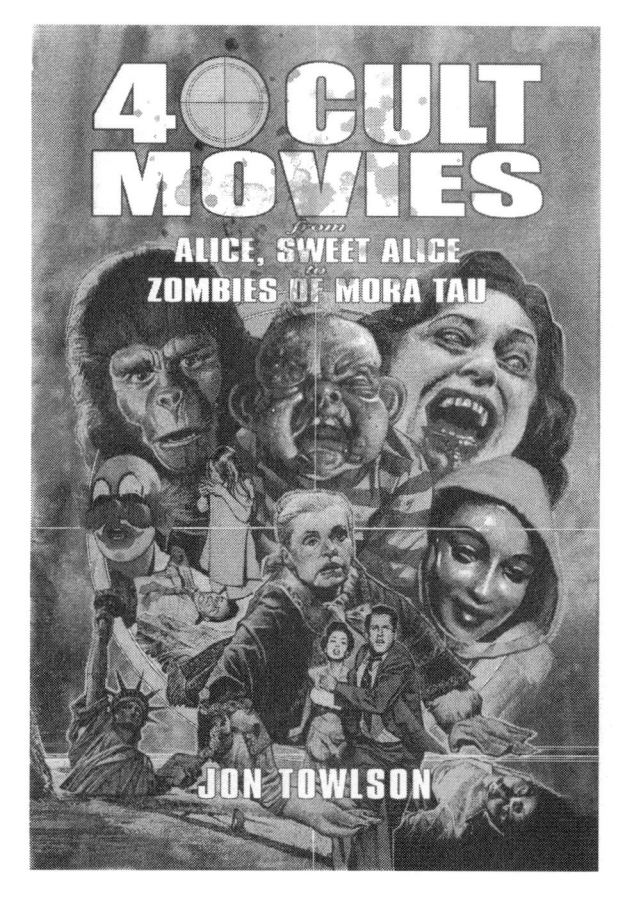

Artwork © Graham Humphreys 2023

40 Cult Movies

From *Alice, Sweet Alice* to *Zombies of Mora Tau*

© Jon Towlson 2023. All rights reserved.

Artwork © Graham Humphreys 2023

ISBN: 9798857160145 (paperback)

ISBN: 9798864931332 (hardback)

The right of Jon Towlson to be identified as the Authors of this Work has been asserted by them in accordance with the Copyright, Designs and Patents Act, 1988.

No part of this book may be reproduced or transmitted in any form or by any means, electronic or mechanical, including photocopying or recording, or by any information storage and retrieval system, without permission in writing from the publisher.

Also by Jon Towlson

Midnight Cowboy (McGill-Queen's University Press, 2023)

Dawn of the Dead (Auteur/Liverpool University Press, 2022)

Global Horror Cinema Today: 28 Representative Films from 17 Countries (McFarland, 2021)

Candyman (Auteur/Liverpool University Press, 2018)

The Turn to Gruesomeness in American Horror Films, 1931-1936 (McFarland, 2016)

Close Encounters of the Third Kind (Auteur/Liverpool University Press, 2016)

Subversive Horror Cinema: Countercultural Messages of Films from Frankenstein to the Present (McFarland, 2014)

Acknowledgments

My heartfelt thanks to the amazing Graham Humphreys for his wonderful artwork. Special thanks to the equally amazing Joanne Rudling for her help with the layout and design of this book. Huge thanks to Richard Cooper at *Scream*, Martin Unsworth at *Starburst* and Allan Bryce at *The Dark Side*. Extra special thanks to Arrow Films, Eureka Video, Second Sight Films and 101 Films.

I dedicate this book to anyone who ever had a tape snarl up inside their VCR.

Follow me @systemshocks

Introduction	5
Alice, Sweet Alice (aka Communion, 1976)	6
Asylum (1972)	12
Audrey Rose (1977)	16
The Blair Witch Project (1999)	20
The Boys Next Door (1985)	27
Braindead (1992)	32
Chained (2012)	37
Creepshow (1982)	42
Curse of the Undead (1959)	48
Day of the Dead (1985)	53
Dr Terror's House of Horrors (1965)	59
Drag Me to Hell (2009)	63
Edge of Sanity (1989)	67
Enter the Void (2009)	72
Freaks (1932)	77
The Hitcher (1986)	82
Horror Hospital (1973)	86
The House that Dripped Blood (1971)	91
In the Aftermath (1989)	95
Invasion of the Body Snatchers (1956)	100
The Legend of Hell House (1973)	104
The Man with the X-Ray Eyes (1963)	107
Martin (1977)	112
Mary Shelley's Frankenstein (1994)	117
Mr Vampire (1985)	122
The New Kids (1985)	127
Night of the Living Dead (1968)	132
Phantom of the Paradise (1974)	135
Planet of the Apes (1968)	139
Pumpkinhead (1988)	142
Rabid (1977)	147
Re-Animator (1985)	153
The Redeemer: Son of Satan (1978)	157
Rock 'n' Roll High School (1979)	165
A Serial Killer's Guide to Life (2019)	170
Shivers (1975)	174
Suburbia (1984)	182
Toto the Hero (1991)	187
Upgrade (2018)	192
Zombies of Mora Tau (1957)	197
Index	202

Introduction

This book arose from a curious realization on my part. For the past ten years I have written articles and essays on films for magazines like *Starburst, The Dark Side* and *Scream* and Blu-ray/DVD booklets for *Arrow* among others. At the time, I thought that the films I wrote about were a pretty disparate bunch ranging from science fiction and horror movies to entries in World Cinema. Only recently have I come to see that the movies I chose to essay could all be described as 'cult' films. It seems that I am by nature drawn to this kind of cinema (the type of films that TV presenter Jonathan Ross once described as "incredibly strange") and it stands to reason that readers of this book are drawn to them too. The question is: why do we like these movies so much?

I can only say that what appeals to me about movies like *Alice, Sweet Alice* (1976) and *Zombies of Mora Tau* (1957) — and the other films discussed in this book — is that they arouse in me a sense of curiosity. How did the makers of these odd films come up with their ideas? Why are these films so unusual? And why do they exert such a strange fascination on their audience?

I have approached each of the 40 essays contained in this book with this same sense of curiosity. Each essay is an investigation into a cult film and what makes it 'cult'. I have avoided any kind of film studies theory to do with cult cinema: eg. what is a cult film? How do we define cult cinema? That is not the kind of book you hold in your hands. Instead, this is a collection of writing on cult films that — hopefully — adds up to more than the sum of its parts.

I trust that this book will introduce you to some films that you may not have seen, and for those that you *have* seen, I hope it makes you look at them afresh. Some of the movies like *Night of the Living Dead* (1968) are old favourites, others you may not have heard of. In writing about these films over the years, I have tried to say something new, something a little different to what is usually said, maybe shed new light or offer new insights on the movies.

You may not necessarily agree with everything I write in these pages, but that's ok! Above all else, I have tried to convey the enthusiasm for cult movies that we all share. So, if after reading, you feel the need to watch some of these movies again or seek out any you haven't seen yet, then I will have succeeded in making you curious, too.

Alice, Sweet Alice (aka Communion, 1976)

Alfred Sole's *Alice, Sweet Alice* is ripe for re-discovery. I would venture to call it one of the best 'Catholic' horror films — alongside *The Exorcist* (1973) and George A. Romero's *Martin* (1977). *Alice, Sweet Alice* has had a chequered release over the years, under various different titles, so chances are you may have caught it on VHS or DVD at some point. I first read about it in a back issue of *House of Hammer* magazine. The reviewer at the time, Tony Crawley, hated it but went on to admit that *Alice, Sweet Alice* (titled *Communion* on its first release) had earned lots of plaudits and praise from the great and the good.

Alice, Sweet Alice won awards at a number of festivals including at the 1976 Chicago Film Festival, and among its admirers were veteran Hollywood directors Joshua Logan and Robert Wise. Industry commentators, including famed critic Roger Ebert predicted great things for director Alfred Sole, and Christopher A. Wood went as far as saying that Sole was "destined to become one of the most important directors of our time". *House of Hammer* critic Crawley was sceptical, claiming that as a director, Sole was too self-conscious, that in *Alice, Sweet Alice* 'there is an over-emphasis on camera position and not story exposition'. It was an opinion shared by George A. Romero, who saw *Alice, Sweet Alice* at the 1977 Cannes Film Festival. In a conversation between Romero and Crawley, the two agreed that Sole's visual style was a distraction from the film and the characters. "He tries too hard," Crawley complained. "He's designing still — not directing. Yes, there is a difference." Crawley would ultimately be proved right — in one respect at least: Alfred Sole was not destined to become a major director — in fact — after *Alice, Sweet Alice* he made only two more movies [*Tanya's Island* (1980) and *Pandemonium* (1982)] and the 1984 TV flick *Cheeseball Presents* before embarking on a successful career as a production designer in U.S. television. But for me, it's Sole's sense of design that makes *Alice, Sweet Alice* such a memorable horror movie, one that captures perfectly the sense of musty Catholic rites and repressions in a middle-class suburb of Paterson, New Jersey.

Alice, Sweet Alice is probably best known for its star, Brooke Shields, making her movie debut as Karen Spages, the sweet, pretty youngster brutally murdered during her first communion by a sinister figure in a yellow plastic rain mac and painted mask. High on the list of suspects is Karen's plain and clearly troubled older sister, the titular Alice (Paula Sheppard). After Shields became famous for playing a child prostitute in *Pretty Baby* (1978), *Communion* was re-released as *Alice, Sweet Alice*; and then, when

Shields had a box-office hit with *The Blue Lagoon* (1980) it was released again as *Holy Terror* in 1981.

Alice, Sweet Alice is very much Alfred Sole's movie: he co-wrote it and directed it using his own money, and even did all the production design chores himself. And yes, he designed and storyboarded all the shots himself, too. *Alice, Sweet Alice* grew out of Sole's love of the movies, especially Alfred Hitchcock films, and draws on his own childhood growing up in Paterson, New Jersey in the 50s and early 60s. His family was Italian and his grandmother, a devout Catholic, lived next to a church. Although his parents weren't strict Catholic, young Alfred was made to attend church regularly on pain of having his legs broken otherwise. You can see where the idea for *Alice, Sweet Alice* might have come from!

When he wasn't in church, Alfred went to the movies. Downtown Paterson had two picture houses, and Alfred would spend every Saturday afternoon watching movie double-bills. A film that made a big impression on him was the Henri-Georges Clouzot classic *Les Diaboliques* (1955). Sole was so impressed by the film's style that he knew then and there that he loved horror films.

At first, Alfred thought that he wanted to be a painter and got a scholarship to The Cooper Union for the Advancement of Science and Art, a private art college near New York's East Side. But his parents worried that he might end up a drug addict if he went to the Big Apple. So, instead, Alfred managed to persuade them to let him study in Florence, Italy. He enrolled at the Academy of Fine Arts to take design and architecture. Meanwhile, he kept going to the movies and soaked up Italian cinema and foreign movies. At the back of his mind was the knowledge that his idol Alfred Hitchcock had started out as a draftsman and a production designer before taking to the director's chair. And just as Hitchcock learned his craft at the UFA studios in Berlin, Alfred Sole learned much of his in Florence.

Returning home to Paterson, Alfred got a job as an interior designer, and then opened his own architect firm. The company did well, and Sole had some big clients. But he started to get bored, and that's when he caught the movie bug. He bought himself a 16mm clockwork Bolex camera and set out to make a little film. His three-minute short, *Daydreams*, won a prize at the New York Film Festival, and that's when the movie bug really bit. But Alfred Sole's next film would see the fledgling filmmaker blacklisted by the city of Paterson and facing a possible 15 to 20-year jail sentence!

Deep Sleep (1972), his first feature film, was an X-rated movie meant to cash in on the box office success of hard-core porn hit *Deep Throat* (1972). Sole cast the movie with a mix of professionals and family and friends. The star of the film was a local actor called Joe Rose, who went by the stage name of Willard Butz. Sole shot the sex scenes in a New York studio using, in his words, "struggling actors working to pay their bills". The hard-core scenes were added at the request of the distributor, and Sole showed the movie at the New York Erotic Film Festival where it won first prize. It was at this point that that the proverbial s**t hit the fan for Alfred Sole. The publicity that *Deep Sleep* started to generate around Paterson caused a backlash against the movie and against Sole. Alfred was blacklisted by his friends and pretty soon he was facing trial for Transportation of Pornographic Material — a federal offence. It was only when The Playboy Foundation stepped in that the case against Sole was dropped, but not before the Catholic Church excommunicated Sole from the Diocese of Paterson.

One of his neighbours in Paterson remained sympathetic to what Sole was going through. Her name was Rosemary Ritvo. She was an English teacher who fancied trying her hand at screenwriting. One day Sole told her an idea he had for a horror movie. He had a vision of a young girl being killed on her first holy communion. Ritvo, who was also a Catholic and a regular churchgoer, loved the idea of making a horror film about the rituals of the Catholic Church and she agreed to write the script, incorporating Sole's ideas with her own point of view as a woman involved with the Church. A big inspiration to Sole was Nicolas Roeg's 1973 masterpiece, *Don't Look Now*, and it's from that film that Sole stole the idea of a murderer in a shiny red rain mac.

Meanwhile, Sole went cap in hand to his family for money to make *Alice, Sweet Alice*. He managed to raise $25,000 seed money, and it was then that the art director in Sole started to work his magic. During his day gig as an architect Sole had been involved in the restoration of a number of historic buildings in Paterson, and found ways to incorporate them into the script of *Alice, Sweet Alice*. He and Ritvo had decided to set the story in 1961, and this would involve period costumes for the actors. Sole himself shopped for the clothes for the characters, as well as finding props for the main locations — including Alice's home, an abandoned building which he and his friends decorated to look like a drab 1960s tenement. For *Alice, Sweet Alice*, Sole wanted a dark, dreary look, and his use of locations, props and costumes capture this brilliantly. Some of the Paterson locations that Sole was able to bag for the film included the Rogers automotive building, a factory that made steam trains. Sole uses this warehouse building for a creepy scene in which Alice's father (Niles McMaster) is murdered by the masked killer.

For scenes set in the church, Sole used the chapel of the Cheek funeral home, as he wasn't able to persuade any church to let him film a murder scene on consecrated ground. For the church exteriors he had to shoot at St Michael's in Newark, New Jersey, as he was still excommunicated from The Roman Catholic Diocese of Paterson. The Paterson police department did allow Sole to film in a local police station in Paterson, though, and this is where the scenes involving Detective Spina (Michael Hardstock) were shot.

Casting, like the rest of pre-production, was handled by Sole himself and he managed to pull off a couple of coups. The biggest one, of course, was landing a twelve-year-old Brooke Shields. At the time Shields was a child model with little acting experience. Sole spotted her photograph in a magazine and saw in her the kind of child that would make her sister envious, which is the relationship in the movie between Alice and Karen. Whereas Brooke Shields was twelve years old but seemed older, Paula Sheppard was nineteen but looked much younger. Sole managed to track Brooke Shields down because she lived in New Jersey, and persuaded her mother to let Brooke have the role of Karen.

Playing Karen and Alice's mother is Linda Miller, daughter of Jackie Gleason, mother of Jason Patric [*The Lost Boys* (1987)] and wife of Father Karras himself, Jason Miller. Linda Miller didn't go on to do a great deal after *Alice, Sweet Alice*, although she did star opposite James Brolin in *Night of the Juggler* (1980). Sole found Miller difficult to work with and quite emotionally unstable. Production of *Alice, Sweet Alice* had to be halted briefly when Miller slit her wrists on the set. Despite her fractious relationship with the director, Miller gives a good performance [and looks very similar to Greek actress Olga Karlatos in Lucio Fulci's *Zombie*, (1979)!]

Another piece of inspired casting on Sole's part was having Alphonso DeNoble play Alice's sleazy, obese landlord, Mr Alphonso, the cat-loving paedophile who tries to feel Alice up in the movie. With his piss-stained pants, giant stomach hanging over his filthy vest, and his shaven eyebrows, Mr Alphonso is a truly repulsive figure, despite his love of classical music. Sole discovered DeNoble working as a bouncer in a gay bar in Paterson. According to Sole, DeNoble had a racket going on in a nearby cemetery where he would pose as a priest, and say a prayer for people's loved ones in return for a small donation 'to the Church'. After *Alice, Sweet Alice*, DeNoble went on to feature in two films for the cult director Joel M. Reed, the notorious *Blood-Sucking Freaks* (1976) and *Night of the Zombies* (1981). Of course, Mr Alphonso gets his comeuppance in the film, and his death is set to the ironic strains of Kay Kyser's 'Three Little Fishies' ("Down in the meadow in a little bitty pool swam three little fishies and a mama fishie too"). It's a truly grotesque moment, one of many in the film: another character is bundled inside a coffin during a church ceremony and set alight; later on, a priest has a knife thrust into his throat; and, in a wince-worthy scene, a woman is stabbed in the foot. In these scenes, Sole uses elements of the bizarre for horrific effect.

Sole admits that many of ideas in *Alice, Sweet Alice* were stolen from other movies, such as Fritz Lang's *M* (1931), Orson Welles' *The Lady from Shanghai* (1947) and, as previously noted, Nicolas Roeg's *Don't Look Now* (1973), but Sole combines them in such a way as to make *Alice, Sweet Alice* a truly memorable horror film. Sure, to an extent *Alice, Sweet Alice* can be criticized for rehashing other horror movies. Tony Crawley made the comment that for 'all its old tricks and old connections', *Alice, Sweet Alice* can't disguise the fact that it is a rather obvious whodunit. Crawley has a point there, but what Sole does do well — and one of the reasons why *Alice, Sweet Alice* has gone on to become a cult film — is that it takes a classic theme in horror and explores it very effectively. The 'evil child' horror trope dates back to *The Bad Seed* made in 1956, the story of an eight-year-old girl who happens to be a sociopathic killer. Numerous horror films have used this theme since then, including *Orphan* (2009). In the seventies, after the success of *The Exorcist*, diabolical variations on this theme became popular and the 'evil child' became a literal 'devil child' in films like *Carrie* (1976), and *The Omen* (1976). In *Alice, Sweet Alice*, Sole plays on our expectations of the genre in the character of Alice, who we are constantly kept guessing about — is she the killer or isn't she? As Sole told Joseph Stargensky, "The whole thing about Alice was if she didn't get enough love and attention because she wasn't pretty, she would either grow up to be a killer or she'd grow up to be…well, she'd never be normal". The final shot of *Alice, Sweet Alice*, which holds on Alice's face after the final murder, plays into this idea that, even if Alice is innocent of the crimes committed in the film, she will never be normal.

This leads us to a question that numerous critics have asked — is *Alice, Sweet Alice* an anti-Catholic film? For his part, Sole says no. He claims that he didn't make *Alice, Sweet Alice* to condemn religion. Even though issues like divorce and paedophilia are touched upon, Sole maintains that these things are there because he took them from other murder-thriller movies. But that hasn't stopped scholars from discussing *Alice, Sweet Alice* in terms of its heavy use of religious symbolism and its less than flattering portrayal of the Roman Catholic Church.

One of the most perceptive reviews of *Alice, Sweet Alice* was by the filmmaker Chris Petit. He praised it as a film of many layers, whose numerous parallels and cross-references neatly bind it all together. *Alice, Sweet Alice* 'delights in confounding expectations as it conducts three separate enquiries. The plot investigates the murder; the film examines the family's self-destruction; and the film-makers construct a running commentary on the films of Alfred Hitchcock: against a carefully evoked background of Catholicism emerge twin themes of repression and guilt'. Petit's reading of *Alice, Sweet Alice* certainly draws the film's many facets together, and provides some clues as to what makes this 70s cult shocker so great.

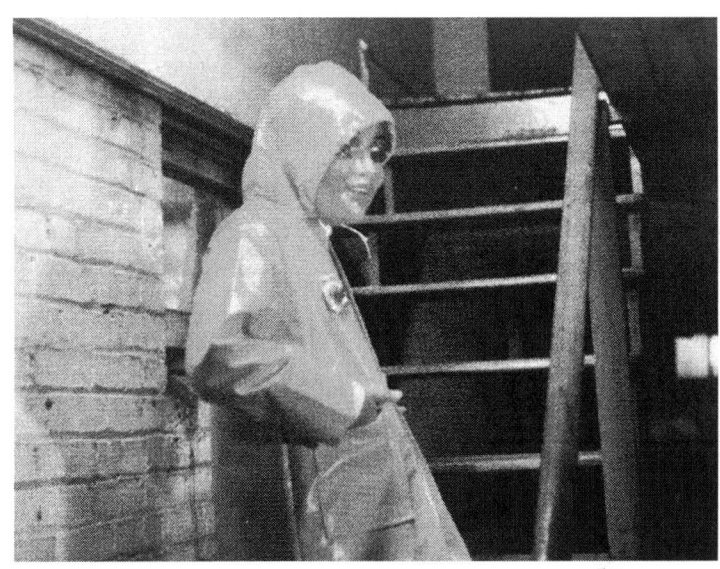

The masked killer in *Alice, Sweet Alice* (Allied Artists Pictures, 1976)

Asylum (1972)

American author Robert Bloch's five-film tenure as scriptwriter at Amicus began in 1966 with an adaptation of his own unpublished story, *The Psychopath*. If the title sounds overly derivative of Alfred Hitchcock's *Psycho* (1960), it won't come as a surprise that Bloch was, at that point in his career, best known as the author of the source novel on which Hitchcock's film had been based. After penning a prodigious number of short stories and several novels, Bloch had moved to LA in 1959 to commence a second career as a screenwriter in television, writing scripts for a number of anthology shows such as *Thriller* and *Alfred Hitchcock Presents*. He broke into the movies with an adaptation of his novel *The Couch* (1962), and two scripts for producer-director William Castle: *Straight-Jacket* and *The Nightwalker* (both 1964). That same year, Amicus producer Milton Subotsky acquired the rights to Bloch's short story *The Skull of the Marquis de Sade* (1945), which Subotsky adapted into *The Skull* (1965). Bloch was then engaged to script *The Psychopath* and *The Deadly Bees* (1966); but it's arguably in his Amicus anthologies, based on his short stories, that Bloch came into his own as a screenwriter.

The first of these, *Torture Garden* (1967), established the Bloch-Amicus formula: Subotsky would select four of Bloch's short stories and weave them into a framework, devising a wrap-around story that would showcase the four tales thematically. Bloch would then write the full dialogue script. *The House That Dripped Blood* (1971) took that formula and developed it in terms of sheer entertainment value; *Asylum* (1972) perfected it, resulting in a film that is not only pure Amicus but pure Robert Bloch. Indeed, Bloch considered *Asylum* his best film adaptation of all, remarking later that it was the one that came closest to what he had intended. Largely this is thanks to the film's director, Roy Ward Baker, who had the good sense to shoot Bloch's screenplay as written, with few changes. As Baker told *Cinefantastique* in 1973, "In *Asylum* what attracted me was a good script. It was not fantastically new, but it was beautifully carpentered and soundly constructed. I liked that because it appealed to my sense of pattern".

Subotsky must also take credit for selecting four of Bloch's most powerful tales in *Asylum*; stories which have a psychological element, but which also leave the viewer with a sense of ambiguity. Witchcraft, occultism, mysticism and necromancy all feature in *Asylum*, but may be nothing more than figments of the imagination: fever dreams of the inmates who are telling their weird tales to the incumbent psychiatrist, Dr Martin (Robert Powell). Madness is the underlying theme of the film, as it is in much of Bloch's work, but what gives *Asylum* its sense of 'pattern' is the unity of the stories themselves: each tale explores the boundaries between insanity and superstition - are the uncanny events of *Asylum* really happening or simply taking place in the mind? It is fitting that in an early sequence Baker has the camera dwell on old asylum drawings hanging on the hospital wall, showing the horror of Victorian bedlams, evoking bygone times when mental illness was thought to be supernatural in nature.

Asylum begins in the portmanteau tradition popularized by *Dead of Night* (1945), establishing a link story by which the tales can be told. Dr Martin is tasked with identifying which of four mental patients is actually the hospital's director, Dr Starr — who has himself gone insane. Martin is all-too-ready to assign glib psychiatric diagnoses to each of the inmates, whose stories comprise reanimated body parts, magic suits that bring the dead to life, divided personalities that take the form of murderous apparitions, and tiny clockwork automata that carry out the will of their maker. "Those poor devils up there can't be cured", rebukes the wheelchair-bound Dr Rutherford (Patrick Magee), who has taken over from Dr Starr as the head of the institution, "they can only be confined…and kept from being dangerous".

The first tale, 'Frozen Fear', told by the female inmate Bonnie (Barbara Parkins) is based a Bloch short story first published in *Weird Tales* in 1946. A time-honoured tale of infidelity, murder and madness, Richard Todd plays the errant husband who tries to 'off' his wife (Sylvia Syms) so that he can elope with his younger mistress (Parkins). But he hasn't counted on the voodoo-infused trinket, a symbol of life force, given to Syms by an African witch-doctor, which has the power to revive the woman's corpse even after Todd has chopped her into tiny pieces.

Bloch's dialogue in the story is heavy with meaning but handled with typical aplomb. "There are natural forces that are stronger than life or death," Syms warns her murderous hubby, to no avail. Bloch's tale of marital strife stems from a time when divorce laws in the USA were much stricter than they are now, when murder as a way out of an unhappy marriage could be more easily justified dramatically in tales of fiction without losing sympathy for the trapped spouse/s. In his adaptation, Bloch updates the Todd character to be more venal than the husband of the original short story is - and the wife is made more possessive and spiteful. "You're a weak, vain, selfish opportunist," she tells him. "You're content to live off my money. But you are *mine*. And I will never let you go. Never!"

Bloch was particularly pleased with this first sequence of *Asylum*, remarking to Darrell Schweitzer in 1993, that it "came off exactly as I wanted it to come off". 'Frozen Fear' had originally been intended as the third segment of the film, but the decision was taken to place it first. Arguably, it overpowers the sequences that follow, whereas Bloch had wanted the film to build up to it. Neither was Bloch happy with the additional footage of "limbs crawling across the floor", although it is difficult to imagine how else the sequence could have been filmed. Baker claims that he shot what was written in the script, and in fact praised the scene for its cinematic restraint. As he told *Cinefantastique*, "Everyone has remarked that this is a particularly good sequence. Although there is nothing explicit in it… [I]t's gruesome because you care about Sylvia Syms, who has been chopped up, and you care about her husband, Richard Todd. That's why it works".

Critics tend to rate *Asylum*'s second story as the best. 'The Weird Tailor' is based on Bloch's short story of the same name, first published by *Weird Tales* in 1950. The tale of a penurious tailor (Barry Morse) who accepts the task of making a suit for the mysterious Mr Smith (Peter Cushing) Bloch had adapted it once before, in 1961, for *Thriller*, expanding the original story's plotline and adding characters. In the *Thriller* version, Bloch tells the tale from Smith's perspective, laying out the back-story of Smith's dead son, and the distraught father's desperate turn to the occult in a bid to bring the boy back to him. In *Asylum*, though, Bloch shifts the perspective to that of the tailor, thereby creating a sense of mystery: who is this strange Mr Smith? What is the special suit that he wants the tailor to make for him? And who does he want the suit for, if not for himself? In *Asylum*, Bloch keeps us guessing, and this version of 'The Magic Tailor' is all the better for it.

'Lucy didn't sound like she was arguing with me. She knew. That's because Lucy is smarter than I am. Lucy wouldn't have started the drinking and gotten into such a mess in the first place. So it was about time I listened to what she said.'

So begins Bloch's short story, 'Lucy Comes to Stay', first published in *Weird Tales* in 1952. Substitute 'Lucy' for 'Mother' and we can clearly see this story paving the way for *Psycho* as a typically Blochian exploration of two sides of the same divided personality, one side goading the other into murder. Written in the first person, the author withholds this split-personality revelation until the end, as he does in *Asylum* (although it has now become such a well-worn trope that most viewers will guess the pay-off way before it happens).

'Lucy Comes to Stay' is the most psychological of Bloch's stories in *Asylum*, and draws on the 'paranoid woman' genre of the 40s. Recovering from her stay in the asylum, Barbara (Charlotte Rampling) starts to believe that she is being gaslighted by her brother [James Villiers, evoking his role in

Repulsion (1965)] and her live-in nurse (Megs Jenkins). In her bid to escape their evil clutches she is abetted by her mysterious friend, the titular Lucy (Britt Ekland). When scissors come into play there can be only one outcome! Baker even includes a nod to *Psycho*, involving a stabbing atop a flight of stairs, but the ethereal mood of 'Lucy Comes to Stay' is more akin to Robert Altman's *Images* (1972) made the same year as *Asylum*.

Despite, or perhaps because of, the shift in the order of stories from how Bloch had intended them in the screenplay, the implicitly psychological approach of 'Lucy Comes to Stay' segues neatly into the film's final segment. We are returned to the framing story and Dr Martin's bid to identify the elusive Dr Starr (another 'divided personality') from amongst the inmates. *Asylum* is unusual as an Amicus anthology in that the link story is itself based on a Bloch tale. 'Mannikins of Horror', first published in *Weird Tales* in 1931, told of a mental patient called Colin, an ex-surgeon who had developed *dementia praecox* after serving in the British Red Cross in Ypres during World War 1.

At the hospital, he starts to sculpt tiny figures of clay, anatomically accurate even down to their miniature brains and internal organs. One day, Colin notices the tiny clay men move! In his adaptation of the story for *Asylum*, Bloch has his mad sculptor, Dr Byron (played by Herbert Lom) 'will' his figurines to life and use them to exact revenge on his enemies, including the other doctors in the asylum. Finally, in another Blochian twist involving divided personalities, the true identity of Dr Starr is revealed. 'Mannikins of Horror' would have life breathed into it again in 1989, when TV screenwriter Josef Anderson adapted Bloch's story for the Richard P. Rubinstein-produced *Monsters*. However, *Asylum* remains the best version of the tale, not least for its enduring image of a miniature scalpel-wielding Herbert Lom.

Patrick Magee in *Asylum* (Amicus, 1972)

Audrey Rose (1977)

On its initial release in 1977, critics were quick to dismiss Robert Wise's *Audrey Rose* as a rip-off of films like *The Exorcist* and *The Omen* (1976). Arriving as it did on the tail of these two barnstorming Hollywood studio movies, it seemed like déjà vu to critics. The story of a young girl reincarnated by the spirit of a dead child (the Audrey Rose of the title), despite being based on the best-selling novel by Frank De Felitta, the movie was greeted with lukewarm reviews. *The New York Times* called it 'The soul of The Exorcist instantly recycled'; while *Newsweek* complained that 'it lacked any sign of intelligence.' Even such a venerable personage as Alan Frank dismissed the film. In his December 1977 review for *House of Hammer* magazine Frank wrote 'Audrey Rose should be a major horror film. Sadly, it cannot decide whether it's an out-and-out supernatural shocker…or whether it is trying to make a believable case for reincarnation. It fails on both counts.' *Saturday Review* echoed Frank's sentiments claiming *Audrey Rose* 'starts out as a titillating little thriller, but after 20 minutes, it bogs down in a series of mini-lectures on reincarnation that wipe out whatever dramatic potential the story might have had'. Perhaps most damning of all was *Cinefantastique*'s verdict that 'although Audrey Rose is an honourable film, it isn't particularly memorable or even an important one.'

Interestingly, though, critics are now beginning to reconsider *Audrey Rose* and the film is enjoying a growing reputation among horror fans and scholars alike. Film critic Adrian Schober describes *Audrey Rose* as one of Robert Wise's most underrated films. 'In eschewing sensationalism and gratuitous special effects,' according to Schober, 'Wise sought to tell his story in a very realistic and believable milieu'. Other critics see *Audrey Rose* as a key title in the 'Devil Child' subgenre; and in locating the source of story's horror as situated firmly within the modern American family, *Audrey Rose* also stands with 1970s classics like *It's Alive* (1975) and *The Amityville Horror* (1979). It's certainly a film that deserves closer examination.

Audrey Rose follows the story of Bill and Janice Templeton (John Beck and Marsha Mason) two wealthy New Yorkers who live in a grand Central Park West apartment with their thirteen-year-old daughter Ivy (Susan Swift). Their seemingly idyllic lives start to unravel when Ivy is stalked by the enigmatic Elliott Hoover (Anthony Hopkins) who claims that she is the reincarnation of his own daughter, Audrey Rose, who died in a car accident on the day Ivy was born. As Ivy starts to become 'possessed' by the spirit of Audrey Rose, the increasingly desperate Templetons turn to Hoover for help — with tragic consequences.

As Alan Frank wrote in his review of *Audrey Rose* reincarnation was a subject that had been largely ignored by filmmakers at that point in time. There were the various films of H Rider Haggard's *She* which employed the theme of reincarnation, and it was a key plot element in the 1932 Universal version of *The Mummy* as well as the 1959 Hammer remake. As Frank points out, it was treated seriously, but dully, in *The Search for Bridey Murphy* in 1956, and less seriously the following year when the heroine of *The Bride and The Beast* turned out to be the reincarnation of a gorilla. 'In 1970,' writes Frank, 'the subject received the musical treatment with Barbra Streisand in *On a Clear Day You Can See Forever*, and the last major film *The Reincarnation of Peter Proud* was appallingly bad.'

De Felitta and United Artists might have brought in a lesser director than Robert Wise to make *Audrey Rose*, but the thinking was that to bring in a strong director — the same way that Blatty brought in William Friedkin for *The Exorcist* — was more likely to result in a movie that audiences would want to see - a well-directed, effective horror movie. *Rosemary's Baby* (1968) set a precedent here. Paramount and producer Robert Evans brought in an exceptionally skillful director for that film in Roman Polanski and they reaped the rewards of doing so at the box office. And of course, *Jaws* (1975) had trumped *The Exorcist* financially, thanks, in large part to the virtuoso directing of Steven Spielberg. Robert Wise was not a only a veteran of screen horror, having directed classics like *The Haunting* (1963) but he had a number of huge box office hits to his name, including *The Sound of Music* (1965). In fact, at that point he was probably one of the most highly respected directors in Hollywood.

In his review of *Audrey Rose* for the *Monthly Film Bulletin*, Richard Combs writes that it displays 'a dramatic rationale and figurative substance that makes it at least as diverting as *Rosemary's Baby*, and a cut above the special effects hocus-pocus of its nearer predecessors in the demonology genre.' It is worth noting that by the release of *Audrey Rose* in April 1977, the Devil Child or Evil Child trope had become fairly well established in horror cinema as it had in horror fiction. *The Omen*, released in 1976, solidified this subgenre in a melding of *Rosemary's Baby* and *The Exorcist* to give us, in the child Damien, a literal spawn of the devil. Independent filmmakers were quick to jump on The Exorcist-Omen bandwagon with such titles as *The Child* (1977), *Cathy's Curse* (1977), and *The Redeemer: Son of Satan* (1978) all made around the same time as *Audrey Rose*.

But the evil child trope had been around since the 1950s, with the release in 1956 of Mervyn Leroy's *The Bad Seed*. Based on the 1954 novel by William March, it is the story of an eight-year-old psychopath who appears to have inherited the murderous genes of her serial killer grandmother. You can see how such a story would become popular in the 1950s, the decade in which there was much concern over the issue of juvenile delinquency.

Reviewing the film in *Time Out*, Tony Rayns described *Audrey Rose* as 'notable for centering on the emotional plight of the paranormal malarkey. It is ultimately, in fact, a strikingly sober portrait of the incompatibilities of marriage.' One of the major themes of Devil Child movies is the breakdown of the modern American family, and *Audrey Rose* is quite obsessive in its exploration of this theme. Suffusing *Audrey Rose* is a sense of loss and grief. Elliott Hoover has lost his wife and child Audrey Rose in a car accident. This left him searching for a sense of purpose and harbouring the desire to believe in the afterlife — in the possibility that the soul of his lost daughter Audrey might still reside on Earth in Ivy's body. In a similar way Bill and Janice fear losing their child, Ivy, to forces they do not understand, and through the story they feel Ivy increasingly slipping away from them, until, they, like Elliott are left only with the vague hope that Ivy's soul still survives after her death.

At the same time, Janice and Bill's marriage starts to disintegrate and here too we are left with a sense of loss and the feeling of a family in a state of crisis. In this way we can see *Audrey Rose* picking up where *The Exorcist* and *The Omen* left off. *Audrey Rose* deals with the disintegration of the perfect upper-middle class American family — the Templetons are aspirational white Americans living the dream in a beautiful Manhattan apartment. He is a successful advertising executive; she a devoted wife and mom. As the story unfolds, we gradually get to see the incompatibilities of this couple. In documenting the breakdown of a marriage, what Blatty made the backstory of *The Exorcist* is made the front story of *Audrey Rose*. De Felitta makes the disintegration of Bill and Janice's marriage in the face of supernatural threat a bigger part of the story, where in *The Exorcist*, Chris MacNeil's divorce is background rather than in the foreground. What *Audrey Rose* shares with *The Exorcist*, though, is the idea of the family being attacked by supernatural forces.

In classic horror films of the 1930s and 1940s, the family is attacked from outside of the family unit — by monsters, vampires, werewolves or demons that exist outside of normality. By the 1970s, though, the threat was shown to come from within the family itself. In the cases of *The Exorcist*, *The Omen* and *Audrey Rose*, children in the family are vessels by which the supernatural enters the family home, posing a threat to the family unit. There is a sense of creeping paranoia in these movies that mark them as different to the secure worlds presented in traditional horror movies where the monster is always destroyed at the end and normality is always restored. The line of defense against the unknown is easily distinguished. In paranoid horror, like *The Omen* and *Audrey Rose*, the line between the known and unknown is easily blurred, presenting threats that cannot be resolved by restoring normality.

What De Felitta and Wise present in *Audrey Rose* is how even a safe life like the Templetons enjoy, afforded by modern city living, good education, hard work, dedication to child rearing and marriage, can come unstuck when confronted with the fear of the unknown. Both Janice and Bill come to realize that they are woefully unprepared for what is about to happen to them and to their daughter Ivy; that their lives, based on material things and home comforts, lack the spiritual dimension, and this leaves them ill-equipped to deal with the possibility that their daughter has been touched by the supernatural, by forces beyond their understanding or control. Maybe the perfect American family is not so perfect after all.

Susan Swift as Ivy in *Audrey Rose* (United Artists, 1977)

The Blair Witch Project (1999)

The Blair Witch Project may be the most influential horror film ever made. Shot on a budget of $60,000 it returned that figure four THOUSAND times over, grossing $250,000,000 at the box office, making *The Blair Witch Project* one of the most financially successful independent films ever. This was at a time when horror was losing its audience, caught as it was in a loop of formulaic repetition. Box office receipts for once profitable franchises like *Friday the 13th*, *A Nightmare on Elm Street* and *Halloween* were flagging due to audience boredom and lacklustre sequels. The franchises suffered diminishing returns financially and artistically, and horror was reverting back to being a niche genre, no longer appealing to wider audiences as it had done in the 70s and 80s.

The huge financial success of *The Blair Witch Project* changed all that, and made horror films bankable again. It kicked off the found footage genre, leading the way for the even more profitable (and popular) *Paranormal Activity* franchise, and inspired a new generation of low-budget filmmakers working on digital to make horror movies.

Of course, this doesn't make *The Blair Witch Project* a masterpiece — or even a great film. While critics were more or less unanimous in their praise on its release in 1999, audience opinion was divided: some found it genuinely scary and others felt it had been over-hyped. But even if you see *The Blair Witch Project* as basically a low budget exploitation movie whose marketing and advertising campaign promised much more than it could deliver, it's still undeniably influential as an exercise in marketing horror. And as a case study in producing no-budget lo-fi horror, even twenty or more years later it's a masterclass.

'Why are they videotaping themselves? It's the thing that every found footage movie fights with, I mean, if somebody is chasing you why don't you throw down the camera and run the fuck away?'

So said Eduardo Sanchez in 2012, decrying the rash of bad found footage movies that appeared after *The Blair Witch Project*'s runaway success. Sanchez should know — after all he co-directed *The Blair Witch Project* with Daniel Myrick, as well as part-found footage *Lovely Molly* (2011) and Bigfoot yarn, *Exists* (2012). It seemed after *The Blair Witch Project* that every wannabe horror director looking for a sure thing was drawn to the found footage genre for the simple reason that it is cheap 'n' cheerful. But very few have the skill to pull off it like Sanchez and Myrick or *Paranormal Activity* director, Oren Peli. For every film that made the found footage approach plausible, like *Cloverfield* (2008), there were plenty [like *Tape 407*

(2012)] that failed miserably in the conceit. Over seventy found footage movies were released in the twelve years following the heady days of *The Blair Witch Project*, and with only a few worth a damn, that made for a lot of tedious camcorder, kids-lost-in-the-woods-type dross (remember *A Night in The Woods*, 2012 anyone?)

Of course, a successful franchise like *Paranormal Activity* will keep churning 'em out, and most of them managed to be quite scary. When done well the found footage approach really can draw us into the horror and make us believe what we see is real (or at least partially forget what we are watching is a movie). But the found footage movie is also rife with clichés, and easily spoofed, as the atrocious *Scary Movie*-type send-up *Supernatural Activity* (2012) showed. *Supernatural Activity* shamelessly lampooned everything from *The Blair Witch Project* to *Grave Encounters* (2011) to *The Last Exorcism* (2010) showing how dumb the average found footage movie can actually be.

Most critics claim that the found footage horror movie began with *Cannibal Holocaust* (1980), Ruggero Deodato's infamous nasty about a documentary film crew who travel to the Amazon to film a tribe of cannibals and then mysteriously disappear, leaving only their filmed footage behind. But the roots of the genre can be traced back further still to Michael Powell's *Peeping Tom* (1960), the much-maligned British shocker about a psycho-killer who likes to film his victims with his trusty 16mm Bolex. The fact that the killer in the film is also a photographer introduced two key themes into the horror genre that have become staples of the found footage horror film ever since: voyeurism and the nature of filmed fear. Many subsequent films feature characters that just love to film, and seem to love to film fear. This is, of course, primarily a way to get around the main problem that Sanchez so eloquently identifies: why keep filming, why not throw down the camera and run? Often screenwriters throw in a neat bit of dialogue to smooth over the plausibility problem: "Jesus, Thad, how can you keep filming at a time like this?" And although *Peeping Tom* wasn't solely found footage, it featured plenty of through-the-lens-shots to get its point across.

The Blair Witch Project borrowed the mockumentary conceit of *Cannibal Holocaust* ("three filmmakers went missing… a year later their footage was found") cleverly combining 16mm and Hi 8 footage to present not a film-within-a-film as *Cannibal Holocaust* was but a combination of professional documentary and home movie. It also got around another major plausibility problem thrown up by the found footage approach: that of editing. For a movie to work for an audience it has to be edited, but found footage by nature is raw unedited material. All of which presents a dilemma for the filmmaker: how to explain that the footage has been put together for an audience. The best found footage movies manage to give the impression that what we are seeing is raw material (perhaps edited 'in camera') and therefore more real. *Cloverfield* does this very well. Mockumentaries attempt to get around the problem by presenting the film as a documentary edited afterwards but this approach presents another issue. How can the filmmakers edit the film together if they are killed in the course of its making? A plausibility problem that *Diary of the Dead* (2007), *The Last Exorcism* and *The Devil Inside* (2012) almost but not quite managed to pull off.

The Blair Witch Project, of course, featured that famous shot of Heather Donahue crying and drizzling snot into the camera lens ("I'm so fuckin' scared.") and many found footage movies have attempted (and usually failed) to capture the same sense of unseen horror. This has mostly resulted in a lot of obnoxious youths filming each other's hysteria in night-vision (*Evil Things*, 2009), but occasionally yielded some effective results in the classic Val Lewton-esque 'suggested' horror style. *Evidence* (2011) was one that made the most of its found footage conventions in presenting a group of campers set upon by unseen attackers that wreck their RV and pick them off one by one. We are left guessing as to the true nature of the threat until the end of the movie and the hysterical attempt of the survivors to capture the beasts on video against actually adds to the suspense rather than detracts from it.

Another found footage movie that managed to add something new as well as take us into the unknown was *Apollo 18* (2011). Unfortunately, it wasn't very good. But it did, at least, have an intriguing premise: claiming to be classified footage from a secret 70s moon landing that resulted in the mysterious disappearance of three astronauts. During the course of the film the astronauts are attacked by unseen forces that... you get the gist. Despite its initial promise *Apollo 18* took the lazy route to become another *Blair Witch* clone (substitute the moon for the woods and you get the point), and one which broke the rules of plausibility to boot. Why would NASA edit the footage together and then add a movie score?

To see a found footage film that really made a hash of it, check out *Evil Things*. As usual we are informed at the start that the film we are about to see is 'evidence' from the files of the authorities (in this case the FBI). Cue the usual inanities of a group of unsympathetic friends on vacation in the wilderness — handicam in tow - stalked by an unseen attacker. *Evil Things* threw away any logic in the found footage approach. Not only is the footage edited and given a music soundtrack (presumably by some budding

Spielberg at the FBI) but POV footage from the killer's perspective is added for good measure.

If *Evil Things* marked the low point of the found footage genre, *V/H/S* (2012) offered some hope. Granted, a found footage movie that was also an anthology movie might have seemed less than promising at first but *V/H/S* arguably got inside the skin deeper than any found footage movie since *Paranormal Activity*. In the wrap-around story (*Tape 56*) a gang of thugs are paid to break into an old man's house and steal some videocassettes. Things turn nasty as the depravities that the gang visit on others are visited on them. Meanwhile each tale presents a variation on found footage scenarios: in *The Sick Thing That Happened To Emily When She Was Younger* (dir. Joe Swanberg) a Skype-chat becomes the setting for ghostly goings on in a woman's apartment; a couple's holiday video turns into a document of murder in *Second Honeymoon* (dir. Ti West); in *Amateur Night* (dir. David Bruckner) a man dons a hidden webcam in his spectacles hoping to film a sexual encounter, but the tables are turned on him and his two friends in bloody ways.

V/H/S explored and updated the themes of voyeurism and filmed horror that *Peeping Tom* introduced more than fifty years ago. And while the technology may have changed, the twisted psychology remained the same.

In *The Blair Witch Project*, the focus was less on the horror of psychosis, more on fear of the supernatural. But Sanchez and Myrick used the found footage approach to help make that fear believable. It's for this reason (and to overcome the lack of production values) that *The Blair Witch Project* took the form of mockumentary.

In fact, documentaries on paranormal phenomena inspired the makers of *The Blair Witch Project* as much as horror movies where the monster remains 'unseen', such as *The Shining* (1980) and *Jaws* (1975). Myrick and Sanchez have cited the 70s TV series *In Search Of...* as a particular influence. Coinciding with a surge of public interest in mysticism, the paranormal and the unexplained, *In Search Of...* investigated a whole gamut of phenomena that ran from UFOs to the Loch Ness Monster to the Yeti and Bigfoot. The format of interviews, re-enactments and location footage is something that *The Blair Witch Project* adopts in its pseudo-documentary approach.

In *The Blair Witch Project* a group of student filmmakers go in search of the Blair Witch in the woods of Burkittsville, Maryland and mysteriously go missing. Their recovered film footage becomes the movie itself, cleverly blurring the boundaries between reality and fiction, filmic 'truth' and actuality. Part of the film's conceit is to try to convince the viewer that what he or she is seeing is 'true'. *The Blair Witch Project* wasn't the first horror film to claim that the events in the story actually happened [*The Last House on The Left* (1972) and *The Texas Chain Saw Massacre* (1974) both made that claim in their publicity and in the opening titles of films themselves] but it was the first to reinforce that misperception in a raft of ancillary products, such as its website and accompanying documentary *The Curse of The Blair Witch* (1999).

The purpose of this, of course, was to start a debate on the internet as to whether *The Blair Witch Project* was a real-life documentary or a work of fiction, but it also served to fulfil the basic requirement of plausibility to the success of a horror film. For any horror film to work viewers must suspend their disbelief. To help achieve this, the makers of *The Blair Witch Project* used the tropes of reality TV. In his excellent book on *The Blair Witch Project*, Peter Turner talks about how Myrick and Sanchez constantly make us aware of the use of the camera as a way of giving the film a sense of authenticity. While the viewer is conscious that the film is not real life, they are also drawn into the action by the fact that the person operating the camera is a part of the events taking place on screen. In fact, Myrick and Sanchez had the actors operate the cameras themselves during the entire making of the film. Joshua Leonard, who plays cameraman 'Josh' in the film, was cast partly because he knew how to operate a 16mm camera. Similarly, Heather Donahue was given a Hi8 camera for the duration of the shoot and it's her own faming of herself featuring just the top corner of her face and head that became the film's most famous image.

In another blurring of fiction and reality the characters were given the same names as the actors playing them. Myrick and Sanchez did this partly so that they would be able to use all the footage that the actors filmed, including moments in which they spoke to each other out of character. In his book Turner mentions the film's use of individual to-camera confessions being edited next to footage of group discussions, and how this also reflects reality TV shows like *Big Brother* with its diary room confessions cut into sequences showing the group dynamic of the whole cast. In *The Blair Witch Project* we see the breakdown of the group as they succumb to fear, hunger, lack of sleep and exposure to the wilderness leading to Heather's on-camera confession.

Myrick and Sanchez actually approached directing the film as they might a reality TV series, by creating an improvised situation in which the actors were placed, and controlling it from afar. Leonard, Donahue and Michael Williams ('Mike') were basically sent into the woods for real, and tracked by the directors using GPS. Each day they were given written notes to help them improvise what was to happen to them that day. The directors hunted the actors at night, making scary noises and placing objects outside of their tents. Like 'caught-on-camera' TV shows, this technique gave a sense of random events being filmed by the group, and helped capture authentic responses by the actors to these terrifying happenings.

Originally, the Hi8 and 16mm footage filmed by the actors was planned to be edited together with professional documentary material shot by Myrick and Sanchez, to make *The Blair Witch Project* a more traditional mockumentary. But Myrick and Sanchez decided to go with just the raw shaky-cam footage filmed by the actors, as this fitted in better with the idea of a found footage movie that was at the heart of *The Blair Witch Project* (the stuff shot by Myrick and Sanchez was edited together as *The Curse of The Blair Witch*).

The mix of 16mm and Hi8 amateur footage in *The Blair Witch Project* is what really makes *The Blair Witch Project* work as a pure form of found footage movie. Found footage has its origins in the epistolary novel popular in the nineteenth century. These novels were made up of official documents like letters, diary entries and newspaper clippings. Some of horror's greatest novels, such as Mary Shelley's *Frankenstein; or, The Modern Prometheus* (1818) and Bram Stoker's *Dracula* (1897) were written in this style, to add greater realism to the story and give the perspectives of different characters. Adopting this form gives *The Blair Witch Project* an added air of authenticity and believability: the found footage became like an 'official' document of events, and this helped Myrick and Sanchez overcome a lack of production values, too.

Like any good horror movie, *The Blair Witch Project* starts in the realm of commonplace experience and gradually introduces the supernatural. The camping trip becomes more sinister the deeper into the woods the film crew go, the closer they get to the Blair Witch. The sound of snapping twigs at night leads to the discovery of mysterious cairns, and strange stick figures that appear in the woods outside the group's tent. Really this is all there is to the film, but it builds up a mood of increasing dread precisely by making the unusual mundane and by reducing the supernatural to a home movie.

As one critic wrote, 'Blair Witch is scary, but it lacks surprise, and without surprise, you're left with a bunch of kind-of annoying people shakily filming themselves wandering the woods and reacting to loud noises.' What couldn't be re-captured in the sequels *Book of Shadows: Blair Witch 2* (2000) and *Blair Witch* (2016) - or in most of the found footage films that followed the success of *The Blair Witch Project* - was the phenomenon itself. *The Blair Witch Project* was the first film to be marketed primarily by the Internet, through the website, chat rooms and social media. This was something new to audiences, whose interest was increased massively by their on-line experience. *The Blair Witch Project* was the first film to go viral. In many ways the phenomenon of *The Blair Witch Project* is inseparable from the phenomenon of the Internet which was then still a novelty. You might call *The Blair Witch Project* a fluke, but it's arguably one-of-a-kind. Indeed, an exercise in marketing horror may be the most influential aspect of it.

The original is a laff-in-the-dark — a virtually plotless movie hyped up by the distributors using then new Internet marketing and promotion. But it also plays very forcefully on our fear of the unknown — we never see the Blair Witch herself, but we feel her palpably evil presence throughout. In the words of film critic Lisa Schwarzbaum, 'as a horror picture, [*The Blair Witch Project*] may not be much more than a cheeky game, a novelty with the cool, blurry look of an avant-garde artifact. But as a manifestation of multimedia synergy, it's pretty spooky'.

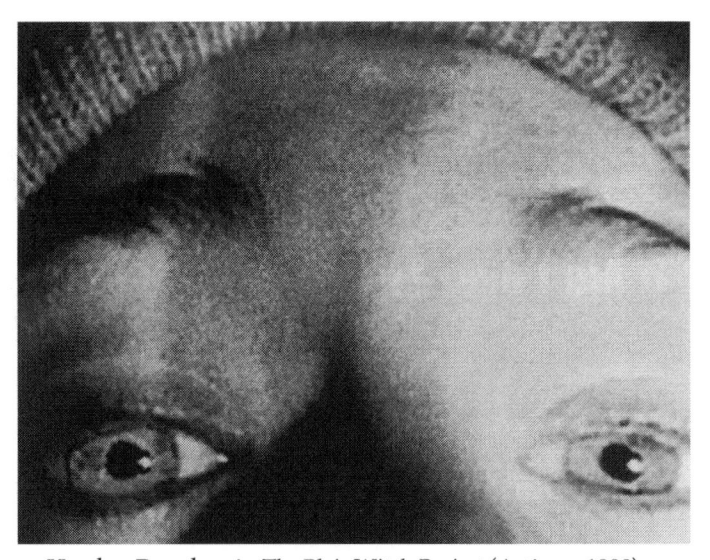

Heather Donahue in *The Blair Witch Project* (Artisan, 1999)

The Boys Next Door (1985)

At first glance, *The Boys Next Door* seems like an oddity in the filmography of Penelope Spheeris. Made two years after the punk-inspired *Suburbia* (1983) and seven years before her first mainstream success, *Wayne's World* (1992), *The Boys Next Door* is pretty far removed from Spheeris' work as a 'rock and roll anthropologist' documenting punk and heavy metal culture in America. This, Spheeris had started to do in the 70s, making music promos via her LA-based production company Rock 'n' Reel, before directing a feature-length music documentary about the Los Angeles punk scene, *The Decline of Western Civilization* (1981).

Produced before the serial killer craze of the 1990s, *The Boys Next Door* stands outside that particular cycle as well, despite its apparent concern with the phenomenon of real-life serial killers (a trait it shares with other low budget movies of the genre like *Henry: Portrait of a Serial Killer*, 1986). Indeed, Spheeris has claimed that "it wasn't that I did *The Boys Next Door* because I really loved serial killer movies. I don't". It was, in her words, "the only thing I could do at the time to get paid". François Truffaut once made the comment that one worries about a director's second feature film, meaning that filmmakers often appear to lose their way after their debut, especially if their first film has been a personal one. That Spheeris would go on, after *The Boys Next Door*, to direct comedy-crime pic *Hollywood Vice Squad* (1986) suggests that she might easily have disappeared into the 80s low budget exploitation mill ("That movie fuckin' blew weenies," Spheeris memorably told Sarah Jacobson and Beth Loudmouth in 1998).

But if you dig a little deeper, *The Boys Next Door* has more in common with Spheeris' 'personal' movies than you might think. In *The Women's Guide to International Film*, Barbara Koenig Quart describes *The Boys Next Door* as dealing with 'violent, disaffected' youth 'within the codes of exploitation film'. This is something it clearly shares with *Suburbia* (both films were distributed by Roger Corman's New World Pictures), and links to a 'fascination with the frustration, despair and violence of the marginal young' that has informed Spheeris' films from *The Decline of Western Civilization* onwards (including its sequels - *Part Two: The Metal Years*, 1988 and *Part Three*, 1998).

What's more, *The Boys Next Door* looks forward to the broadening of Spheeris' output in later years (which would come to include wry comedies and children's movies). Spheeris has proven to be a diverse filmmaker, even as she has remained true to her roots: something she shares with other directors from the Corman stable, such as Martin Scorsese and Jonathan

Demme, who managed to combine the personal and the commercial successfully throughout their careers. At the heart of Spheeris' work there is a humanitarian call for the protection of childhood, kinship and the need for belonging, and this threads through all of her films (even *Hollywood Vice Squad*) regardless of genre and other commercial demands.

The Boys Next Door opens with a montage of portraits showing us a number of real-life serial killers in the style of a true crime documentary speculating on the causes of the serial killer phenomenon. A series of voice overs reflect on the psychological traits that may have contributed to these seemingly 'normal' young men inexplicably becoming killers. We are told that many of these murderers are white males; handsome, charismatic and intelligent. They seem like 'regular kind of guys'. Not the kind of guys that would kill anyone. Dig underneath, though, and they exhibit an inability to see other people (particularly women) as human beings. They cannot differentiate between sex and aggression. The violent society may be to blame. These killers have been so brutalized in their own upbringing that they are incapable of empathy. Killing becomes normal for them. As society becomes more violent, suggests the voice over, the number of serial killers increases. The phenomenon is growing. The scary thing is that a serial killer could be anyone: "seemingly normal people commit these crimes. They can act like anyone. Your friend. Your teacher. The guy next door."

Thus, *The Boys Next Door* sets out its stall right from the start. This is to be an expose of the serial killer phenomenon that was, in 1985, just beginning to take hold of the public's imagination. In other words, Spheeris poses the question: what makes a serial killer? (There have, of course, been no shortage of these films made in recent years and their genre traits are now familiar to audiences.) As the title suggests, Spheeris is concerned with the monster that lurks behind the façade of normality. In the film, Roy (Maxwell Caulfield) and Bo (Charlie Sheen) are two 'normal' good-looking boys who commit unspeakable acts of violence against society. What triggers such antisocial behaviour? This is where Spheeris' concerns as a filmmaker and the edicts of genre seem to converge: *The Boys Next Door* approaches its subject matter ostensibly as a social study of violent, disaffected youth. But there is also a sense throughout *The Boys Next Door* of Spheeris working *against* the material, even as she *appears* to follow it. This is apparent in the wry tone of the movie that undermines it as a sober treatment of male sociopathy. In other words, the director takes the male-orientated subject matter and does a 'Spheeris' on it. In its way, *The Boys Next Door* is just as subversive and 'punk' as any of her other films.

As the title of her 1983 movie *Suburbia* suggests, one of Spheeris' principle concerns is debunking the ideal of American suburbia. Indeed, that film portrayed the collapse of the suburban ideal. A number of filmmakers, including Steven Spielberg, have shown the darker side of suburbia: the cultural shallowness and ethnocentrism that hides behind the serene façade of the white picket fence. But few before Spheeris suggested the extent of its failure. Given that the suburban ideal is one of the West's great social experiments, its failure is indicative of the decline of Western civilization itself. It is no accident that *The Decline of Western Civilization* is the given title of Spheeris' three-part music documentary: ostensibly about American punk music, it is really about a lost generation.

It follows that in *The Boys Next Door* suburbia has nothing to offer young people except the prospect of a dead-end job and a life of boredom and frustration. It is significant that Spheeris' serial killers are products of suburbia. This inverts the usual trope of serial killer movies in which sociopathy is shown as symptomatic of urban blight. The killers of *The Boys Next Door* are dehumanized not by the city but by soulless suburbia.

Roy and Bo's small-town mentality demands that they conform to a toxic masculinity of aggression and misogyny. They exhibit this in frequent displays of male bravado that masks their insecurity. This is taken to extremes later, particularly by Roy who vents his anger and frustration in the city under the cover of anonymity. In *The Encyclopedia of Modern Murder*, Colin Wilson suggests that most cases of seemingly motiveless crime can be traced to feelings of resentment: the criminal is looking for somewhere to place the blame for their own misfortunes. In *The Boys Next Door*, Roy confesses to feeling angry all the time. He is actively looking for the means of channelling his aggression. He and Bo eventually tip over the edge into violence when their masculinity is challenged in a gay bar. Barbara Koenig Quart has described Spheeris as 'a kind of detached anthropologist in the country of alienated adolescent white males who are often outrageously sexist'. In her music films, this sexism is often shown as rock and roll males overcompensating for their effeminate appearance by behaving in a misogynistic way. Similarly, casual sexism is part of Roy and Bo's 'goofiness' in high school; this erupts into violence against women later in film. Spheeris makes clear in her work that racist, sexist and homophobic attitudes are common in 'alienated' white American youth; these attitudes are shared by Roy and Bo in *The Boys Next Door*, and characterize their violent acts later in the film.

If Spheeris' early films chart the collapse of suburbia, it follows that they show the breakdown of the nuclear family as part of the collapse. In *The

Decline of Western Civilization, the youths inevitably come from broken homes. Spheeris herself had a difficult childhood. Her mother married seven times. Most of Spheeris' stepfathers were violent drunks. She lived in trailers throughout her teenage years and was moving around all the time. The punks in *Suburbia* are runaways from domestic abuse. Parents are shown as neglectful at best. In *The Boys Next Door*, Roy's father is uncommunicative to the point of not even noticing Roy is in the room with him. In Spheeris' films, the disaffected young form surrogate families with each other — replacements of their biological families. In *Suburbia*, the punks who squat a tract house together become a kind of family, with the older youths taking on the roles of guardians. Spheeris has commented that rock bands are a replacement family made up of rejected people. In *The Boys Next Door* there is similar kinship between Roy and Bo as a result of their being social outcasts. However, they are more than just 'brothers' - Spheeris has much to say about male relationships and homophobia.

The Leopold and Loeb murder case — in which two wealthy male students kidnapped and murdered a 14-year-old boy in 1924 — has been the basis of several serial killer movies including *Rope* (1948), *Compulsion* (1959), *Swoon* (1992) and *Murder by Numbers* (2002). The serial killer 'double act' has, in fact, become a staple of the genre: underlying the relationship between the two murderers is their repressed homosexual desire for each other sublimated in acts of homophobic violence and homicidal impulse. Spheeris makes use of this genre convention in *The Boys Next Door* but also uses it to highlight the slightly cartoonish 'buddy' relationship between Roy and Bo. In many ways this pair is not that dissimilar to Wayne and Garth in *Wayne's World*. The central male relationship in both films takes precedence over the male-female ones (women are marginalized as a result), and underlying it is an unacknowledged homoeroticism between the two 'buddies'. "I don't want to sound like a fag or nothing, but you are my best friend," Bo tells Roy in *The Boys Next Door*. Their latent homosexuality explodes into homophobic violence when they murder Chris, who they meet in a gay bar (the scene in the gay bar is given particular emphasis by Spheeris). Bo lashes out in a kind of blind panic when he thinks Chris is making a pass at him. However, Roy's behaviour is much more calculated — he has already removed his shirt in order to deliberately provoke a sexual response from Chris — suggesting that Roy is aware of his own latent homosexuality in a way that Bo is not. Indeed, the poster of *The Boys Next Door*, showing a topless Maxwell Caulfield reclining in bed, with a photograph of him with his arm around Charlie Sheen's shoulders, plays up the film's homoeroticism.

Despite the dark subject matter of *The Boys Next Door*, Spheeris constantly undermines the docu-realism that characterizes the serial killer genre. This she does through an irreverent comic tone that emphasizes the absurd male swagger of the two killers. Their dialogue is frequently tongue-in-cheek:

"I've got stuff inside of me." "What, like cancer or something?"

"Fucking dykes really get off calling us fags."

"They're what?" "Anarchists, man. It means they'll fuck anything!"

The effect is to puncture the male ego. Spheeris fights against the material in this respect, subverting what has since become the most male-centric of film genres. In these ways, then, *The Boys Next Door* is a serial killer movie, but also, very definitely 'a Penelope Spheeris film'.

Charlie Sheen in *The Boys Next Door* (New World Pictures, 1985)

Braindead (1992)

The *Los Angeles Times* called it 'the most hilariously disgusting movie ever made. It makes *Re-Animator* seem like a UNESCO documentary about Mother Teresa.' For those who only know Peter Jackson for *Lord of the Rings*, his 1992 splatstick classic *Braindead* is bound to be a bit of an eye-opener. It has been described as 'an orgy of bad taste and splatter humour' (*Variety*), and 'a spoof horror movie…that wins hands-down on excess' (*The Independent*), while the critical consensus on *Rotten Tomatoes* is that *Braindead* is 'extremely gory and exceedingly good fun, thanks to Peter Jackson's affection for the tastelessly sublime'.

The 'gonzo story of a lovestruck teen and his zombiefied mother' set in the suburbs of Wellington, New Zealand, *Braindead* features karate-kicking priests, zombie babies, and the novel use of lawnmower as a weapon with which to pulverize the living dead. It's all in the worst possible taste and features then-state of the art gore effects and puppetry. In fact, it could well be the bloodiest splatter movie ever made! One thing's for sure, *Braindead* is a zillion miles away from Jackson's Oscar-nominated drama *The Lovely Bones* (2009) and his highly acclaimed World War One documentary, *They Shall Not Grow Old* (2018). But it's a showcase for his subversive sense of humour and social satire, and the best work of his splatter phase with which he started his career back in the early years — or as Jackson himself has called them — "the naughty years". The British Board of Film Classification summed up *Braindead* well when they described it as 'Dame Edna Everage meets Norman Bates and George Romero in this glorious zombie extravaganza, which parodies almost every horror movie you ever saw, as well as poking fun at bourgeois pretensions Down Under'.

Braindead was third in a trilogy of Peter Jackson movies that pushed the boundaries of screen gore, bad taste and shock about as far as they could go: *Bad Taste* (1987), *Meet the Feebles* (1990) and *Braindead* sent censors worldwide running for their scissors, audiences for their sick bags, and in the process turned Peter Jackson into a cult director and a national hero. Nowadays, Sir Peter Jackson (he was awarded the New Zealand Knighthood in 2009) may be happy rubbing shoulders with the Spielbergs of this world but his early work in the late 1980 and 1990s has more in common with the splatter comedies of Frank Henenlotter, Sam Raimi and Brian Yuzna than it does with Tin Tin or the Hobbits.

Peter Jackson was born into a working-class family in Pukerua Bay, near Wellington and seemed determined from an early age to rebel against his small-town New Zealand background. Growing up on a diet of Ray Harryhausen movies, *Thunderbirds* and *Monty Python*, Jackson started making films at the age of nine after a family friend gave him a Super 8 camera. There followed a string of homemade Minotaur movies featuring his own special effects. It was his love of model-making kits as much as the movies he watched that really drew him to film. "I just wanted to put my models on film," he told *Dark Horizons* in 2005. "I never wanted to be a director, I just wanted to be a special effects man in movies." Jackson's early films revel in special effects and DIY gore, often fashioned by his own hand. Jackson loves the magical in the movies, the creation of illusion. With the *Hobbit* trilogy, it's the magic of Middle Earth that draws him to make movies but back then it was the magic of make-up effects artist extraordinaire Tom Savini — whom Jackson also lists amongst his influences. Jackson describes New Zealanders as perfectly suited to make films — especially his type of films — because, like Savini, they are 'ingenious'.

Like many of cinema's true visionaries, Jackson had no formal training in film, but learned his craft in the doing. So it was with his first feature, *Bad Taste* which began life as a short film shot at weekends but gradually expanded and grew over a period of four years into a full length 35mm feature. *Bad Taste* can only be described as a 'sci-fi splatter-punk comedy' - aliens invade the small New Zealand town of Kaihoro to harvest humans for their intergalactic fast food franchise. The town is defended by a four-man army - Frank, Ozzy, Barry and Derek. Their unconventional military tactics include exploding sheep with a rocket launcher and alien dismemberment by chainsaw. Early on in the film Derek (played by Jackson himself) finds his own brain leaking from his skull after a massive head injury and results to increasingly desperate measures to hold it in. When a hat doesn't work he tries a belt, and when that fails, he stuffs part of an alien's brain into his head to make up for what he's lost of his own!

Jackson wrote, directed, edited and acted two roles in the film. Like Stanley Kubrick and Ridley Scott he also operates the camera on all his films from *Bad Taste* onwards - that way he can be near the action and more involved. Despite its — um — bad taste, the film caught the attention of the New Zealand Film Commission, which gave Jackson the funds to complete the film and send it to festivals — including Cannes —where it became an instant cult success.

The late 1980s was a watershed time for New Zealand film with directors like the late Geoff Murphy (*Goodbye Pork Pie*, 1981, *Young Guns 2*, 1990, *Free Jack*, 1992) and Vincent Ward (*The Navigator*, 1988, *Map of The Human Heart*, 1992, *What Dreams May Come*, 1998) entering the national and international stage. New Zealanders still remember the buzz around Jackson at the time. He was clearly one to watch even back then.

While he was making *Bad Taste*, Jackson worked full-time as a photo-engraver for a local newspaper, still living at home and spending all his money on 16mm film equipment and film stock. After the success of *Bad Taste*, Jackson began work with long-time collaborators Fran Walsh, Stephen Sinclair and Danny Mulheron on a series of scripts, including a sequel to *A Nightmare on Elm Street* (1984) and the screenplay to what would eventually become *Braindead*. But when the finances for Jackson's proposed zombie movie fell through at the last minute, he turned his sights to making a short film for television entitled *Meet the Feebles*. At first envisaged as a Muppet-style musical comedy, Jackson quickly expanded the idea to feature length after he found a group of Japanese investors who evidently shared his bizarre sense of humour. The finished film has been described as 'Sex, Drugs and Soft Toys' and it's a pretty accurate description.

Meet the Feebles is the behind-the-scenes story of a theatrical troupe (the titular Feebles) and their backstage antics as they prepare for a live TV show that might make them rich and famous. They are a badly-behaved bunch, indulging in vice, pornography and illicit sex. You could think of them as the Muppets' dark alter-egos, with Heidi, the hippo, for example, taking the part of Miss Piggy. Only Miss Piggy doesn't actually have sex with Kermit the Frog, the way Heidi does with her love-rat boyfriend, Bletch in *Meet the Feebles*. And after Bletch does the dirty on Heidi with another feeble, Heidi seeks solace in a giant chocolate cake that causes her such flatulence that she lays waste to the television studio with her wind. Another highlight (!) is the projectile vomiting by Harry the rabbit who is suffering from a suspected STD. You can see why people describe Jackson's second feature as once-seen-never-forgotten.

Jackson and his team of puppeteers made *Meet the Feebles* inside a derelict goods shed in the winter of 1989. Jackson recorded the dialogue of the Feebles first, scene by scene and then matched the puppet performances to the voices. He would listen to the recording at home, "all ninety minutes of it", he recalled, "shut my eyes and just visualize the movie". When it came to filming the puppets in action, Jackson's ingenuity and that of his crew was continually challenged as even the simplest scenes required constantly changing camera angles to hide the strings of the puppets.

Critics called the film 'disgustingly graphic, obscenely offbeat and caustically funny'. Jackson was clearly a filmmaker adept at using shock tactics. "You are showing something so extreme as to be ridiculous, that can't help but make people laugh", he has said of his work.

Extreme is definitely the word to describe Jackson's next film. After the financial success of *Meet the Feebles*, Jackson returned to *Braindead*, rewriting the script to turn it into the most raucous and gruesome zombie movie ever made. Forget Romero, forget Raimi, in *Braindead*, heads and arms aren't just ripped off, flesh is stripped from bone, zombie babies are liquidized, and zombie hordes are chopped to pieces by the spinning blade of a Flymo. It is all so ridiculous you can't help but laugh. "I couldn't make a horror movie that scares people because I just can't take them seriously", Jackson said in 1994, "I find them hilarious".

By the time of *Braindead*, a theme was starting to emerge in Jackson's films - that of using outrageous shock 'n' gore and bad taste to hit out at the parochialism that had dogged Jackson's childhood in small town New Zealand. *Braindead* is set in the 1957 in Wellington where the film's Pee Wee Herman-like hero Lionel (Timothy Balme) battles the will of his domineering mother (Elizabeth Moody) when he falls for the enchanting shopkeeper's daughter Paquita (Diana Peñalver). After mother is bitten by a Sumatran Rat Monkey ('Simian Raticus') during a trip to the local zoo she succumbs to incipient zombie-itis and is soon infecting everyone with the disease. Shamed Lionel is forced to take desperate measures to keep his monstrous mother — and the ever-growing band of her zombie victims — hidden from prying eyes by locking them all in the cellar of his house. But like any dirty secret, this one is bound to come out eventually, and it does so with outrageously gory results during an impromptu party thrown by Lionel's obnoxious Uncle Les (Ian Watkin).

Braindead begins with a close up of the New Zealand flag which then cuts to a shot of Queen Elizabeth II riding a horse, with the British National Anthem playing in the background. It ends with Lionel's zombie mother turning into a giant, Gerald Scarfe-Pink Floyd's *The Wall* — like monstrous matriarch who literally tries to stuff her son back into her uterus. What was Jackson saying about New Zealand under the British monarchy you might ask? Doubtful that Jackson would have been knighted on the strength of *Braindead*! But it did bring him cult status.

Not surprisingly for a film with such extreme gore, *Braindead* met with censorship problems in a number of countries when it was first released in 1993. This caused it to be released in a number of different versions. In Germany the full 104-minute version was banned, and it was eventually released in a heavily cut version that clocked in at a mere 94 minutes. In the

United States it was released in a 94-minute R-rated version under the title *Dead Alive*, and also in a 97-minute unrated cut that kept in most of the gore but lost a few minor scenes that were thought to slow the pace.

Here in the UK, *Braindead* was shown in its full 104-minute uncut glory with an '18' certificate, and the British Board of Film Classification even considered lowering the certificate to a '15', because the censors thought that the film was hilarious! 'I don't much care for horror spoofs,' one BBFC reviewer wrote in his report, 'but this is wonderfully funny — a genuinely entertaining grand guignol farce in which the pace never flags… I was strongly temped to go for "15" despite the endless succession of amputated limbs, torn-off head-skins, beheadings, buckets of blood, dismemberments, pustules bursting, arms being devoured; on and on the comic gore is piled but not without genuine comic structure so that each sight of entire rib cages being torn out, heads being whipped up in a blender and so on is continuously varied by a truly original comic sense.'

The censor goes on to reveal how much he and his colleagues enjoyed the film's sickest scene, featuring Selwyn the zom-baby who gets his comeuppance inside a liquidizer 'The attempt to stuff a wonderfully vicious zombie baby into the blender results in a series of sight gags which had us all in hysterics. In fact, I don't think I've laughed so much at a film all year.'

'In the end I went along with "18" simply on the pragmatic grounds that most people would expect the astonishing amount of gore here to be "18"', the BBFC reviewer concluded, 'But I can't imagine even a sensitive teenager being bothered by this.'

Other BBFC examiners were just as gushing in their praise of *Braindead*, describing how the film's OTT farce and clever editing had the whole team 'rolling about in mirth'. The British censors absolutely loved the film's *Monty Python* humour, for the reason that 'there's none of that undercurrent of cruelty and personalized violence that concerned us in *The Evil Dead* films or *Demons 2*. *Braindead* is played for belly laughs rather than screams or ghoulish chuckles, and it's much less heartless than the recent *Rabid Grannies* (passed "18" uncut).'

Censors, eh? Go figure.

Timothy Balme in *Braindead*
(Wingnut Films, 1992)

Chained (2012)

The emergence in recent years of a number of important women working in the horror genre — Julia Ducournau (*Raw*, 2016; *Titane*, 2021); Ana Lily Amirpour (*A Girl Walks Home Alone at Night*, 2014; *The Bad Batch* 2016; *Mona Lisa and the Blood Moon*, 2021); Jen and Sylvia Soska (*American Mary*, 2012; *Rabid*, 2019); Karyn Kusama (*Jennifer's Body*, 2009; *The Invitation*, 2015); Jennifer Kent (*The Babadook*, 2014) to name but a few — proves that women are taking increasingly influential roles in horror films, both behind the camera and in front of it. There have been notable female horror directors in the past (such as Stephanie Rothman and Mary Lambert) but never before have women been as strong a presence in the genre as they are today. (This goes against the traditional glass-ceiling in the film industry generally.) And as women become more established as a force within horror the range of subject matter that they tackle continues to expand.

Jennifer Lynch's *Chained* shows us that horror films made by women don't necessarily have to be *about* women; on the other hand, the perspective that, as a woman, Lynch brings to the serial killer subgenre is unique.

Shot in just 14 days on a budget of $700,000, *Chained* tells the story of Bob, a middle-aged taxi driver (played by Vincent D'Onofrio) who kidnaps and keeps as prisoner in his farmhouse a nine-year-old boy, Tim (Evan Bird), whose mother he has murdered. Bob attempts to take the boy under his wing and teach him to become a serial killer like himself. As Tim grows to be a teenager (the older Tim is played by Australian actor Eamon Farron), he tries to resist the malign influence of his adoptive 'father' who regularly abducts women to rape and kill. But when Bob brings home a pretty college student called Angie (Conor Leslie) as Tim's 'first time', things start to change.

As her fourth psychological thriller/horror, Lynch made *Chained* in 2012 after *Boxing Helena* (1993), *Surveillance* (2008), and *Hisss* (2010). On its first release, *Boxing Helena* was critically reviled, but its central premise of a person held captive by a 'loved one' is intriguingly reflected in the plot of *Chained*. Love in *Chained* isn't the romantic kind but familial love: it is very much about fathers and sons, and how fathers try to mould their sons in their own image — *Chained* is the ultimate 'bad dad' movie!

Chained started out as a screenplay by Damian O'Donnell (not the one who directed *East is East*) rooted firmly in the torture porn style. Lynch freely admits that she took on *Chained* just so she could work again after the disastrous *Hisss*, a film taken out of her control during editing (Lynch's traumatic experience making *Hisss* was captured in the documentary

Despite the Gods, 2012). However, she took O'Donnell's script and rewrote it herself to reduce its gratuitous violence in favour of a sharper focus on the psychology of the characters: her ambition was to direct a film about "how monsters are made". In this, Lynch succeeds brilliantly: *Chained* is arguably the most intense study of male psychopathy since *Henry: Portrait of a Serial Killer* (1986).

Chained opens with the nine-year-old Tim alone in the isolated farmhouse, looking through a tin of driving licenses. We know immediately that something's afoot: the photos on the licenses are all of different women. The front door smashes open, and Bob enters, dragging with him a girl who is bloody and dishevelled. He throws her to the floor, and there the scene fades. Lynch frames the action in a distancing long shot, to alienate us. She uses this strategy throughout the film.

Much of the action of *Chained* will take place in this farmhouse, in the kitchen area of this pre-title prologue. *Chained* is a very much an interior film; but it never feels less than cinematic, although it is as claustrophobic a chamber-piece as you are likely to see.

A title card tells us it is eight weeks earlier, and we start the story proper as Tim and his mum (played by Julia Ormond) take a trip to the movies. Dad Brad (Jake Weber) has told them to get a taxi home; but tragically for Tim, the taxi they get into happens to be driven by a monster. Pulling off the highway, Bob takes them to his own house and makes short work of Ormond in front of her son. (Lynch leaves us with the image of Tim trapped inside the taxi, hysterically smacking the window with his hands as his mother is dragged away through the garage, through a door and out of sight. It is the last time he will ever see her.) When Bob returns some time later, still spattered with the woman's blood, it is with the news that Mum is dead, and that Tim had better get used to the fact.

Bob lays down the rules. Tim's job from now on is to clean the house: "you will serve me breakfast every morning for the rest of your life." Tim also has to assist in the crimes by cutting out news stories of missing people, store cash from the victims, and keep the driving licences safe. From now on, the farmhouse is Tim's world. Bob re-names him 'Rabbit' (also Lynch's working title for the film), and when Tim tries to escape one day through the attic window, Bob is ready for him. He attaches a long chain to Tim/Rabbit which allows him to move around the house but not flee it.

We cut to nine years later. Tim is now almost fully grown up, and a strange uneasy bond has developed between them. In his own twisted way, Bob can't help but take a paternal interest in the boy: "You are not going to be ignorant", he tells him, "you are going to study and you are going to learn." What Bob gives him to learn, though, is an anatomy text book so that Tim/Rabbit can find out all about the human body, to be an efficient killer just like Bob.

Lynch cast Vincent D'Onofrio because of his ability to play characters who are essentially damaged children, and D'Onofrio gives an astonishing performance as the lumbering, stuttering, semi-literate taxi driver-cum-serial killer. D'Onofrio's Bob is an amalgam of numerous true-life cab driver murderers — David Berkowitz (The Son of Sam), Glen Edward Rogers (The Casanova Killer), Russell Elwood — all of whom used their taxis for finding victims. This lends the character a chilling believability on the surface. On the inside, Bob is not that far away from Private Pyle in *Full Metal Jacket*, 1987 (and there are even shades of *Men in Black*'s Edgar 'The Bug', 1997, in his performance). He is not a natural born killer: he's made into one through the cycle of violence perpetuated in his family.

Although much of *Chained* is from Tim's point of view, Lynch also takes us into the mind of Bob. In an early scene, Bob picks up a father and son in his cab. The pair has an argument, and the domineering father strikes the son. A flash-back shows us that Bob had a tyrant for a father who kept the family in a constant state of terror. As the oldest son, Bob bore the brunt of the abuse. When he reached teenage, Bob's father regarded Bob as a threat to his own position as head of the family. So, Father forced Bob to have sex with his mother to stop him becoming a 'man'. It is Bob's psychosexual problems caused by his father and his family that made him into a sociopath.

Lynch and D'Onofrio invite us to see Bob as a pathetic character rather than as a monster, because even Bob wants to be loved and understood. But what's horrifying is the way that Bob tries to force Tim/Rabbit into the same way of being as himself. He knows only relationships based on pain, damage and abuse.

For the most part, *Chained* is a two-hander between D'Onofrio and Farron. The on-screen chemistry between the two actors is electric. Farron plays Tim/Rabbit as an observer, someone who has learned not to put a foot wrong, because upsetting Bob means risking a beating, possibly far worse. But they are also very much the odd couple. They bicker like a father and son who don't like each other but are forced together because they simply have no-one else. And having somebody — anybody — is better than having nobody. So the sense of identification between them grows, and we start to wonder if Tim/Rabbit may eventually buckle under Bob's will. The Stockholm Syndrome is a psychological condition that can develop in people who are held hostage for long periods of time. They start to form psychological alliances with their captors as a means to survival. We begin to think that this might be happening to Tim/Rabbit in his relationship with his captor, Bob.

When Bob brings Angie home to be Tim's 'graduation present' so comes the crunch. Lynch keeps us guessing as to which way Tim/Rabbit will jump. And later, when Bob allows Tim out of the house to accompany him on a hunt, there is a moment that mirrors the earlier image of the nine-year-old Tim trapped in the taxi as his mother is taken away to be murdered. It's a bookend of sorts for Tim — one that marks the end of childhood, the loss of innocence; and the moment where Tim has to decide upon his own identity.

Lynch suffered problems with the American censor board — the MPAA — with *Chained*. The film was originally rated as an NC-17, which can cause problems for a movie because in the States the NC-17 is still associated with the old X certificate, which was reserved for sexually explicit films: some advertisers and cinemas refuse to show NC-17 films. *Boxing Helena* had been rated NC-17, but changed to an R after appeal. Lynch attempted to appeal for the rating of *Chained* to be changed in the same way, but the decision was upheld. Ultimately, Lynch had to cut the film in order to secure an 'R'. However, the cuts were minimal: reductions were made to a throat slashing scene (the uncut version of the scene is included as an extra 'alternate scene' in the DVD release). But anyone who has seen the documentary *This Film is Not Yet Rated* (2006) knows that these things are often political: explicit or 'disturbing' sex and violence in independent films are often treated differently to the casual violence of big Hollywood studio pictures. As Lynch protests: "Apparently, it's okay for teenagers to see girls getting their breasts chopped off and their heads lopped off if it's funny and slick and sexy, but it's not okay for them to see what real violence is and how hideously quiet and clumsy and haphazard it can be". The delays to *Chained* caused by these censorship problems ultimately delayed the film's release, and Anchor Bay Entertainment ended up putting it out straight-to-DVD.

Chained was only screened theatrically at film festivals, where it has occasionally been programmed in a double-bill with David Lynch's *Eraserhead*. It's tempting to see *Chained* as some kind of riposte to the elder Lynch (critics speculate that *Eraserhead*, 1976, was influenced by David's terror of fathering Jennifer), especially when you consider *Chained*'s controversial twist ending, which undermines our assumption that it was pure fate that brought Tim to be Bob's captive. The film seems to be saying that even 'normal' families can be tainted by abuse. (It's the kind of ending that seems to tie things up a little too neatly on first viewing, but which becomes perfectly logical when you later come to review all the events that preceded it.)

But *Chained* is about much more than just the relationship between a father and child. It ruminates on the way people can come to identify with the aggressor rather than the victim; how the cycle of violence is perpetuated by society's patriarchs. Not a popular message, for sure, especially amongst those newspaper critics who hold 'traditional' values (*The Daily Telegraph* in the UK called it 'a lurid disgrace') — but one that makes for powerful, disturbing viewing nonetheless.

Vincent D'Onofrio in *Chained* (Anchor Bay, 2012)

Creepshow (1982)

'The Most Fun You'll Ever Have Being Scared!" You can count on the fingers of one skeletal hand the number of horror films that are now hailed as classics of the genre but got a lukewarm reception when first released. *The Shining* (1980), for example, now thought of as one of the greatest horror movies ever made, but was panned when it first came out. "Not scary enough", people said back then. Now it's considered plenty scary.

Likewise, George A. Romero and Stephen King's *Creepshow* was deemed only a moderate success when it was released in 1982, to mostly mixed reviews. But it's now enjoying a resurgence of interest thanks to the *Creepshow* web TV series, and the fact that its Michael Gornick-directed 1987 sequel *Creepshow 2* is also getting some love by fans and critics after its initial pasting.

Maybe audiences just 'get' *Creepshow* now, where they didn't back in 1982. Back then it was considered Romero and King's failed experiment, a dry run for the mooted super-production of *The Stand*, a movie long awaited by fans which never happened (not with Romero, anyway, and not as a movie). *Creepshow* was their calling-card to Hollywood, a way to raise the budget and credibility needed for *The Stand*. But *Creepshow* received only a limited theatrical release by Warner Brothers (a three-week run during Halloween season in 1982), and while it was number one in the *Variety* charts for a short while (Romero's only number one hit at the box office), it didn't make back as much money as it could have if it had been given a longer run. Critics compared *Creepshow* to anthology movies of the past, like the ones made by Amicus in the 60s and 70s; they said anthology movies never really work, that they don't do well at the box office, blah blah blah. Very few critics picked up on what Romero and King were actually aiming for — which wasn't a re-run of *The Twilight Zone* or *The Outer Limits*. *Creepshow* was intended as a love-letter to the EC comics that Romero and King had grown up reading in the 1950s — the infamous horror comic books that influenced them to work in the horror genre. *Creepshow* is basically an EC comic brought to life on the movie screen. Not only did the critics fail to understand this, but younger audiences didn't know what EC comics were. They didn't have that frame of reference.

So why the resurgence of interest now? Well, that resurgence has been gradual. *Creepshow* was released in the days before reboots of *The Twilight Zone* and Steven Spielberg's *Amazing Stories* made the TV anthology format popular again. Since then we've had the Laurel (Romero's production company with Richard P. Rubinstein) produced *Tales from the Darkside* and the *Masters of Horror* TV series. The comic book format movie has become immensely popular, of course, thanks to Marvel and DC but also the graphic-novel-brought-to-life techniques of *Sin City* (2005) and *300* (2006) made the live action comic book popular with movie audiences. Their techniques of animating comic book frames, and recreating the inky colour and lighting of graphic novels on film were innovative — but *Creepshow* got there first and people are now beginning to recognize that. More than that, though, *Creepshow* can now be seen as a celebration of the whole EC comic tradition.

Entertaining Comics was founded in 1944 by Maxwell Gaines and quickly gained notoriety for titles like *Tales from the Crypt*, *Vault of Horror* and *The Haunt of Fear*. But it didn't take long to start a backlash against comic books, aimed mainly at EC, which resulted in a Comic Code being formed and the effective ban of horror comics. EC comics went out of business in 1956. But its tradition lived on in the Amicus films made in the 60s and 70s (two of which were based on EC titles), and in the Grand Guignol horror of the 70s like *The Texas Chain Saw Massacre* (1974) which owes a debt of gratitude to EC. In fact, we might look at EC as the missing link between the Parisian Theatre du Grand Guignol, the gruesome horror movies of the 30s like *Mad Love* (1935) and *The Raven* (1935) and the moralistic slasher films of the early 80s.

George Romero himself has said that what he — alongside Stephen King — took from EC was "the irreverence and uninhibited presentation" of the graphic horror on display. In the 50s EC provided an alternative for its youthful audience reacting against materialism and the conformity of the Cold War. The 50s was the era of the teenager and the 'juvenile delinquent'. (In fact, the word 'teenager' did not exist before that era.) After the Second World War, in America, people had money to spend, including young people who often had jobs of their own. Youths started to drive cars and listen to rock 'n' roll. They had much greater independence than ever before. They started to question their parents' beliefs about politics and religion. Youth rebellion started a moral panic about juvenile delinquency and comic books were blamed for corrupting the minds of younger teenagers. When Bill Gaines took over EC from his father Maxwell, he started to engage writers and artists who were veterans of World War Two, who took a cynical view of the Cold War culture and its anti-Communist doctrine.

EC writers started to give their stories socially conscious, progressive themes that anticipated the American Civil Rights movement and 60s counterculture. They offered satirical antidotes to the hypocritical conformism of the McCarthy era. Comics like *Shock Suspense* engaged in social criticism that was considered un-American, condemning militaristic patriotism and lynching. Many EC stories included 'shock endings' that involved decaying corpses rising from their graves, or ironic gruesome twists that served as poetic justice for their characters. EC comics often contained moral elements, showing everyday people who did bad things, getting their just desserts.

EC wasn't afraid to mock its readers, either, who revelled in the gruesome irreverence of stories. The satire of EC was aimed squarely at them, to whom it referred as 'boils and ghouls'. While mainstream culture glorified white suburban domesticity as the American Dream, EC comics chipped away at it, exposing its cracks.

This was all too much for the moral crusaders of America, who blamed EC for the corruption of youth. In 1954, Dr Frederic Wertham, a clinical psychiatrist concerned about the effects of media violence on the minds of children, wrote a book called *Seduction of The Innocent* which levelled the blame for 'juvenile delinquency' directly at comic books of the time. A US Congressional enquiry into the effects of comics was set up, and this led to the Comic Code which required all comics to be given approval before publication. As part of the Comic Code no comic was allowed to use the words 'horror', 'terror' or 'weird' on its cover. Gaines refused to join the Code, and instead stopped publication (with the exception of the long-running satirical *MAD* magazine).

Part of the allure of EC comics was their notoriety and the fact that they were vilified by adults. It made teenagers want to read them all the more. Both Romero and King were avid readers of EC comics when they were kids, and the influence on their work in the horror genre is arguably as great as the 50s B-movies and Gothic horror novels that they also used to love.

In 1987, King elaborated to Paul R. Gagne on what he thought made EC so special. "EC was the last gasp of romanticism in American literature after World War Two. In the EC stories you have these horrible people who actually do the 'nasty' — the husband kills his wife, the bad guy kills the saintly second baseman — but they couldn't let it go at that. The scales were always put back into balance, even if it meant that this decomposing, rotting corpse had to get out of the ground and go after the people who killed him." Essentially King saw EC comic stories as morality tales, and would take that line with *Creepshow* (almost all of the six stories involve characters or things coming back from the grave or out of crates to dish out retribution against the bad guys). During the production of *Creepshow,* King would wear a T-shirt emblazoned with the words: 'A Laurel comic is a moral comic.'

Creepshow's wrap-around story that shows a young boy (played by King's son, Joe — now better known as the author Joe Hill) being punished by his father (played by John Carpenter regular Tom Atkins) for reading EC comics sums up perfectly the illicit lure of the 50s comic book. The boy reads them as an escape from his bullying father (who has his own secret stash of 'girly magazines' in his bedroom drawer). Banished to his room after his father throws the comic book (called *Creepshow*) into the trash, the boy conjures up a spectre — a skeletal figure outside his bedroom window — that is going to make sure Dad gets what's coming to him.

The spectre flies away from the boy's bedroom window to retrieve the *Creepshow* comic from the trash can. At this point the magic happens as live action turns to cartoon animation (courtesy of long-time Romero associate Rick Catizone) and the credit sequence takes the form of a flick through the pages of the cartoon *Creepshow* comic — showing us what we are about to see in the movie. The cartoon sequence is a joy to behold as a celebration of the look and atmosphere of EC.

According to King, the first story — *Father's Day* — is "a deliberate EC pastiche. To my mind, it's the archetypal EC story, with the dead guy coming back and relentlessly offing his family, one after another." The dead guy in question is Nate Grantham, whose family, led by Sylvia Grantham, gets together every year to celebrate his passing. Viveca Lindfors plays Bedelia, the spinster aunt who looked after Nate for most of her life. On his last birthday, Nate's demands of "where's my cake?" finally made Bedelia snap. So, she bludgeoned the old man to death. Now, every year she visits his grave with a bottle of booze to wallow in remorse. The highlight of the story has got to be Nate literally coming out of the grave to strangle the drunken Bedelia to death. Also on Nate's murderous roll call is Ed Harris (fresh from playing King Billy, the idealistic leader of a modern medieval re-enactment troupe in Romero's underrated *Knightriders*, 1981) as Sylvia's son-in-law. In true EC fashion Ed gets his head squelched when he falls into Nate's newly vacated grave and the tombstone falls on *him*. *Father's Day* ends with a classic EC-style still frame of Nate's rotting corpse holding a platter with Sylvia's head on it decorated with candles. "I got my cake!" he cackles victoriously. Nate has become so iconic you can even buy an action figure of him — complete with 'hinged jaw, interchangeable hands, and a head cake accessory!'

Father's Day sets the tone perfectly for *Creepshow*'s EC homage, and *The Lonesome Death of Jordy Verrill* comes next. Stephen King plays the farmer who discovers a meteorite on his land and unwittingly becomes infected by its spore that turns everything — including Jordy — into virulent vegetation (Jordy evidently never saw *The Blob*, 1958, on his old black and white TV, otherwise, he'd know not to mess with 'meteor shit'). Pretty soon green weeds start to sprout all over his land, and on his fingers and tongue too, and gradually take over his whole body, eventually turning him into a kind of walking Christmas tree. King makes us feel quite sorry for poor old Jordy, who doesn't really deserve this fate worse than death. All he wanted was to make a few bucks by selling the meteorite to the local university's 'Department of Meteors' so that he could pay off the loans on his farm. But *The Lonesome Death of Jordy Verrill* strikes the kind of comic-tragic notes that make it a worthy homage to the more mournful aspects of EC-type satire.

Something to Tide You Over sees *Creepshow* back in classic EC territory. Leslie Neilsen plays the jilted husband of Gaylen Ross (who played Fran in Romero's *Dawn of the Dead*, 1978), a ruthless TV producer who sets up a nasty revenge on her and boyfriend Ted Danson (of *Cheers* fame). This involves burying them both up to their necks in sand on a deserted beach, with cameras and TVs set up so they can watch each other drown. Naturally, this being EC and all, the dead don't stay dead, and Neilsen finds himself suffering the same watery fate.

Creepshow's most celebrated segment, *The Crate* is based on King's short story of the same name. *The Crate* works so well as a piece in itself, it's almost like its own mini-movie. Hal Holbrook plays an academic who dreams of offing his obnoxious wife (a show-stealing Adrienne Barbeau). He gets his chance when an old crate of relics housed in the archaeology department of the university (next door to the 'Department of Meteors' presumably) turns out to contain a slathering beast with very sharp teeth that resembles the Tasmanian Devil in the Looney Tunes cartoons. What makes *The Crate* so good is that Romero and King invest it with time to build suspense, to develop the characters and for the story to twist and turn in an intriguing and supremely satisfying way. It's a perfect EC-type tale — with the promise of comeuppance for the wrong-doers just hinted at in the very final frame. Whatever was in the crate may well be back…

The final segment of *Creepshow* is pure Grand Guignol. *They're Creeping Up On You* features a reclusive millionaire (E.G. Marshall) holed up in his sterile New York apartment battling his phobias of germs and bugs. He's a foul-mouthed rotten old bastard as we can tell by the way he treats the bug man (David Early) who arrives to treat a cockroach infestation. Of course, the bugs don't go away — in fact more and more of them turn up, and soon they're all over the apartment, inside his computer, and eventually inside *him*. King lives up to the 'visceral' horror of EC in the final scene, in which the roaches erupt *out* of Marshall's body. All in all, *Creepshow* keeps the EC comic tradition very much alive.

Creepshow (Laurel/Warner Bros, 1982)

Curse of the Undead (1959)

'*Curse of the Undead* is an oddity in that it combines the characteristics of the horror picture with those of the Western. The combination is a well-contrived one that should widen the film's audience since the production draws upon the interest of two extensive categories of motion picture addicts' (*Film Daily*, June 29, 1959).

Telling the story of a preacher, played by Eric Fleming, who is pitted against a vampire (Michael Pate) in the Old West, *Curse of the Undead* is indeed a novel idea for a movie. It is often described as the first Vampire-Western (pre-dating *Billy the Kid Versus Dracula*, 1966, by seven years!) and it pretty much set the template for future Horror-Westerns in the way it manages to combine the two genres. In *Curse of the Undead*, we have a mysterious stranger (Pate) who insinuates himself into the life of the ranch-owner's daughter (Kathleen Crowley), and her fiancé, the preacher, who is the only one to know the truth about the villain. Pate is both a vampire and a dangerous gunslinger. He's on the wrong side of the law, and the enemy of good Christian folk. He preys on the townspeople, including the rogue lord baron who's trying to steal Crowley's land, the town's ineffectual sheriff, and the quack doctor who's mystified by the vampire-murders afflicting the town's women folk. Like every good Western there's a showdown between the good guy and the bad guy, but here it's a shoot-out with a twist as the preacher has imbedded his bullet with a tiny wooden cross...

As *Film Daily* said in its review, 'the elements of the horror film and the Western have been astutely welded into a story that unwinds smoothly and swiftly and that sustains the attention uncommonly well.' *Curse of the Undead* shows us just how much the horror film and the Western have in common. But *Curse of the Undead* is also less of an oddity than *Film Daily* would have it. It wasn't the first Horror-Western, for example, and definitely not the last. *Bone Tomahawk* (2015) may have brought the Horror-Western to many people's attention, but this hybrid genre has been going since the silent days. In fact, some fans and scholars claim the Horror-Western to be part of a wider hybrid, the Supernatural Western (which can be said to be part of the Weird Western!) of which there are numerous examples (I count at least seventy American movies that belong to the Supernatural/Weird Western). Some notable ones are *Black Noon* (1971), *High Plains Drifter* (1972), *White Buffalo* (1977), *Ghost Town* (1988), *Ravenous* (1999), *The Quick and the Undead* (2006), *The Burrowers* (2008) and *Jonah Hex* (2010), amongst others.

As mentioned, the Horror-Western dates back to the silent era (with *Haunted Range*, 1926); it enjoyed a heyday of sorts in the late 50s (*Curse of the Undead*; *The Living Coffin*, both 1959) and a brief resurgence in the late 60s/70s (*And God Said To Cain*, 1970; *Black Moon*, 1971) before re-emerging again in the 90s with films such as *Grim Prairie Tales* (1990) and *Phantom Town* (1998). Since then there have been a steady trickle of titles, like *The Dead and the Damned* (2011), *Exit Humanity* (2012) and *Blood Moon* (2015). When you consider how tied up with themes of 'good vs evil' horror films and Westerns are, it's not so surprising how closely the two genres are linked.

According to an article in *Midnight Marquee*, *Curse of the Undead* started as a tongue-in-cheek satire cooked up by husband-and-wife writing team Edward and Mildred Dein, a 'Western horror story about a fag vampire running around the desert eating little boys'. It's difficult to believe such a claim, given that a story like that would certainly have been vetoed by the Production Code Administration, and that Universal International producer Joseph Gershenson on hearing about the story from his wife, purportedly phoned Edward Dein immediately, telling him that he wanted to make the picture based on the bare-bones idea alone. More likely is that Gershenson and Dein managed to sell Universal on the concept of a Vampire-Western following the success of the Gershenson-produced *Monster on the Campus* (1958) for Universal the previous year. Gershenson (who was also a highly successful musical director for Universal) had also been a producer on *House of Dracula* (1945) and therefore had some background in the horror genre. Dein had started as a scriptwriter in B-movies in the early 40s, penning gangster scripts for the Producers Releasing Corporation (PRC) before working on the dialogue of *The Leopard Man* (1943) for Val Lewton at RKO. He later co-wrote the screenplay of the 1946 version of *The Cat Creeps*. Dein had graduated to directing in 1952 with romantic drama-thriller *Come Die My Love*, shot in Spanish and starring a young Honor Blackman. His previous film to *Curse of the Undead*, as director, had in fact been a Western called *Seven Guns to Mesa* (1958).

The Affairs of a Vampire (the working title of *Curse of the Undead*), was shot in eighteen days on the Universal backlot, with the standing set of a Western town doubling for the Texas-Mexico border village where the story takes place. The opening credits feature a view of a stucco mission house with a Spanish-style doorway, on which has been placed a wreath. We then see views of the village cemetery, and its many tombstones and crosses. Pate's vampire, it is revealed later in the film, is in fact a Spanish nobleman called Drago Robles, who committed suicide after killing his own brother in an argument over a woman. Right from this credit sequence *Curse of the Undead* manages to link the imagery of the classic Western, as well as the typical characters and story scenarios of Westerns, with those of the classic horror movie. Most obvious, of course, are the references to Bram Stoker's *Dracula* — no doubt Hammer's *Horror of Dracula* (1958) was in Universal's mind too. As the titles close, a horse-drawn carriage ferries Dolores (Crowley) to a ranch house where the local doctor is taking care of a patient — a young woman, Cora, who has been mysteriously drained of her blood. There also is Preacher Dan Young, whose ministrations have helped keep the woman alive — at least for the time being. The situation and characters (as well as the flat way that Dein films the action) are perfectly in keeping with the black and white Westerns of the 50s; but they could just as easily be substituted for Bram Stoker — with Preacher Dan as Van Helsing/Jonathan Harker, Dolores as Mina and Doctor Carter (50s horror/science-fiction stalwart John Hoyt) as Doctor Seward ministering over stricken vampire victim, Lucy. Dr Carter informs us that this is "an epidemic affecting only young girls. If I was superstitious, I'd say it was more like a curse." When the trio leaves Cora alone for a moment, to drink coffee down in the kitchen (the very picture of a frontier family!), there is a blood-curdling scream! Preacher Dan hot-foots it back into Cora's bedroom just as the window blind clatters shut and finds Cora dead in her bed — two tell-tail bite marks on her neck.

Only the clothes and set dressings tell us that this is the Wild West and not Victorian England, but the gothic theme ties the genres together seamlessly. And in classic Westerns, as in gothic horror, Christianity saves the day. Interestingly, for this reason, *Curse of the Dead* almost wasn't made at all, because the Production Code Administration had serious misgivings about having a Protestant preacher carry a gun and slay a vampire! In a letter addressed to Universal's legal department, George A. Heimrich, the PCA's West Coast director wrote:

'After a careful review of your screenplay, "The Affairs of a Vampire," it is our opinion that it is a picture which the vast number of Protestants would object to. The characteristics and portrayal of Preacher Dan for one thing is certainly not true as to the belief of the vast majority of Protestants.' Heimrich directed Universal to a specific scene in the script in which 'it is definitely inferred by Preacher Dan that it is the Will of the Lord that a man should be murdered. Nothing could be further from the truth. Protestants also do not believe that a preacher should be placed in the position of putting a gun "into a man's gut" and pulling the trigger, as on page 69, scene 169. We definitely believe that it is most offensive when you have a preacher using such words as "Business, Hell!" as on page 40, scene 88.'

Also offensive to Heimrich, who seemed to take on the role of Protestant spokesman, were Preacher Dan's words in the same scene, "You quivering lump of lard!" and later in the script a line where Preacher Dan retorts to Drago, "I'll see you dead!"

Summing up his letter, Heimrich concluded that Universal 'would be much better off if you did not involve a preacher in this screenplay at all.'

While Universal was told that *Curse of the Undead* would be offensive to Protestant audiences, the Roman Catholic Church, on the other hand, had no problem with it! When the film was released in May 1959, the Legion of Decency, an organization dedicated to combatting movies objectionable to the Roman Catholic Church, classified it as 'morally *un*objectionable' and approved it for an adult audience, despite the vampires and the gun-toting preacher.

Horror had, by this time, become carefully regulated under the Production Code (which was about to change when Hitchcock's *Psycho* was released the following year in 1960). The Code itself had been reduced to a checklist which each film was subjected to. *Curse of the Undead* went before the PCA in January 1959, and it ticked several boxes in terms of censorship concerns. Interestingly, in terms of genre, the PCA categorized it as a 'Melo (drama)-horror', but acknowledged its time period as the 'development of the West', with settings listed as 'Western town-Homes-Sheriff's Office-Saloon-Western Exteriors-Mausoleum-Cemetery'. In terms of its 'portrayal of "races" and nationals', Drago raised some concerns, marked as unsympathetic, with his race being prominently featured in the film. Balancing this out in the PCA's eyes, though, were the crimes he committed — 'killings by vampire' — and that the story tended not to enlist the sympathy of the audience for the criminal, and that his fate was to be killed at the end. The ending was thus marked 'happy'!

Despite any censorship objections that *Curse of the Undead* might cause, or any offence to Protestant audiences, the critics received the film on the whole quite favourably. This was thanks largely to the novelty of the script. Amongst the best moments in the film are, without doubt, the scenes in the mausoleum where Drago returns to his coffin as the sun goes down. Dressed all in black, like the gunslinger he is, with his black Stetson and his six guns holstered, as he lifts the lid of his coffin, ready to climb in, Pate makes for a striking figure, the perfect but totally unexpected juxtaposition of Western movie and horror iconography in the same frame: incongruous but at the same time making perfect sense to horror addicts and Western aficionados alike.

There can be little doubt that *Curse of the Undead* had an influence on the Horror-Westerns that followed it. If we think of the horror film as the Western's dark shadow, then the Horror-Western, of course, makes perfect sense. Western movies traditionally portray the American Dream, Horror movies embody our nightmares. Those two worlds are the flipside of each other. They coexist in our subconscious and it's not hard to imagine one quickly turning into the other. As Preacher Dan himself might say, "There's somethin' mighty strange goin' on in this here town…"

Michael Pate and Kathleen Crowley in *Curse of the Undead* (Universal, 1959)

Day of the Dead (1985)

'To me it is a matter of some urgency that *Day of the Dead* receive at last the attention and respect it deserves. It is if anything more important today than it was when it was made. If not quite about the end of *the* world, it is clearly about the end of *ours*, which it now seems that little short of a universal miracle can prevent.'

When film critic Robin Wood wrote those words about the third in George A. Romero's zombie trilogy in 2003, he was bemoaning a film that had all but sunk without trace on its release in 1985 and which had met with little enthusiasm from the critics. Audiences and film reviewers didn't seem to appreciate its commentary on militaristic macho-ism in the Reagan era. One critic even called it a "cesspool of vile filth produced by a sick mind for sick-minded people." Thankfully it's now regarded by fans and critics alike as one of Romero's best — a movie that stood in opposition to the jingoistic multiplex blockbusters of the 80s like *Top Gun* (1986). As Wood wrote, 'It was an extraordinary film to come upon in the midst of the *Rockys*, the *Rambos*, the *Back to the Futures*, that dominated the era: it still seems extraordinary today.'

I first came upon *Day of the Dead* in a cinema in Rome in 1986 (where it was released under the title *Il Giorno Degli Zombi*). The movie house was filled with overexcited Italian teenagers. They talked loudly through the whole movie except for the Tom Savini gore scenes where they cheered, whistled and stamped their feet. Then they would go back to talking amongst themselves until the next gore scene when they'd cheer some more. The movie was dubbed into Italian. I don't speak Italian, but it was pretty clear to me that *Day of the Dead* was a talky film, and that a lot of that talk seemed to be deeply philosophical. It was also clear that Tom Savini's effects went far beyond what had ever been seen in a movie before in terms of their sheer, bloody wizardry. It was only when I got back to England and *Day* was released in cinemas here about four months later (in September 1986) that I actually got to understand what the characters were talking about, and that some of the gore effects had been censored by the BBFC.

It's true that *Day* is a very dialogue-heavy film. Paul R. Gagne, who wrote the excellent book *The Zombies That Ate Pittsburgh* chalks up the poor reviews for the film to disappointed critics "who wanted more than a couple of gory zombie attacks and a lot of arguing and preachy philosophy". But time has been good to *Day* and what seemed like a lot of arguing and preachy philosophy then now seems like claustrophobic tension between characters and pretty relevant philosophy, actually, about the way we humans have brought about the end of the world through our aggression towards each other.

Famously, the version of *Day of the Dead* that Romero made was a stripped-down version of the original screenplay that Romero had intended to be the third part of his trilogy. That version had been budgeted at a cost of $6.5 million. The financier United Film Distribution Company told Romero and his producer Richard Rubinstein that for that price they would have to deliver a movie that would be guaranteed an 'R' certificate by the American censor, the MPAA. But UFD had put *Dawn of the Dead* (1978) out as an unrated film because of its ground-breaking gore, and *Day of the Dead* was set to be just as gory — if not gorier — than *Dawn*. To avoid being given an 'X' — which at the time was box office poison — *Day* would have to be released without an MPAA rating like *Dawn*. This was still a problem because some newspapers and theatres refused to show or feature the unrated film, thereby impacting on box office revenues. The bottom line was that UFD didn't think they would make their money back on an investment of $6.5 million if they put *Day* out unrated; and Romero and Rubinstein knew that to cut the gore out in order to get an 'R' would disappoint their fan-base and result in a movie that people didn't want to see. In the end Romero had little choice but to compromise and re-tailor the script to a smaller budget ($3.5 million) if they were going to keep the gore intact. In order to make *Day* fit into this budget parameter, Romero had to rethink the screenplay altogether. At the time he regretted doing this as *Day* turned out to be a completely different movie to what he had originally intended — the storyline had to be changed. And a lot of fans also lamented that the original screenplay for *Day* could not be used. In fact, it's possible to argue that the message of *Day* never really changed — the film version still carries the same social commentary as the original screenplay. In my opinion, it's maybe a bit sharper than the original screenplay in this respect. To see how Romero's message stayed the same even though *Day*'s script changed, we need to look closer at Romero's idea for his zombie trilogy.

Romero claimed to have first got the idea for a trilogy sometime in the 60s, before he even made the ground-breaking *Night of the Living Dead* in 1968. He had read a book called *I Am Legend* by the sci-fi horror writer Richard Matheson and saw in it a metaphor for a revolutionary society overturning the currently functioning society, but thought that Matheson had not followed through with the implications of the idea. *I Am Legend* was about the last survivor on Earth after a virus had turned everyone into vampires. Romero changed vampires to zombies and, according to him, wrote a short story about the end of civilization as we know it: the living dead rising up against living and taking over. He wrote it as a short story of three parts.

The first part — which eventually became *Night* — saw the beginning of the revolution — with the zombies beginning to grow in numbers, but with the humans basically staying on top of the situation. In the second part, the zombies are beginning to take over, but it's still undecided who is going to win out. In the final part of the story (which only existed as a couple of sentences in the short story) the zombie society has become the dominant one, with only a few human survivors left.

While the first part of the story became *Night* (co-written with John Russo), Romero took the middle part and developed it into *Dawn of the Dead*. This was ten years after his first film and Romero wanted the metaphor to be relevant for America in the 70s as *Night* had been for the 60s — so *Dawn* became the commentary on consumerism that we all know and love. Romero and Rubinstein produced *Dawn* independently and sold the American distribution rights to UFD in 1978. By then, Romero had already started to think about a third film and knew that he wanted to bring the story to a kind of full circle. While the human survivors were in the minority and had set up their own mini-society as a refuge against the zombies (who had by then basically taken over the world) nothing had really changed in the way that human society was being run. The human 'sell outs' were feeding the zombies in a bid to control them and turn them into an army so that a megalomaniac tyrant could use them against his enemies in a bid to rule the world (or what's left of it).

Romero's original screenplay of *Day* is available on the internet, and makes for a fascinating comparison with the film version that Romero eventually shot.

The script starts in Florida. It's now five years after the zombie outbreak of *Night* and *Dawn*. We are introduced to a boatful of human survivors making their way to an island off the Florida coast. These survivors are called Sarah, Miguel, Tony, Chico and Maria. A fight with other humans at the city marina sees Tony die from gunshot wounds and returning as a zombie to bite Maria, who commits suicide rather than become one of the living dead. Miguel also gets bitten, but Sarah cuts off his arm before the infection can take hold.

Arriving at the island, Sarah, Chico and Miguel discover a huge military installation populated by a group of soldiers led by Captain Rhodes. Rhodes and his men have already trained a number of zombies to become soldiers. Rhodes is able to control them by feeding them human meat from refrigerated cartons. But where is this meat coming from? Sarah, Miguel and Chico battle Rhodes and his men — Miguel is killed, Chico is captured.

Sarah manages to escape and is rescued by a Caribbean islander called John and his friend McDermott. These two turn out to be inhabitants of the island, too, but they are on a lower social rung than the soldiers. Sarah finds out that the island has been divided into sectors. The lowest sector (to which John and McDermott belong) is made up of ethnic minorities, Irish, political dissidents (like the mad scientist Dr Logan), and disabled people as well as social undesirables — drug addicts, criminals, prostitutes. It is this sector of human beings that is being used as zombie meat to feed the military-trained living dead. The next social level up comprises a team of scientists — headed by Mary and Dr Fisher. They are studying zombie behaviour in a bid to control the living dead. Their star pupil is 'Bub', an intelligent zombie who seems to have formed a close attachment to Mary. In the original script the scientists are basically in hock with the soldiers — at first they don't question the morality of what they are doing. Instead they follow military orders and do what they do 'in the name of science'.

At the head of it all is one man: former Florida Governor Henry Dickerson. He has complete control of the island's complex, and has set up a lifestyle of luxury for himself complete with a harem of beautiful women who wait on him hand and foot. Dickerson (who is nicknamed Gasparilla after a pirate) has made his empire a stronghold of the living dead, and has plans to conquer not only the rest of America but the entire world with his growing army of zombies!

Sarah, John and McDermott eventually join forces with Mary and the others to start a rebellion against the island's tyrannical regime. In the ensuing battle, the zombies are accidentally unleashed and start eating their way through the residents of the complex. Sarah and the other rebels (which includes a bunch of *Mad Max Beyond Thunderdome*, 1985, — type kids) flee the island and find their own — a tropical paradise where they start up afresh as an equal society. At that point it also becomes clear that the recently dead are no longer returning to life — the zombie plague is finally over!

Fans of Romero's movies will probably recognize elements of this story in his other films. For a long time after *Day*'s release there had been rumours of Romero making a fourth zombie movie. Fans started to call it *Twilight of the Dead*, although Romero always denied that he was working on a film with this title. With the backing of Universal Studios, Romero made *Land of the Dead* in 2005. Romero actually went back to his original *Day* script and used a lot of the story situations: this time, though, he set the story in Pittsburgh (actually, shot in Toronto) and substituted a swanky high-rise condo development complete with boutique shopping mall instead of the underground facility of the *Day* script. This he called Fiddler's Green, and its main occupant was a Gasparilla-type called Kaufman. Kaufman still lords it over the denizens of Fiddler's Green including a ghetto of poor people, and mercilessly puts down any attempts at rebellion. Eventually, though, Kaufman's core people start to turn against him and plan a fresh start in Canada. Meanwhile a legion of the living dead, led by the intelligent zombie, Big Daddy, lay siege to Fiddler's Green as revenge for Kaufman's slaughter of the zombies.

Land of the Dead and the final film in Romero's zombie series, *Survival of the Dead* (2009), followed the themes of the original *Day* script faithfully. We have the rich tyrants who exploit the zombie apocalypse for their own benefits, and the strict segmentation of the surviving human society by class divisions. And we have the rebellion that takes place alongside the zombie revolution itself. We have the people we can identify with who want to start afresh and put the old society's ways into the past: those who want to build a new, fairer society and those who want to hold on to the values of the old one.

Day of the Dead as it was actually filmed has elements of all of these things, but they are not quite as pronounced as they were in the original *Day* script (or in fact in *Land*). *Day* takes place solely inside the military facility somewhere in Florida. The character of Sarah (Lori Cardille) is a combination of Sarah and Mary from the original script. She is the lone woman among the male survivors, a scientist who follows orders but tries to be the voice of reason throughout. She believes in her mission to try to find out what caused the zombie virus and therefore to find a cure and a way of stopping it. Gradually, though, she comes to see the situation around her as hopeless. The macho Rhodes is a gung-ho soldier who has staged a coup to put himself in charge — he is more a military dictator than a politician (interestingly, we never find out who the higher authority is in the film — who Rhodes took his orders from before he turned renegade). John and McDermott are still Sarah's allies in the film version, but they are soldiers too. The film shows gradually how Sarah, John and McDermott become rebels against Rhodes. The focus of this change is Sarah, as she slowly starts to abandon her mission of seeking a cure for the virus, giving up hope of saving society as it used to be, and instead begins to see the way forward of setting up a new society no longer based on macho war-mongering values. It is her inner strength that makes Sarah the true leader of the people in this respect. In this she has a mentor in John who gradually persuades her to take up that role. A lengthy dialogue exchange between them becomes *Day*'s beating heart:

John: We don't believe in what you're doing here, Sarah. Hey, you know what they keep down here in this cave? Man, they got the books and the records of the top 100 companies. They got the Defence Department budget down here. And they got the negatives for all your favourite movies. They got microfilm with tax returns and newspaper stories. They got immigration records, census reports, and they got the accounts of all the wars and plane crashes and volcano eruptions and earthquakes and fires and floods and all the other disasters that interrupted the flow of things in the good ole U.S. of A. Now what does it matter, Sarah darling? All this filing and record keeping? We ever gonna give a shit? We even gonna get a chance to see it all? This is a great, big, 14 mile tombstone! With an epitaph on it that nobody gonna bother to read.

Now, here you come. Here you come with a whole new set of charts and graphs and records. What you gonna do? Bury them down here with all the other relics of what once was? Let me tell you what else…You ain't never gonna figure it out, just like they never figured out why the stars are where they're at. It ain't mankind's job to figure that stuff out. So what you're doing is a waste of time, Sarah. And time is all we got left, you know.

Sarah: What I'm doing... is all there's left to do.

John: Shame on you. There's plenty to do. Plenty to do, so long as there's you and me and maybe some other people. We could start over, start fresh, get some babies…and teach 'em, Sarah, teach 'em never to come over here and dig these records out.

It's a strongly written speech by Romero, beautifully delivered by Terry Alexander as John, and it could almost be thought of as the centrepiece of Romero's zombie films — their key message.

As Robin Wood said in his praise of *Day of the Dead*: the power of the film lies in the way that John, Sarah and McDermott start out as being connected or belonging to the authority group headed by Rhodes, but 'in the course of the film they progressively dissociate themselves, by their actions and their attitudes, from these nominal allegiances, forming an oppositional group of their own'. Like in *Star Wars*, it's the rebellion against the Empire that gives us hope. *Day* shows how such a rebellion might start. For Romero, the future of humanity depends on people like Sarah, John and McDermott. While those with the military mentality like Rhodes are destined to perish — torn apart and eaten by zombies.

Dr Terror's House of Horrors (1965)

Think of Amicus, and you will most probably picture those wonderful British anthology horror movies of the 60s and 70s with tongue-in-cheek titles like *The House That Dripped Blood* (1971), *Asylum* (1972), *Tales from the Crypt* (1972) and *Vault of Horror* (1973). More camp than Hammer, Amicus was, nonetheless, for a time that studio's main competitor in the UK horror film industry. From 1965 to 1976 Amicus churned out a slew of product for the international market (many titles distributed by American International Pictures) that, as well as horror pictures, included thrillers (*The Psychopath*, 1966), science fiction (*The Terrornauts*, *They Came from Beyond Space*, both 1967), *Dr Who* spin-offs (*Dr Who and The Daleks*, 1965; *Daleks' Invasion Earth 2150 A.D.*, 1966) and Edgar Rice Burroughs adaptations (*The Land that Time Forgot*, 1975; *At the Earth's Core*, 1976).

But it's for their seven portmanteau horror films that Amicus is best remembered. Although Amicus didn't invent the portmanteau horror (that honour must surely go to Paul Leni's *Waxworks* made in Weimar Republic Germany in 1924) or even set the template for compendium horrors (the British film *Dead of Night* did that in 1945), they did popularize the form with movies like *Torture Garden* (1967) and *From Beyond the Grave* (1974). And it was an Amicus production that started it all back in 1965: *Dr Terror's House of Horrors*.

Milton Subotsky's screenplay for *Dr Terror's House of Horrors* was, in the writer-producer's own words, "a beautiful package of entertainment", featuring a compendium of five stories in the horror vein. Subotsky's script had originally been intended as a TV series, and, according to some sources, written as early as 1948. If this was indeed the case, then it goes to prove that in the movie business timing is everything. By 1965 the public was ready for a portmanteau horror film and *Dr Terror's House of Horrors* would mark the turning point for Amicus.

Dr. Terror plays like a classic anthology horror. Five men board a train heading for the fictional town of Bradley. On board they encounter the mysterious Dr Schreck (Peter Cushing), who offers to read each man's fortune using tarot cards (which Schreck calls his 'house of horrors'). We see the men's stories in turn, each of which is marked by supernatural or fantastical events: an architect returns to his ancestral home to discover a werewolf stalking its halls; an intelligent plant threatens a family trapped inside their summer home; a jazz musician steals the music of a voodoo witch doctor and pays the price; the severed hand of an artist plagues an arrogant art critic; and a young doctor comes to suspect that his new bride is a vampire. Each story ends in a fate worse than death for the man whose fortune is told. Later, Schreck informs them the only way each can avoid his terrible fate is by dying first.

Even from this bare bones outline we can see the influence of two previous landmark portmanteau horrors. *Waxworks* is notable for its casting of German stars Emil Jannings (*Faust*, 1926), Conrad Veidt (*The Man Who Laughs*, 1928) and Werner Krauss (*The Cabinet of Dr Caligari*, 1920) in a trio of stories about a wax museum and a writer hired to imagine the tales of the exhibits there. Only one of the stories, 'Jack the Ripper', about the waxwork figure of Spring-Heeled Jack which comes alive and stalks the writer in the halls and corridors of the museum, can really be described as 'horror'. The other two stories are a mix of Arabian Nights adventure and historical drama. But the conventions of anthology horror films are there in other ways, including in the twist ending of the framing story, in which the writer wakes up to realize that being chased by Jack the Ripper was a dream. *Waxworks* is imbued with German Expressionism, and its style would influence many filmmakers to come, especially in the Universal classics of the 30s and 40s.

Dead of Night is even more influential. Produced by Ealing Studios, it boasts not only five stories, but four major directors of the era: Alberto Cavalcanti, Robert Hamer, Charles Crichton and Basil Dearden. The segment that everyone remembers, though, is one of Cavalcanti's, 'The Ventriloquist's Dummy', which stars Michael Redgrave as a ventriloquist who becomes convinced that his dummy is alive. But Hamer's episode 'The Haunted Mirror' — about a man who buys an antique mirror only to find it casts a ghostly reflection — is memorable too. In fact Amicus would remake the story in their final anthology, *From Beyond the Grave*: a fitting tribute to *Dead of Night*. This black and white Ealing classic still manages to raise a chill. It starts with a man awaking from a nightmare, from which he flees to a weekend party at a friend's country house whose assembled guests he has seen before in a recurring dream. The guests tell each other their tales of the supernatural and we see each one unfold in turn. The film ends where it began, with the man awakening from what he takes to be a bad dream, before driving off to the manor house where the cycle will begin all over again in a never-ending nightmare. The influence of *Dead of Night* is apparent in the premise and structure of *Dr Terror*, the queasy mix of comedy and horror, the framing story with the twist ending, and even in some of the detail: both films feature architects who visit country houses.

Dr Terror's House of Horrors begins as each of the five passengers board the train for Bradley. In some ways this introduction to the main characters is the one of the film's most effective sequences, much because it is done visually, with almost no dialogue. There's some nice business with the carriage door that won't close, and with the ways that the men try to manoeuvre around each other for a seat without disturbing the haughty Christopher Lee, who is first one on. Then a hand outside wipes off the steam from the train window and we glimpse — alarmingly — Peter Cushing with bushy eyebrows peering in. "Room for one more?" he asks as he embarks — a nod to *Dead of Night*'s segment with a bus conductor whose repeated cry is "Room for just one more inside."

Once the men are settled in the carriage, director Freddie Francis and his director of photography, the ever-versatile Alan Hume, stage the first of the film's many visual coups. As Cushing looks from one man to the next, the camera moves around the back of his head, framing each man in turn — sizing up the subjects for the fateful tarot reading. It is just one of several visual flourishes that add immensely to the suspense in the film. In later sequences, such as 'Werewolf', Francis uses a similar creeping camera movement that tracks across the rooms or hallways, searching for the source of terror or point of interest. In the 'Voodoo' vignette, as Biff Bailey (Roy Castle) walks home through darkened empty streets, Francis stages a vivid suspense sequence that reminds the viewer very much of 1942's *Cat People*. There's even a Val Lewton-like 'bus' moment as the door of a telephone box swings open shockingly into the frame. Even if Francis was not altogether the greatest director (as some of his later Hammer films show), there is no doubt that he was a brilliant visual stylist whose talent with the camera adds immeasurably to *Dr Terror*.

Subotsky would later claim that he preferred short stories to novels or novellas in his Amicus adaptations for science fiction and horror films, as he felt the short form worked better for those genres than longer fiction works. There may be some truth in that but the main weakness of *Dr Terror* — and of most anthology horrors — is precisely the lack of story and character development. With each segment lasting only fifteen minutes, there is very little time to build character, suspense or mood. Maybe because of that reason, the format lends itself too readily to clichés and to becoming formulaic. But one could easily level this criticism to horror anthology movies and TV shows outside the Amicus stable, even to the format itself.

The portmanteau horror film, as numerous critics have pointed out, is by nature uneven and inconsistent. While all the stories in *Dr Terror* are entertaining, only one — 'Disembodied Hand' — is (if you'll excuse the pun) genuinely gripping. Christopher Lee gives a fine performance as the uptight art critic fighting hysteria as the severed hand keeps reappearing in his life after repeated attempts are made to destroy it. He tries to burn it, drown it, but the damn thing keeps coming back to stalk him. Eventually it gets caught in his windscreen wipers as Lee is driving home in the pouring rain, causing a tragic accident in which Lee gets his comeuppance. The severed hand with a life of its own is an old idea, of course, dating back to Robert Florey's 1946 *The Beast with Five Fingers* by way of Thing in *The Addams Family*. In 1981, Oliver Stone borrowed the concept for *The Hand*, starring Michael Caine as a comic book artist whose appendage takes to murder after he loses it in a car crash. (Perhaps the most amusing variation on the theme is Patrick McGrath's 1988 short story, *Hand of a Wanker*.) Still, it's a creepy idea, and the crawling mechanical hand itself, which cost Amicus £400 to build, is eerily effective.

The weakest segment, by contrast, is 'Creeping Vine', which never manages to be convincing. More science fiction than horror, it seems out of place in a horror anthology. Intriguingly, Freddie Francis reputedly directed several scenes of 1963's *Day of the Triffids*, including some of those featuring special effects, so it may be that 'Creeping Vine' was included partly for that reason. Like *Day of the Triffids* it includes a sequence where people are trapped inside a house, and Hitchcock's *The Birds* (1963) had been a recent hit, which might also explain Amicus's enthusiasm for the segment. Also, with a small cast and a confined location, it would have been relatively inexpensive to film, and this would have been a consideration too. But in many ways it's the framing story of *Dr Terror* — the tarot reading scenes set on the train — that really holds the film together. A strong story in itself, it's also an effective and memorable linking device for the individual segments.

More blackly comic than Hammer, more playful and prone to send themselves up, Amicus proved itself with *Dr Terror's House of Horrors* to be a distinctive company in its own right, and a worthy rival to Britain's most eminent horror studio. Amicus would go on to make films in a number of genres, including classic non-anthology horror movies like *The Skull* (1965), but for most fans, it's the portmanteau films that really stand out. And for many of us, anthology horror will always mean, first and foremost, Amicus.

Roy Castle in *Dr Terror's House of Horrors* (Amicus, 1965)

Drag Me to Hell (2009)

The Guardian called it recession-era horror: 'bank worker refuses Hungarian crone more time to pay her mortgage, resulting in a curse, three days of demonic torture and the prospect of eternal damnation'. Director Sam Raimi himself claimed that the credit crunch was a coincidence; that he just wanted to tell "the story of a person who wants to be a good person but who makes a sinful choice out of greed, for their own benefit, and pays the price for it." But *Drag Me to Hell* marked a return to form both for Raimi and for the horror genre. Appearing soon after thousands of Americans lost their homes in the worst financial crisis since the Great Depression, *Drag Me to Hell* saw Raimi make not just his *first* horror movie since *Army of Darkness* (1992) but one that seemed to key directly into the times. Casting Alison Lohman as the hapless bank loans officer who suffers the consequences for having a gypsy woman's house repossessed, Raimi crafted a good old-fashioned morality tale about society's greed and selfishness, and how greed leads to destruction.

Drag Me to Hell, from an original screenplay by Raimi and his brother Ivan, seems at first glance to reprise much of what made *The Evil Dead* trilogy so popular with fans. There's the wildly kinetic camera style. The splatstick comedy mixed with genuinely creepy horror. There are gross out moments. There's even a few eyeball *boings* á la The Three Stooges. But look closer and the themes of *Drag Me to Hell* tie in closely with those of Raimi's *A Simple Plan* (1998). In that movie, the discovery of a stash of money in a backwoods community leads to lies and deception, turning brother against brother, bringing misery and murder. As in *Drag Me to Hell* the lust for money leads to a living hell for our characters, and the moral of the story is that greed destroys everything that it touches — family, community, friendship, trust and brotherly love.

Ivan and Sam actually started work on the screenplay of *Drag Me to Hell* in the late 1990s, after Raimi's neo-western *The Quick and the Dead* (1995) and around the time of *A Simple Plan*. Back then the script was called simply 'The Curse'. The story grew out of the brothers' fascination with curses and the idea of what might happen to an ordinary person if they were cursed by a witch — what lengths would they go to get the spell lifted? In the script, that person is Christine Brown (Lohman), a young loan officer trying to get ahead in her job, cement her relationship with boyfriend Clay (Justin Long) and generally make a go of her life. When she is approached for a loan extension by the elderly Mrs Ganush (Lorna Raver), Christine faces a difficult choice. Should she try to impress her boss (who's considering her for promotion) by showing him that she can make tough decisions? Even in the knowledge that if she denies the loan extension to Mrs Ganush, the bank will foreclose and the woman's house will get repossessed? When Christine decides to go the selfish route and deny the loan, her world falls apart: she becomes victim of forces beyond her control. According to Raimi, "she does one bad thing. She's makes a choice to sin; it sets the ball in motion, and the movie's about payback to her…She's put into a situation where her punishment does not fit her crime".

In most of Raimi's films the protagonists — from Ash in *The Evil Dead* (1982) to Peter Parker in the *Spiderman* movies — are reluctant heroes, and have to be dragged kicking and screaming into action. So it is with Christine, whose curse pulls her into a fantastical, supernatural world where she has to deal with all kinds of weirdness and horror: an unseen presence that seems to pervade her home, a sudden gushing nosebleed that appears out of nowhere, and the phantom of Mrs Ganush herself, transformed into a hellish vengeful ghostlike figure.

Raimi fashions the film so that we are with Christine every step of the way, drawn into her fracturing world, sharing her point of view. We identify with Christine's predicament, even as she is forced to take extreme action in order to survive her terrifying ordeal. As he does in *The Evil Dead*, Raimi is not afraid to take us down dark paths as Christine is driven, in Raimi's words, "to make choices that could alienate the audience, darker and darker choices, so that she can survive this terrible ordeal she's going through."

In the screenplay, Sam and Ivan drew on the M. R. James story 'Casting the Runes' (made into the classic film *Night of The Demon* [Aka *Curse of The Demon*] in 1957). In both works, the victim suffers a curse for three days that can only be lifted if it is passed on to somebody else. In the James story the curse is passed from person to person by a physical object — a parchment on which a rune is written. In *Drag Me to Hell* the object is a button from Christine's coat upon which Mrs Ganush has placed a curse, which Christine desperately tries to pass back to the woman later on.

Another 'borrowed' feature is the demon itself that purses the accursed victims in an attempt to devour them. In *Drag Me to Hell*, Raimi makes this demon a 'Lamia', a mythic beast that has taken many shapes and forms throughout history, sometimes portrayed as a child-eating monster in Greek literature, or a serpent-like succubus who devours young men in later classical periods. But the one thing that the legends have in common, according to Ivan Raimi, is that the Lamia "is a demon that, when awoken in anger, drags its victims down to hell screaming!"

What sort of horror film did Sam Raimi set out to make? In an interview with *Post Magazine*, he set out his stall: "A horror film with lots of wild moments and lots of suspense and big shocks that'll hopefully make audiences jump. But I also wanted to have a lot of dark humor sprinkled throughout." One thing that does separate *Drag Me to Hell* from Raimi's previous horror films, though, is that gore does not play as big a part. Raimi tried to make a movie that his *Spiderman* audience would be able to see, and that meant a PG-13 certificate. For Raimi, this was also a way of doing something different to the *Evil Dead* trilogy, turning *Drag Me to Hell* into more of a supernatural suspense thriller than a gorefest.

Casting Lohman as Christine turned out to be a good move on Raimi's part. We can believe her as a twenty-something professional, just starting out, eager to make good, but up against the realities that were just then starting to face those of her generation. How do I keep my job? How do I advance? Will I ever be able to afford my own home? We share Christine's sense of insecurity. Even if the credit crunch context of the film was just a coincidence, as Raimi maintains, the financial hardships facing Christine resonates with the film's audience, then as now.

For Raimi, much of the attraction of making *Drag Me to Hell* was the chance to get back to small-scale filmmaking. Let's not forget that he had started out as a fully hands-on filmmaker in *The Evil Dead*. Back then, Raimi and his tiny crew would do everything themselves, from working the camera, to blowing artificial blood through tubes for the make-up effects, to playing 'fake Shemps'. As Raimi said later, "it's refreshing and wonderful to be reminded that, as with most filmmakers, the best way to do it is yourself, with a tight team doing the main jobs." Members of the tight team on *Drag Me to Hell* included Peter Deming, a cinematographer who had started out with Raimi on *Evil Dead II* and gone on to work with some of the greatest American independents like David Lynch, David O. Russell and the Hughes Brothers. Master of the dark and brooding look, it's no surprise that Deming has a number of other horror films on his CV including two instalments of the *Scream* franchise and Drew Goddard's *Cabin in The Woods* (2012). For *Drag Me to Hell* Deming followed a lighting design that saw the film get progressively darker as Christine is drawn further into the supernatural. The heightened sense of realism that Deming and Raimi were trying to create was aided by KNB's visual effects, which used puppetry rather than CGI where possible. But this doesn't mean that on *Drag Me to Hell*, Raimi wasn't keen to use all of the tools at his disposal — including CGI.

An example of a sequence in *Drag Me to Hell* enhanced by CGI is the final showdown in the railway station. In his usual way, Raimi had storyboarded the entire sequence the way he saw it in his mind's eye. The problem was, according to Raimi, "When I wrote it, I had a misconception about how train stations work. I thought they were all like the ones in New York where the platforms are very high and the train is on the tracks on a bed many feet below. But in LA at Union Station where we shot, the tracks are only six inches lower than the platform, so all the visuals in my mind of how this scene would work, and all the storyboards I'd worked on with my artists, were all really wrong-headed."

Rather than redesign the sequence to fit the reality of the existing railway station, Raimi used CGI to change the reality so it fitted his pre-visualization of the scene. "The visual effects had to be created to correct all that and make the station look like I'd originally imagined it. And those were visual effects that were needed for almost every shot in the station, and people probably won't even realize they're effects shots. I mean, who'd spend the time and money making such effects shots?" But if anything sums up Raimi's filmmaking it's exactly that — he always bends reality to fit his imagination. Raimi's movies are nothing if not storyboards brought to life in the zaniest way possible!

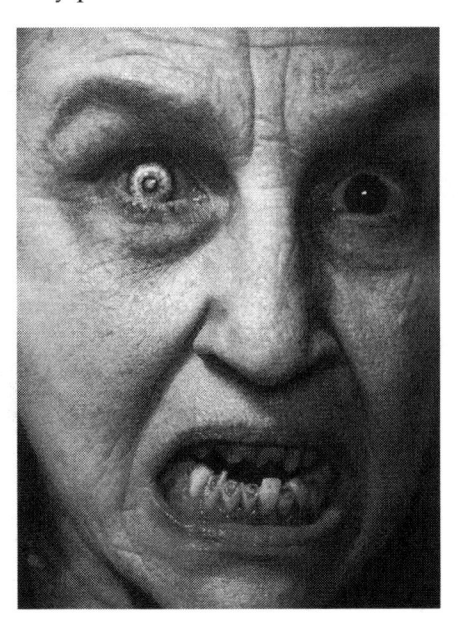

Lorna Raver in *Drag Me to Hell* (Universal, 2009)

Edge of Sanity (1989)

By 1989 the horror genre was going through one of its periodic lulls. This tends to happen when international censorship strikes at horror's excesses. We might first evidence such a hiatus in the 30s with the tightening up of the Hollywood Production Code, which effectively removed 'gruesomeness' from the screen; simultaneously, the introduction of the 'H' certificate in Great Britain in 1936 helped to take horror films off studio rosters for three years until *Son of Frankenstein* (1939) restarted production of (admittedly tamer) horror pictures. Something similar (if less drastic) happened in the 70s after the financial successes of independently produced flicks like *The Last House on the Left* and *The Texas Chain Saw Massacre*. These renegade movies undermined the Motion Picture Association rating system, putting pressure on the MPAA to make changes, pressure which the regulatory body resisted for a number of years but which eventually resulted in the replacement of the X-rating with the NC-17.

In the meantime, the MPAA's Classification and Rating Administration (CARA) slapped a number of horror films with X certificates as a way to discourage the genre, and brethren at the (then-titled) British Board of Film Censorship got handy with the scissors on a number of titles like *Dawn of the Dead* (while denying certificates to others). The aim was simple — to dissuade small independent distributors from taking a punt on problematic horror pictures that might cause controversy and create competition with Hollywood studio product.

However, the mid-80s saw the worst threat to the genre's financial viability with the introduction of the Video Recordings Act (1984). Draconian censorship of the genre in the UK, prompted by the media's attack on so-called 'video nasties' (and mirrored by continuing antagonism by the MPAA) cut off its markets domestically and abroad; and even European horror production by the likes of Dario Argento and Lucio Fulci was affected by the tightening of international censorship in the 80s and the 90s following the scandal. The intention was nothing less than to bury the genre.

Given this context — the stifling of horror by the mainstream establishment — can it be any coincidence that the key works of this period — movies like *Hellraiser* (1987) and *Santa Sangre* (1989) — have at their hearts an inexorable return of the repressed? As Freud tells us, that which is repudiated, demonized, denied and potentially annihilated — as horror was in the 80s -inevitably seeks a monstrous return. Gérard Kikoïne's 1989 cult curio *Edge of Sanity* fits squarely into this canon of 80s horror movies that seem to be fascinated by a symbolic return of the repressed. Indeed, in terms of its immediate subject matter and its production context, it is a particularly striking example of a horror film that centres on repressed energy and its explosive reappearance in monstrous form. The mere existence of these films, at a time when attempts were being made to stamp out the genre, speaks to the protean nature of horror: you just can't keep the genre down. Throughout cinema history, it always keeps coming back.

The genre itself, then, is an example of that which society represses or makes 'other', returning in the form of the monster. Horror movies serve that function. They are essential Freudian projections of antisocial sentiment syphoned off as harmless entertainment but nevertheless problematic to bourgeois sensibility. Horror movies by their very nature are the return of that which polite society represses or oppresses. However, some horror films, such as *Edge of Sanity*, make repression and the process of monstrous return the actual focus of their story. *Edge of Sanity* uses as its basis perhaps the most canonical literary source of all in terms of the nature of repression — Robert Louis Stevenson's 1886 novella *The Strange Case of Dr Jekyll and Mr Hyde*. Stevenson was prompted to write the novella as an inquiry into the dualistic nature of man — his propensity for both good and evil. The numerous stage and screen adaptations of the story have tended to foreground the theme of Victorian repression, drawing from the historical setting and the supposed hypocrisies of the Victorian age. In order to be 'good', Jekyll must banish his sexual impulses to his unconscious, where they take the shape of the degenerate Edward Hyde. In the same way, society in the 80s banished horror movies to the collective unconscious where they ultimately festered until making a return the following decade in the more acceptable form of the libidinous psychological thriller (*Silence of the Lambs*, 1991).

In *Edge of Sanity*, Henry Jekyll represses his sadomasochistic desires fostered in him by childhood experience. Like many sexual psychopaths of 80s horror (*Maniac*, 1980, *Nightmares in a Damaged Brain*, 1981) his psychosis is activated by memories of the primal scene. The young Henry witnesses a man and woman having sex in a hayloft. The woman first titillates him and then taunts him as he watches from a trapdoor above. Henry makes his presence known when he accidently tumbles into the hayloft only to be humiliated by the man who pulls down Henry's pyjama bottoms and slaps his bare arse. The woman takes obvious pleasure at Henry's humiliation, and thus womankind thereafter becomes for Henry the object of his equal lust and disgust, sublimated into Hyde's murderous desire.

In this, *Edge of Sanity* draws on a myriad of adaptations of Stevenson's novella, but the most obvious point of comparison arguably remains Rouben Mamoulian's 1931 classic, itself a 'return of the repressed' masterwork. As critic Tom Milne has commented 'the first thing that strikes one about Mamoulian's *Jekyll and Hyde* is its unequivocal sexual basis.' Indeed, Mamoulian turned Stevenson's classic into a story of the 'struggle between Victorian sexual repression and sexual expression'. The original impulse of Jekyll is a noble one. He starts out by rightly rebelling against the narrow conventions of the Victorian period and especially against the sexual repression. Jekyll's idea is that, if he can somehow separate the animalistic from his nature, he will become all one — totally spiritual and good. However, his Mr Hyde is corrupted by human weakness and his human brain, which on one hand aspires to purity and on the other wallows in depravity. As the film goes on he begins to refine his unorthodox pleasures — cruelty, sadism and murder. Gradually Hyde changes from an innocent animal into a vicious human monster, a monster that is part of us but which we usually keep under control.

Screen adaptations have provided Hyde with a focus for his enmity, usually in the form of a prostitute with whom both Jekyll and Hyde become fixated. The character of Ivy (played in the 1931 film by Miriam Hopkins), a dancehall prostitute who becomes the focus of Hyde's sadistic attentions, did not, in fact, feature in Stevenson's story, but originated in Paramount's 1920 version, appropriated from Oscar Wilde's *The Picture of Dorian Gray* (1890), and remained a staple of Jekyll and Hyde adaptations ever since. The Ivy character brings a certain thematic symmetry to the story in terms of Victorian morality: Jekyll is engaged to the virtuous Muriel, but harbours desire for Ivy, a woman of ill-repute; Hyde embodies the eruption of this repressed sexual desire in degenerate, sadistic form. Likewise, in *Edge of Sanity*, Henry abandons his wife Elizabeth (Glynis Barber) in favour of a series of Whitechapel prostitutes whom resemble the woman who scarred his childhood and who, in his adult life, returns to him in a recurring dream.

Edge of Sanity touches base with a number of later Jekyll and Hyde adaptations that provide variations on a theme. Perhaps the most unusual of these remains Hammer's *Dr Jekyll and Sister Hyde* (1971) in which the titular doctor is transformed into a sensual woman who enjoys a spot of murder, an intriguing comment on the oedipal trajectory that prefigures *Edge of Sanity*. Another is Walerian Borowczyk's *Le cas étrange de Dr Jekyll et Miss Osbourne/Docteur Jekyll et les femmes* (*Blood of Dr Jekyll*, 1981), which shares *Edge of Sanity*'s overt condemnation of Victorian morality. Like Borowczyk, Gérard Kikoïne's background in the erotic film industry presupposes an opposition to censorship and the kind of prudery that was taking over in the early 80s with the rise of neo-liberalism in the West. *Edge of Sanity*, like Borowczyk's version of the Stevenson novella, might be seen as an allegory about the increasingly repressive climate in which European filmmakers working in pornography found themselves by the early 80s. Finally, *Edge of Sanity* shares a particularly intriguing conflation of mythology with the Hammer movie: both incorporate elements of the Jack the Ripper case into the Stevenson story; point of fact being that *Edge of Sanity*'s Mr Hyde is named not Edward but Jack.

Of course, Jack the Ripper is our culture's original serial killer, the basis of which so many cinematic sociopaths have been formulated. A major coup for Kikoïne was managing to secure Anthony Perkins for the role of Henry Jekyll/ Jack Hyde — a classic horror conjunction of Ripper/Jekyll and Hyde/Perkins' oedipal conflation. In *Psycho* (1960), Norman Bates personified the ultimate return of the repressed monster — the ultimate human monster à la Jack the Ripper. By 1989, Perkins was enjoying a comeback of sorts, reprising his signature role in Richard Franklin's belated sequel *Psycho II* (1983), playing a psychotic amyl-sniffing sex pest priest in Ken Russell's *Crimes of Passion* (1984) and appearing in the little-seen 1988 slasher *Destroyer*. A further foray as Norman Bates in *Psycho III* (1986) (which he also directed) seemed to cement Perkins' image as the public's favourite psycho of the 80s, an indication perhaps of the cultural repression of that decade. There is no getting away from this in *Edge of Sanity*. Perkins' sexual psychopath screen persona suffuses the film and even the ad line on the poster alludes to it, claiming 'Anthony Perkins hasn't been himself lately…'

The poster image shows the two faces of Perkins in the film, his Dr Jekyll persona and his hideous Jack Hyde visage. The latter — with his pallid face, red-rimmed eyes and lank black hair — resembles none other than Conrad Veidt's Cesare, the somnambulistic murderer of Robert Wiene's *The Cabinet of Dr Caligari*. This visual association underlines how *Edge of Sanity* takes as its subject the horror genre itself and how it has been repressed. From its opening shot, *Edge of Sanity* exhibits as a film at least partly in the *Caligari*-style. Its highly exaggerated lighting design, its myriad canted and Dutch Tilted camera angles, its emphasis on Expressionism as a projection of subjectivity and fractured mental state reminds us of the origins of horror cinema. It is rare for a film to hark back to the very beginnings of genre in such a marked way. One thinks of Dario Argento's *Suspiria* (1977) and E. Elias Merhige's *Shadow of the Vampire* (2000).

Praise should be given here to *Edge of Sanity*'s cinematographer, Tony Spratling B.S.C. Spratling and Kikoïne in fact give *Edge of Sanity* two contrasting visual styles. In the scenes depicting Henry's 'good' persona as the Victorian doctor, the cinematography favours realism. Many of the exteriors were shot on location in London. In the scenes featuring Hyde, (interiors filmed in a studio in Hungary) the visual design becomes highly stylized. It is as though the opium dens, brothels and gin palaces that Hyde frequents during his nightly jaunts threaten to burst through the sunny façade of mews houses at any moment. It is a strikingly executed visual expression of the theme of the return of the repressed, made all the more so by the anachronistic touches which mark the film. *Edge of Sanity* may be about repressive Victorian morality but it perfectly reflects the time in which it was made. With its hyper-saturated colour palette, and its takes on drugs and gender and sexual decadence, *Edge of Sanity* is very much of a late 80s vibe.

Anthony Perkins in *Edge of Sanity* (Allied Vision, 1989)

Enter the Void (2009)

London, September 24th, 2010. After a preview screening of *Enter the Void* at The Rio Cinema, Dalston, the audience sat largely silent, as they had throughout the film. Gaspar Noé, who was present for the post-screening Q&A, stood on stage at the front of the auditorium, squinting into the spotlight, trying to gauge the reaction. Judging from his look of dismay, cinema's foremost provocateur was not used to such a quiet crowd. Only a few short years ago, critics at the Cannes festival had walked out of *Irreversible* (*Irréversible*, 2002) in protest at its scenes of rape and violence, making the film a *succés de scandale* and earning Noé the reputation of *enfant terrible*. Why, then, was this London audience not cheering and/or booing Noé as he took the stage? Why did *Enter the Void* not provoke a single walk-out or even a fainting? Why was the audience seemingly so unresponsive to Noé's provocations this time around?

Could it have been that the condescending tone of the movie critic who introduced the film had displeased the crowd? ("I'm so *jealous* that you're seeing this film for the *first* time!") Or was the audience simply showing its defiance in the face of Noé's provocations — as if to say: "You can't shock us! We know your game!" The truth may be more complex. It's likely that the audience at the Rio Cinema that night had not yet forgiven Noé for *Irreversible*. With that film, Noé had trampled on so many screen taboos. In its broadest sense, cinematic shock is concerned with subverting the traditional morality of a society in unconventional, unexpected ways. Noé's films are intentionally constructed to instil shock in an audience by attacking their fundamental values. They are, in other words, deliberate shocks to the social/sexual/ideological system — and not always progressive ones (many critics attacked *Irreversible* for its pervasive homophobia — a claim difficult to refute).

Of course, directors have been utilizing their power to shock since the earliest days of cinema (one thinks of Edwin S. Porter's startling introduction of the close-up in *The Great Train Robbery*, 1903) and many have pushed the boundaries of acceptability to emphasize the message they are presenting. What an audience experiences as shock reveals the conditions of a particular society at a particular point in time, its fears and taboos. The use of shock by Gaspar Noé is — at least in part — ideologically motivated (consider Noé's extraordinary feature debut *I Stand Alone* [*Seul contre tous*, 1998] — arguably one of the screen's most powerful indictments of fascism since Pier Paolo Pasolini's *Salò, or the 120 Days of Sodom*, 1975). The intention is nothing less than to address the traumas that society seeks to deny. Audiences know all this going in, of course, but it didn't seem to prepare them for *Irreversible*: for the low frequency sound deliberately designed to make an audience feel sick; for the ten-minute single-shot real-time rape sequence that offers the viewer no escape from what is taking place on screen; for the fire extinguisher that crushes a man's head to a pulp in the opening scenes of the same film.

With *Irreversible*, Noé actively sought to *hurt* his audience; and the audience had not forgotten this. At least, that was my impression that night at the Rio. Certainly, *I* had watched the film in trepidation, wondering what trauma lay ahead. I had avoided *Irreversible* altogether for that reason — and to this day cannot bring myself to watch it. Indelible in my mind, too, was the horse so shockingly slaughtered for meat in the opening scene of Noé's early short film *Carne* (1991) (with no warning to the viewer of what they were about to see); while I had found *I Stand Alone* traumatizing to the degree that I thought I was going to have a full-blown panic attack right there in the cinema as I was watching the film.

Enter the Void, then, caught audiences on the defensive — certainly it did on the night of the Rio Cinema preview. Still reeling from the shock of his previous films, we were unprepared for its phantasmagoria. Our silence was the result of being blindsided by this fabulist vision of the afterlife; our struggle to reconcile such flights of fantasy with the cold formalist brutality we had come to associate with Noé; the realization that we were witnessing another side of Gaspar Noé, one hitherto unseen in his films.

In his Q&A, Noé revealed that the idea for *Enter the Void* had first presented itself to him when he was a teenager. This came as no surprise to those of us who, up to that point, had considered Noé the bastard offspring of William Castle and Georges Franju. From the latter, it seemed to us, Noé had inherited the *épater la bourgeois* sensibility of the French Decadent poets by way of the Surrealists; from the former, a huckster's sense of schocksploitation.

Certainly, Franju's *Eyes without a Face* (*Les yeux sans visage*, 1960) continues to exert a strange fascination on filmmakers and world cinema audiences alike. As with much of Noé's output, it was reviled on first release — it met with international disgust and was slammed by critics — but has subsequently grown in acclaim. Like Noé's movies, Franju's masterpiece is at heart an attempt to cash in on the success of exploitation films — but emerges as much more. We might draw comparisons between the two filmmakers in terms of artistic temperament. Franju was engaged as director of *Eyes without a Face* on the strict proviso that he avoided three things so as not to upset European censors: gore, animal cruelty and mad scientists. Of course, he ended up including all three in the film. Noé, without doubt, would have done the same. Like Noé, Franju started out directing short films, two of which — *Hôtel des invalides* (1952) and *Blood of the Beasts* (*Le sang des bêtes*, 1949) — intersect horror and modernity in much the same way as does Noé in *his* work.

A further point of comparison: Franju's films address, albeit in allegorical fashion, the atrocities of fascism, and a Europe stained by the horrors of war. Franju turned government-sponsored documentaries about war veterans, factories and meat processing plants into virtual snuff movies, showing the industrialized slaughter of the modern world. In *Blood of the Beasts*, Franju contrasts the dispassionate butchery of animals with the seemingly oblivious bourgeois normalcy of the surrounding Parisian suburbs. Gasper Noé would achieve much the same effect in the shocking butchery of the horse at the start of *Carné* and throughout much of *I Stand Alone*.

Fantasy film and art cinema have, of course, always been closely connected. Franju's movie has its precedents in Louis Feuillade's silent films, and in the early works of F.W. Murnau, as well as in the Universal horror movies of Tod Browning and James Whale. Likewise, Noé has sought to splice his films with the kind of shock effects favoured by exploitation merchant William Castle. (Think of the warning that flashes up before the climax of *I Stand Alone*, advising squeamish audience members to leave the cinema: what is about to follow might be too much for their nerves to take!)

Channelling Franju and Castle (not to mention Kubrick and Gerald Kargl, whom Noé has named as conscious influences), Noé has pretty much mined the cinema of all its varieties of shock: visceral, perceptual, moral, emotional, ideological. Indeed, it is difficult to think of another contemporary director able to combine the types in such potent ways (only Lars von Trier comes close). Of course, it is easy to shock an audience — if all you want to do is shock an audience. What makes Noé such an intriguing and provocative filmmaker are the glimpses of utopianism — however fleeting — that one gets in his work (even *Irreversible*, by virtue of its back-to-front-narrative, ends [begins] on a grace note). As *Cinemaaxis* noted of *We Fuck Alone* (Noe's entry in 2006's *Destricted* — an anthology of short films by different directors exploring the impact of pornography on society), while 'very dark in tone, there was also a strange air of childlike innocence that flowed throughout the film'.

All of which brings us back to Feuillade, Murnau and *Enter the Void*. It is fitting that Noé should have conceived of *Enter the Void* as a teenager, fantasy often being the richest form of juvenilia. After all, who, as a teenager, hasn't fantasied about having an out-of-body experience; about astral projection or being able to travel through time and space without the need of a body? It's a sweet, romantic idea closely tied to a pervasive sense of teenage angst. Francis Ford Coppola included such a sequence in *Rumble Fish* (1983), his Cocteau-esque *Bildungsroman*, where Rusty James (Matt Dillon) floats out of his body after being injured in a gang fight; his soul hovers above the people in his life as they mourn his tragic and premature demise. They'll miss him when he's gone, right? In the same way, Noé's drug-dealer protagonist, Oscar, leaves his body after being shot by the police, to float as a discarnate entity above the Tokyo streets, observing the aftermath of his death.

Enter the Void adopts the fantastic realism of Feuillade, whose great contribution to the development of cinema was to detail the impossible in crime serials like *Fantômas* (1913), *Les Vampires* (1915-16) and *Judex* (1916). Feuillade's work has been described as the 'social fantastic', and this applies equally to *Enter the Void* as it does to other *auteurs* of the fantasy school — Clive Barker, for example (whose stories often deal with out-of-body experience). The great German Expressionist F.W. Murnau dreamt of freeing the camera from physical restraint, in much the same way as an astral body is capable of travelling outside the physical body. His ambition was partly realized by cinematographers Karl Freund in *The Last Laugh* (*Der letzte Mann*, 1924) and Charles Rosher and Karl Struss in *Sunrise* (1927). Murnau envisaged a camera that was free to move through the architecture in his films in much the same way as Oscar's disembodied soul floats freely through the city of Tokyo.

Indeed, the spirit of Murnau hovers over *Enter the Void*, not least in the extensive use of the subjective camera. Murnau had encouraged his cinematographers to utilize the moving camera in such a way as to take the point of view of his characters, most notably in *The Last Laugh* where Freund attaches his camera to a bicycle to see through the eyes of Emil Jannings; and in the magnificent scene in *Sunrise* where errant farmer George O'Brien goes to meet his mistress, the Woman from the City, by a moonlit lake (Karl Struss would also make good use of the subjective camera in the first scene of Rouben Mamoulian's 1931 version of *Dr Jekyll and Mr Hyde*).

But how many films have taken the step of using the subjective camera to present an entire movie exclusively through the eyes of the main character: a feature film length POV shot? Prior to *Enter the Void* only one springs to mind: Robert Montgomery's *Lady in the Lake* (1947). Dismissed by critics of the time as a gimmick — as an example of juvenile filmmaking — the subjective camera would remain thereafter in the domain of avant-garde and experimental cinema (featuring prominently in such works as Kenneth Anger's *Fireworks* [1947] and Alexander Hammid and Maya Deren's *Meshes of the Afternoon* [1943]). François Truffaut was amongst those who refuted *Lady in the Lake*, claiming that the subjective camera is the opposite of subjective cinema: the viewer identifies with the people seen on screen. He has a point, of course. However, what better way to join protagonist and viewer together in a shared subjective experience? ("You and Robert Montgomery solve a murder mystery together" promised *Lady in the Lake*'s publicity.) And what better way to evoke astral projection, as Gaspar Noé does in *Enter the Void*?

Enter the Void, then, is juvenilia, but it is rich juvenilia nonetheless. Its influence can be seen in at least two noteworthy films made afterwards. Franck Khalfoun's *Maniac* (2012) is distinguished by its use of POV camera throughout, drawing us inside the psychosis of a serial killer while at the same time critiquing the traditional use of POV camera as Slasher trope. And would Alejandro González Iñárritu's Oscar-winning crowd-pleaser *Birdman* (2014) have come into existence without the inspiration of *Enter the Void*?

Paz de la Huerta in *Enter the Void* (Wild Bunch/IFC Films, 2009)

Freaks (1932)

Freaks may well be the most notorious horror film ever made. Tod Browning's 1932 masterpiece — with its scenes of real-life circus freaks rising up against the people who exploit them — was considered too shocking for viewers on its initial release and quickly withdrawn from cinema distribution. In England it was banned for 30 years. It was only in the 60s, when the term 'freak' took on a whole new meaning for the hippy generation that *Freaks* found an audience in the counterculture of the day as a Midnight Movie in America and Europe. Now it's viewed by film fans and scholars very differently to how it was initially received in the 30s. Rather than being an exploitative movie that held up disability as a thing of horror — as *Freaks* was thought of in 1932 — it's generally now seen as a compassionate film about people who might look different to the norm, but inside are every bit as worthy of respect as everyone else. One thing's for sure, for anyone who has watched *Freaks*, it remains an experience never to be forgotten.

Freaks came into being because of the success of *Dracula* in 1931. Studios were all dusting off their murder-mystery-thrills scripts, or looking for stories that could be given some kind of terror angle, so that they could muscle in on the horror cycle that *Dracula* had started. At MGM boy wonder producer Irving Thalberg had been tailoring a short story property called *Spurs* into a screenplay with a horror slant. *Spurs*, written in 1923 by Tod Robbins, is about a circus dwarf who enacts revenge on the 'big woman' who marries him for his money and then tries to poison him. Thalberg was keen to outdo rival studios with a shocker that would be more horrible than all the rest and commissioned screenwriter Willis Goldbeck to work up a suitable script, with instructions to "give me something more horrible than *Frankenstein*" (which was then in production at Universal).

As was his way with most films at MGM, Thalberg took overall control over the script for *Freaks*, and developed the story with Goldbeck and Browning before sending off Goldbeck to write the screenplay. Legend has it that when Thalberg read the resulting script, he held his head in his hands. "Well, I asked for something horrible," he sighed. "And I got it!"

Freaks uses the basic plot of *Spurs* but develops it into an even more lurid tale of revenge. The story revolves around Hans (Harry Earles), one of the little people in the circus, and his infatuation with the beautiful trapeze artist, Cleopatra (played by Olga Baclanova). At first Cleopatra is revulsed by Hans's advances, but when she discovers that he is wealthy, she and circus strong man Hercules hatch a plot. As in the original short story, Cleopatra agrees to marry Hans, and then starts to slowly poison him while convincing him to leave his money to her. Realizing that Hans is becoming ill, the other freaks listen in to Cleopatra and Hercules and discover their secret. One stormy, rain-soaked night, the freaks exact a terrible revenge on Cleopatra and her strongman lover, mutilating the once beautiful trapeze artist and turning her into a grotesque chicken-woman. The film ends with Cleopatra transformed into a freak.

Some scholars have suggested that Browning didn't like it that Thalberg and Goldbeck had taken the melancholic short story and turned it into a wild tale of revenge. Browning had originally wanted a narrative fade out to *Freaks* that would underscore the sadness of the freaks, who could never be accepted by the outside world, but Thalberg had forced the macabre ending on him. If this is true you can understand why, given that the film studios were suffering in the Great Depression as audiences had no money for movie-going, Thalberg had enormous pressure on him to get box office takings from sensational subject matter, and that need would override any artistic aspirations that Browning may have had for *Freaks*.

In fact, it was to be the casting of real-life disabled performers in leading roles — which Thalberg saw at the time as a great publicity stunt and novelty attraction — that proved to be the undoing of *Freaks*. Preview screenings in the early months of 1932 met with a violent response. A letter sent to the editor of *Photoplay* (May, 1932) by a reader from San Diego claiming to having seen it expresses how preview audiences must have felt: 'I certainly think that whoever directed it should be ashamed to have put his name to it," wrote the viewer. "I didn't mind its gruesomeness so much, but its cheap vulgarity is something that left a bad taste in my mouth'.

Freaks plays very much like a parable. It opens on a circus sideshow as the carnival barker exhorts the crowd to see some unseen monstrosity in a pit. As the onlookers gasp in horror, the barker begins to tell us the story of the freak in the pit and how she became the way she is. *Freaks* then flashes back to an earlier time in the circus. We see the daily lives of the freaks and how like everyone else they have their own problems. These almost soap opera vignettes succeed in making the normal out of the 'abnormal'. As numerous critics have pointed out, *Freaks* is, at heart, a morality tale, a story of retribution against the bad people of this world like Cleopatra and Hercules, who would seek to exploit and hurt others. *Freaks* moves towards this conclusion in its still-disturbing later scenes of the freaks slithering through the rain and the mud to take revenge on those who would seek to cause harm to their own.

After the disastrous previews, Thalberg ordered Browning to cut the film's most offensive scenes, including the opening which introduced the freaks playing like children in a country estate, and the gruesome ending involving the castration of Hercules by the freaks. Browning himself hastily wrote the framing device of the carnival barker introducing the freaks, which served to bridge the missing sequences.

Although it's often claimed that what was cut from *Freaks* was just background, a closer look at the script (the missing footage was destroyed) reveals that much of what MGM cut is likely have been thought risqué by the Hays Office censors. For example, the original script presents Venus as a 'fallen woman' trying to reform; but scenes which established this were taken from the film during the preparation of the revised 64-minute version. The revised version of *Freaks* was no more than a damage limitation exercise on the behalf of Thalberg and MGM.

MGM had originally mounted an exploitative ad campaign for *Freaks*, playing on Browning's reputation for the bizarre. Early trade adverts for *Freaks* billed it as the big exploitation novelty sensation of the year, with teasers asking: 'Do the Siamese Twins make love?...Can a full-grown woman truly love a midget?...Do the Pin-heads think?... What sex is the Half-Man, Half-Woman?' The studio would try to downplay these sideshow angles of *Freaks* in its later advertising, promoting it instead as a 'thrilling and astounding love drama'. But its initial box office was generally poor, badly hit by almost universally negative reviews.

Another factor that contributed to the overall poor reception of *Freaks* in 1932 was the growing backlash by church groups, parent-teachers' associations, and other pressure groups against Hollywood films in general, especially gangster movies and sex pictures. To this sector of the public, *Freaks* seemed like a new low for Hollywood, and *Freaks* became a scapegoat. MGM desperately tried to play up the film's daring approach to the taboo subject matter: 'Do we tell the real truth on screen? Do we dare hold up the mirror to nature in all its grim reality?' MGM even tried to convince critics that *Freaks* was really a compassionate film: 'What about abnormal people? They have their lives, too! What about the Siamese twins — have they no right to love? The pinheads, the half-man, half-woman, the dwarfs! They have the same passions, joys, sorrows, laughter as normal human beings. Is such a subject untouchable?'

All in all, the film intended as more horrible than all the rest had turned into an embarrassment for Browning, Thalberg, MGM, the Hays Office and the industry in general. By the time *Freaks* resurfaced at the Cannes Film

Festival in 1962, it had been mutilated almost beyond recognition. Even so, that showing in Cannes brought about a critical reappraisal: *Freaks* began to attract attention in France and in the United Kingdom (although its English ban would be lifted in May 1963, it would remain very difficult to see until its VHS release in the mid-1990s). In the United States, it started to gain a reputation on college campuses and in repertory cinemas where it was often billed alongside films like *Night of the Living Dead*. In 1994 it was inducted into the National Film Registry as a film worthy of preservation. *Freaks* has since had a new lease of life on DVD where thanks to Warner Brothers and Turner Entertainment it's been released (in 2004) with its various endings included as DVD extras.

Freaks has been interpreted by scholars and critics in many ways — as sideshow exploitation, as a fable or fairy-story, as a grim morality tale, even as a comment on Hollywood itself and the way it uses and abuses talent — but it is definitely a film that sticks in the mind. So, what makes *Freaks* endure as a horror classic?

Looking back to the time of its production, the shock value of *Freaks* clearly owed something to breaking the taboos that arose at the time of the Great Depression. But, at the same time it speaks to values that are universal. *Freaks* is essentially the story of an underclass of people exploited by their assumed superiors. Even in the early sequences of the film where the freaks are introduced to the viewer, taboos of physical deformity are broken by Browning's explicit presentation of the freaks, creating — in the audiences of 1932, at least — a response of both fascination and horror. But then *Freaks* quickly begins to undercut this. We forget the physical deformity of the freaks and become intrigued by their domestic lives. How will Roscoe learn to live with his sister-in-law who is literally joined to his wife's hip? How will Frieda win Hans back when he is so obviously smitten with Cleopatra? As these intrigues unfold, we begin to empathize with the freaks, whose problems are really not that different to our own. Once we are re-introduced to Cleopatra and Hercules, the outwardly beautiful but rotten-inside people, the values of society are turned on their heads.

The impact of *Freaks* on popular culture has been enormous. Its influences range from songs inspired by the film (*Pinhead* by The Ramones) to other films (David F. Friedman's *She-Freak* made in 1967 is a kind of sequel) to specific references in the media and in television shows like *The Simpsons*. *Freaks* is a film that makes us look closely at issues of difference and disability, and for that reason it's still an uncomfortable film for many. It asks us to see freakishness as something normal. But at the same time, it makes us look at the normal world afresh, through the eyes of those who are different. For those reasons, despite its many flaws and imperfections, *Freaks* remains Tod Browning's masterpiece and one of the most controversial horror films ever made.

Freaks (MGM, 1932)

The Hitcher (1986)

"The film was an allegory. The passenger represented evil... It was the devil talking." So Rutger Hauer told *The Los Angeles Times* in 1990. Modern viewers may well see Hauer's titular hitchhiker-cum-serial killer, John Ryder, as *The Hitcher*'s personification of evil — the devil probably (even the character's name suggests a metaphysical element — he hitches rides and he kills, and that's all he does). Ryder's cunning and manoeuvring verges on a supernatural level. This element of *The Hitcher* may not have been as apparent to critics on the film's first release as it is now. *The Hitcher* has only grown in stature, and part of the reason for that is a greater appreciation of the film's influences and its place in a small pantheon of road movies that involve the game of cat-and-mouse between an everyman and a diabolical adversary.

If *The Hitcher* brings to mind urban legends and folktales of spooky hitchhikers thumbing rides from hapless motorists up and down American highways throughout history, so it should. Eric Red's screenplay draws heavily on American folklore, in particular the myth of the Vanishing Hitchhiker, an eerie tale told down the generations and dating back to the 1870s. Variations on the story abound but the general gist is the ghostly passenger thumbing a ride from an innocent motorist and suddenly vanishing, leaving behind some garment or scrap of information that alerts the poor driver to the fact that the hitchhiker was actually the spirit of someone recently deceased.

The Vanishing Hitchhiker is pervasive as an urban legend and variations of it exist in the folklore of many countries; but there is something about it that remains particularly suited to the haunted highways of the United States with its four million miles of roads. The tradition of 'hitching a ride' is a peculiarly American one as well, and first gained popularity in the days of the Great Depression as a form of free transportation for people who had little or no money. Although Hollywood cinema of the 30s took a benign view of the hitchhiker in comedies like *It Happened One Night* (1934), newspapers of the era increasingly printed stories of kindly motorists picking up passengers only to fall victim to heinous crimes at the hands of a creepy hitchhiker. The fact that laws were subsequently passed to protect the motorist from such crimes — sponsored by transportation companies who were losing money due to hitchhikers getting free rides — speaks equally to the folklore of the hitchhiker in American culture as it does to actual road crime. After all, such legends as the Vanishing Hitchhiker are, at their heart, cautionary tales about not picking up strangers; and the same could be said for the films which draw upon them — including *The Hitcher*.

But if the press and the lawmakers of the 30s were overly concerned with crime on highways, then much of that concern arose from fear of a modern folk devil who rose to prominence in that decade: the psychopath. From the origin of the concept, the psychopath was perceived as a drifter, an unemployed man living on the fringes of society. It took *film noir* to conflate such criminality with hitchhiking and the social evil of psychopathy — presenting a new spin on old legends from which John Ryder would ultimately emerge.

Edgar G. Ulmer's *Detour* (1945) marks something of a progenitor in this respect. It starts with a hitchhiker (played by Tom Neal) who has the misfortune of thumbing a ride with a man who proceeds to drop dead at the wheel almost as soon as he gets into the car. Realizing that he'll probably get pinned with murder if he comes clean, the hitcher swaps identities with the deceased and continues his journey as the driver. He, in turn, picks up another hitchhiker — a woman (Ann Savage) this time — and a *femme fatale* to boot. She's onto Neal immediately and blackmails him mercilessly. *Detour* kicked into gear a number of tropes that would recur throughout the genre, including in *The Hitcher*, such as the (largely) innocent man framed for murder and the (in this case) borderline sociopathic passenger who enjoys wielding power over him. *The Devil Thumbs a Ride* (1947) revved things up a bit by making the hitchhiker a psychotic killer who, in the words of the film's publicity, will 'Kill Until He Dies!'

Sound familiar? Lawrence Tierney's psychopath has the future John Ryder down to a tee in terms of his determination to kill off everyone except the upstanding driver (Ted North) just for shits 'n' giggles. While Felix Feist's quota quickie nails the essence of this genre in its title, it's the justly celebrated *The Hitch-hiker* (directed in 1953 by Ida Lupino) that really puts the pedal to the metal. Two men on a fishing trip unwittingly pick up a serial killer who proceeds to hold them at gunpoint; it's the unrelenting sadistic pleasure that he takes in tormenting the hostages that makes *The Hitch-hiker* such a powerful — and seminal — film. As critic John Knewson noted, at its heart *The Hitch-hiker* is the story of 'two utterly average middle-class American men slowly psychologically broken by a serial killer'. In a similar way, John Ryder tries to break his hostage Jim Halsey (C. Thomas Howell), but, as we all know, what doesn't break you makes you stronger, right?

'When was the last time you invited death into your car?' asked *The Hitch-hiker*'s poster blurb, edging us closer to what these films are really all about. Almost twenty years later Steven Spielberg's *Duel* (1971) returned the genre to its mythic roots, depicting the unseen truck driver playing cat-and-mouse with Dennis Weaver's milquetoast motorist as a protean force, like John Ryder himself. Nothing, it seems, can stop him (assuming it's a he!) *Duel* set the template for the roadkill thrillers that followed, including *Breakdown* (1997). Here, it's Kurt Russell as the mild-mannered driver whose wife, Kathleen Quinlan, is kidnapped and ransomed by fiendish trucker JT Walsh. The mistake Quinlan makes is to hitch a ride with Walsh in the first place — doesn't she know never to accept a ride from strangers?

John Dahl's *Joyride* (AKA *Roadkill*, 2001) fires on all cylinders as brothers Paul Walker and Steve Zahn unwittingly spark war with a psychotic trucker who goes by the handle of 'Rusty Nail' (like in *Duel* we never see his face, but we hear his voice — courtesy of Buffalo Bill himself, Ted Levine). No hitchhiking involved but what we do have is the hulking eighteen-wheeler of *Duel*, combined with Rusty Nail's almost supernatural-level cunning and manoeuvring of which John Ryder would be proud. Indeed, the ghost of *The Hitcher* seems to haunt *Joyride* in the way that Rusty Nail shares Ryder's apparent omniscience (and omnipotence) and enjoys taunting his victims in a truly evil manner.

A couple of international movies in the 70s drew on the Vanishing Hitchhiker legend while putting their own wheel-spin on it. Inverting the by-now-well-established-tropes of a motorist couple victimized by a solitary hitchhiker, *Nifas Diabólicas* (*Diabolical Nymphs*, 1978) directed by John Doo, comes across as a haunted highway movie replete with sex, death and magic. Two women hitchhikers, Circe and Ursula (Patrícia Scalvi and Aldine Müller), who seemingly share a telepathic link, are picked up by family man Rodrigo (Sergio Hingst). He drives them to a deserted beach, where the women take turns to seduce him. Jealousy inexplicably flares up between Ursula and Circe, each of whom appears to want Rodrigo for her own. A fight develops in which Circe, with the help of Rodrigo, seemingly murders Ursula with a rock. As Circe and Rodrigo flee in the car, the bloody figure of Ursula materializes in the back seat, causing a crash in which the viewer assumes all three characters are killed.

But shortly afterwards, in an enigmatic twist, both women mysteriously appear again, completely unhurt (although Rodrigo is presumably dead). They swap clothes and personas, and in what now seems to be some kind of never-ending diabolical game, resume their hitchhiking once more to find a new male victim. Filmed vérité-style on the mountain roads of Brazil, *Nifas Diabólicas* is an odd, unsettling movie, all the more so because nothing is explained. It takes the oft-used pornographic male fantasy of women hitchhikers picked up by lone men (cf. *The Hitchhikers*, 1972), and turns it on its head.

Pasquale Festa Campanile's 1977 thriller, *Autostop rosso sangue* (*Hitch-Hike*) in which escaped bank-robber David Hess takes a married couple (played by Franco Nero and Corinne Cléry) hostage, further twists the notion of good versus evil that has become the pitstop of the hitchhiker thriller. As *Hitch-Hike* progresses, the couple prove themselves just as morally corrupt as the murderous hitchhiker, and the film ends with Nero, having used the kidnapping as an opportunity to kill his despised wife, stealing Hess's money, and effectively taking his place on the open road as the eponymous 'hitchhiker'. A subversive twist on the black and white morality of Lupino's *The Hitch-hiker*, from which Campanile clearly takes his inspiration.

It took a Doo and a Campanile to fully uncover the sense of absurdism that powers the engine of this genre, which *The Hitcher* knowingly jams the ignition key into. *The Hitcher*'s Jim Halsey is at the mercy of a force he doesn't understand. Existence is meaningless; fate is capricious. It's not surprising that a director such as Roman Polanski would make a variation of the married-couple-pick-up-a-hitchhiker narrative in *Nóz w wodzie* (*Knife in The Water*, 1962), setting the action in the confines of a sailing yacht rather than inside a car on the open road. There follows a series of bizarre power-plays between the three and a shifting of identity. Phillip Noyce provided his own take on this nautical nightmare in *Dead Calm* (1989), pitting Sam Neill and Nicole Kidman against psycho Billy Zane who they pick up from a sinking ship at sea. Several years earlier, the made-for-TV movie *Satan's Triangle* (1975) saw the hapless crew of a schooner rescue the survivor of a shipwreck who turns out to be the Devil himself! Even in the ocean, the rule applies: no good deed goes unpunished.

A constant in all these movies is the fight for dominance between the motorist and the hitchhiker. Both parties literally and metaphorically want to be in the driving seat. However, for the motorist, it is a question of fighting not just for survival, but for control of their own fate. The Vanishing Hitchhiker is really about fearing the Reaper; by picking up that hitchhiker, we might just be inviting death into our car. With the hitchhiker as the personification of death, these cautionary tales embody our coming face to face with the Reaper and trying to resist him. Do we have the courage to face him down? Do we have the resilience to defeat him? Can we last the journey? Jim Halsey in *The Hitcher* is the modern everyman who realizes that he must fight the Reaper alone. Like the biblical Everyman, he learns that when you are brought to death and placed before God, all you are left with are your own good deeds.

Horror Hospital (1973)

The 70s certainly produced some oddities in British horror cinema. Take *The Wicker Man* (1973), an all-singing, all-dancing folk horror musical. Or the three-plot genre mash-up *Scream and Scream Again* (1970), a queasy mix of espionage thriller and vampire killer story chased up with sewn-together superhuman Frankensteins. But one of the oddest horror films made on British soil in the early 70s has to be *Horror Hospital* (1973). Produced by the great B-movie stalwart Richard Gordon, directed by avant-garde filmmaker/ exploitation distributor Antony Balch and starring 70s cheeky-chappie Robin Askwith alongside Amicus veteran Michael Gough, *Horror Hospital* is a Marmite movie if ever there was one. Too strange and eerie to be a comedy, too spoofy and tongue-in-cheek to be straight horror, it's a film that has its fair share of admirers, but also more than a few detractors. Those who love it do so for its irreverent approach to traditional horror tropes and its parody of movies like *Horrors of the Black Museum* (1959) and *Circus of Horrors* (1960). Those who hate it think it preposterously amateurish, especially in the dialogue and acting departments. There's no arguing *Horror Hospital* throws everything into the mix — from mad scientists to rebellious youths, zombified victims, evil dwarves — even motorcycle thugs à la *The Damned* (1962). Though whether it's an intentional 'deconstruction' of British horror films (and of narrative cinema generally) or just the mad-cap work of an eccentric one-off (Balch) is a matter of opinion.

The story itself is slightly bonkers. Askwith plays Jason Jones, a jaded young songwriter who signs up with a company called Hairy Holidays to go on a country retreat at Brittlehurst Manor, a health farm/ medical facility run by the wheelchair-bound Dr Storm (Gough). Pairing up with Judy (Vanessa Shaw), whom he meets on the train going there, they discover that Storm and his dwarf helper Frederick (Skip Martin) are turning patients into zombies and sex slaves.

Robin Askwith would become best known for his role as Timothy Lea in the 'Confessions' series of sex comedies starting with *Confessions of a Window Cleaner* (1974) and we can see him playing a similar character here of the long -haired layabout who just wants to get his leg over with the 'birds'. This makes his casting, at first glance, to be a bit strange to say the least. 'Jason' was the kind of character that Askwith had already played in the film spin-off of *Bless this House* (1973) — the popular middle-England image of liberated youth more interested in pop music, sex and political protests than in finding gainful employment, and very much at odds with traditional lower-middle class values. But then Askwith's film persona at that time is just one of the many things that *Horror Hospital* sends up: Balch himself had made a living as a distributor of sex comedies in the early 1970s, importing foreign sex films and releasing them with raunchy titles and lurid advertising campaigns.

Dig a little deeper though, and you'll see that including Askwith in the cast is not that strange after all. Earlier in his career Askwith acted in films by British-sexploitation-merchant-turned-horror-auteur Pete Walker — *Cool It Carol* (1970), *The Four Dimensions of Greta* (1972) and the giallo-esque *The Flesh and Blood Show* (1972) — in the latter he's the unwitting victim of a maniac killing off the actors in an end-of-pier seaside show. As well, he appeared in the cult horror favourite from 1970, *Tower of Evil*, in which he ends up impaled to a wall with a spear. In *Horror Hospital* he's cast as both a sex comedy type Jack the Lad and a horror victim, an unashamed bid by Balch and producer Richard Gordon to capitalize on the two most popular genres in British exploitation movies at that time — horror films and sex farces — while also sending up both kinds of film.

What makes Antony Balch such an intriguing figure in British cinema is that as both a distributor and filmmaker he embraced the avant-garde movement with equal fervour as he did exploitation movies (often distributing art house movies as though they *were* exploitation pictures). Instrumental to this was his friendship and collaboration with Beat novelist William Burroughs, whom he met in Paris in 1960. Burroughs was inspired by a technique called the 'cut-up' whereby he took passages of prose and literally cut them up and pasted them back together in random order. Balch and Burroughs made two short films together using this method, *Towers Open Fire* (1963) and *The Cut-Ups* (1966). In *The Cut-Ups* Balch chopped each shot into one second long strips and had his editor reassemble them in a completely random order. The result was so disorientating that some patrons of the Cinephone on Oxford Street, where it was shown for two weeks, are said to have walked out of the cinema in such a daze that they left behind their hats, coats and umbrellas!

Horror Hospital, of course, doesn't stray as far into experimental cinema as Balch's early shorts, but there is still a sense of randomness about much of the film, especially in some of its dialogue and the music score. There are moments in scenes which definitely seem to have been made up on the spot while the camera was rolling and the De Wolfe music is often wildly inappropriate.

Balch saw himself as a complete filmmaker, someone who would be his own distributor, cinema-exhibitor and businessman. In 1963, he bought the UK rights to Tod Browning's *Freaks* (1932) after the film had been 'rediscovered' at the Cannes Film Festival the year before. Balch opened *Freaks* in London in a private cinema club, and that marked the start of his career as a distributor. Over the next fifteen years, working from his Piccadilly flat and his office in Golden Square, Soho, Balch distributed cult movies like *Haxan: Witchcraft through the Ages* (1922), *Don't Deliver Us from Evil* (1971), *Truck Stop Women* (1974) and *Supervixens* (1975).

At the same time, Balch worked as the manager of two London cinemas, an exploitation cinema in Piccadilly called The Jacey and a repertory cinema called The Times in Baker Street where Balch would programme movies seemingly at random. One week it would be Roman Polanski, the next a Fred Astaire/Ginger Rogers musical, the next a surrealist classic by Luis Bunuel. The owner of the Jacey Cinema Group John Neville Cohen remembers Balch on his website: 'He was both fascinating and amusing, keen to experiment, he succeeded in distributing cheap foreign films, without any stars, that were made popular by his clever titles and catch lines.' As the manager of the two cinemas, Balch was typically hands-on, doing everything from programming the films, to designing the publicity, to overseeing the projectionists. It's not surprising that his personal touch and love of everything about the movies made Balch move toward directing his own feature films.

Gordon and Balch met at the Cannes Film Festival, and Gordon agreed to invest in a movie called *Secrets of Sex* (1970) — with Balch putting up the other half of the budget from his own money. *Secrets of Sex* is typically bonkers Balch. It was released in America under the apt title *Bizarre* and it's actually an anthology of bizarre vignettes revolving around the theme of sexual pleasure. There's a secret agent who likes to crack safes while she's topless; a female photographer who loves to torture her male models; a young man who hires a prostitute to have a three-some with him and his pet lizard. The film is narrated by an Egyptian mummy. 'Dead for 1000 years… he rose from the crypt' the movie poster informs us, 'to reveal strange and sinister passions.' Sexy, disturbing and very odd indeed, the British censor cut nine minutes when it was released, but that didn't stop *Secrets of Sex* from becoming a box office hit.

Balch wrote the script of *Horror Hospital* with his friend Alan Watson (who makes an uncredited appearance early in the film as a transvestite in a nightclub). Gordon engaged casting director Thelma Graves to cast the unusual roles. Diminutive actor Skip Martin was cast as Frederick. Martin had previously appeared in Roger Corman's Poe adaptation *The Masque of the Red Death* (1964) and Hammer's *Vampire Circus* (1972) and would make only one more film, *Son of Dracula* (1974). In between film assignments,

Martin reportedly worked as a tobacconist. Veteran actor Dennis Price was known for playing upper crust characters in the 40s but by the time of *Horror Hospital* had become reduced by alcoholism to taking parts in low-budget horror movies — including several by Jess Franco. In *Horror Hospital* he plays a travel agent in cahoots with Dr Storm, procuring unwitting victims for the evil doctor's experiments. When he later tries to blackmail Storm, he gets his just desserts. Sadly, *Horror Hospital* would be one of Price's final films; he died in 1973. Another interesting actor in *Horror Hospital* is Kurt Christian, who plays Abraham, a young hippy who drifts into Brittlehurst Manor looking for his girlfriend who, unbeknown to him, has become one of Storm's zombiefied victims. Christian (whose full name was Baron Kurt Christian von Siegenberg) later appeared in *The Golden Voyage of Sinbad* (1973) and *Sinbad and the Eye of the Tiger* (1977), but his career never really took off.

Horror Hospital starts memorably with a scene which perfectly sets up the film's offbeat feel. Two patients of Brittlehurst Manor, a young man and woman, flee the grounds of the hospital and into the surrounding woods. Their heads are swathed with bloody bandages (which we later realize is because of the brain surgery performed on them). Dr Storm and Frederick are in a limousine observing the escapees. "We need to make a clean job of it," Storm tells Frederick. "The car was washed this morning." As the limo speeds toward the couple, Frederick presses a button and a long lethal black blade appears from the side of the car and slices the couple's heads clean off!

After this attention-grabbing opening we cut to a nightclub where Jason and a group of hippies are watching a progressive rock band. Jason is aggrieved because the band stole his song. A punch-up ensues between Jason and the band's lead singer, and Jason ends up with a bloody nose. Staggering away from the club, one of his friends suggests Jason needs a holiday and hands him a leaflet for Hairy Holidays. "I fancy something hairy," he snorts. So far so random.

Hairy Holidays is run by the creepy Mr Pollack (Price) who seems more interested in getting into Jason's pants than in selling him a holiday. Jason makes a quick exit, and next thing he's on a train to Brittlehurst, where he encounters Judy who is on her way there too, to visit her aunt who lives and works at the Manor. By this point in the film, you are either intrigued by the bizarrely wooden performances and outlandish dialogue, or you're about to turn *Horror Hospital* off. But I urge you to stick with it as there are delights in store.

Jason and Judy arrive at Brittlehurst railway station, and after being given directions by the station guard (who you just know is in on the conspiracy) they start to walk to the clinic. On their way they get caught in the rain but are saved by a pair of leather-clad guys on motorbikes who also work for Dr Storm. Delivered to Brittlehurst Manor, they are met by Frederick who shows them to their room. On the way we get our first glimpse of horror as they pass by an open bedroom door. Glancing in, Jason and Judy see that the bed is soaked in blood. "Nothing to worry about," Frederick tells them. "We all have our little accidents."

Making themselves comfortable in their own room, there's the inevitable rumpy pumpy before the couple go down to dinner. It's at this point that *Horror Hospital* really kicks into gear as Jason and Judy take their seat in the dinner hall with the other residents. All of them have the pale-faced, glassy eyed look of zombies, and what's more, large scars on their heads from where they appear to have been lobotomized.

Realizing that something is seriously amiss, Jason and Judy decide to do a little investigating (after a bit more bedroom time together) and soon find themselves at the mercy of Dr Storm who has rather nasty plans for the young couple. Escape soon becomes the order of the day. But can they escape Dr Storm's scalpel?

Revealing any more of the plot would involve too many spoilers, and I urge you to seek out *Horror Hospital* for yourself. You'll find it fascinating and infuriating in equal measures. It's fascinating because it does include so many 70s horror tropes: it's basically a 'generation gap' horror movie, not unlike Michael Reeves' *The Sorcerers* (1967) and *Witchfinder General* (1968) in that it's about the older generation preying on liberated youth, trying to get a little of what the young people are having (sex and drugs, mostly), things that the older generation were deprived of in their own youth. Dr Storm is a bit like that in wanting to turn his patients into his sex slaves! *Horror Hospital* also bears more than a passing resemblance to Pete Walker's work in the 70s, namely *House of Whipcord* (1974) in that the youths are 'imprisoned' in an institution where they are experimented on for the sexual gratification of those in charge.

The House that Dripped Blood (1971)

Robert Bloch's career as a screenwriter began in 1960, although contrary to popular belief, he was already well on his way to writing for film and TV by the time *Psycho* (which was based on Bloch's 1959 novel) was made by Alfred Hitchcock that same year. Born in 1917 and raised in the Midwest, Bloch spent much of his youth in cinemas. A screening of Lon Chaney's *Phantom of the Opera* (1925) made a big impression on Bloch as a young boy and led to a lifelong obsession with fantasy, horror and science fiction. Bloch became a professional writer at the tender age of seventeen with a short story sale to *Weird Tales* — numerous short stories and novels would follow — but Bloch had his eye on Hollywood early on, and in 1959 an invitation to write a detective series for syndicated television brought Bloch to L.A. where he would become a scriptwriter on shows like *Alfred Hitchcock Presents*, *Thriller* and *The Alfred Hitchcock Hour*.

Television in the 1960s — before the networks took over — gave Bloch a great deal of artistic freedom, with any changes made to his scripts the result of constructive criticism on the part of producers of the shows. It was the sort of relationship that Bloch would later come to enjoy with Milton Subotsky at Amicus — for the most part, at least.

Before his tenure at Amicus, though, Block was to receive a lesson in the exigencies of low-budget horror from legendary B-movie producer-director William Castle for whom he wrote two psychological thrillers, *Straight-Jacket* and *The Nightwalker* (both 1964). *Straight-Jacket* was based on Castle's own story of a female axe killer released from the local asylum, but Bloch's screenplay played up the suspense and turned Castle's routine pot boiler into a series of virtuoso murder set pieces. *The Nightwalker* was Castle's first picture for Universal and another attempt on his part to move from the kind of gory shockers he had become famous for in the 50s towards psycho-thrillers. Bloch's reputation was built on horror, but he would remain a versatile writer throughout his career. An acolyte of H.P. Lovecraft, Bloch had started out writing cosmic horror in his early short stories, but gradually moved into territory that was more psychological. (He also wrote science fiction and even contributed three episodes of *Star Trek*.) Bloch's versatility, his ability to write to order and his extraordinary productivity made him a natural for low-budget horror movies, although he would have mixed feelings about working at this level, often suffering script changes due to budgetary restrictions. As he later remarked in his autobiography, "a low-budget film always operates on the same principle, that is to say, no principle whatsoever except saving a buck, even if it means losing the potential of the picture".

Producers nevertheless knew that Bloch was a craftsman in the genre and a talented writer of dialogue and character. He was modest to boot, claiming in 1969, "empathy is the only strength I have — the ability to put myself inside the characters and understand their motivations". Bloch's sense of story realism attracted producers like Castle and Subotsky, filmmakers looking for an alternative to Gothic horror, following the trend set by *Psycho*.

What's more, Bloch had a strong sense of the cinematic in his writing, and according to Subotsky, it was this visual sensibility that attracted the producer to Bloch's short story, *The Skull of the Marquis de Sade*, first published in *Weird Tales* in 1945. "What I liked about it," Subotsky told *Cinefantastique* in 1973, "was that I saw we could do the last four reels without any dialogue, which is just the way we did it". Subotsky wrote the screenplay for *The Skull* (1965) himself but his script follows Bloch's short story closely. So much so that Subotsky's script is said to have been only forty minutes long (with director Freddie Francis claiming to *Shivers* in 1995 that "we had to expand it to 85 minutes on the set").

Despite any misgivings that Bloch himself may have had about *The Skull*, he signed up with Amicus as screenwriter of *The Psychopath* (1966), based on his own original unpublished story. With the working title of *Schizo*, it's not hard to see that Amicus was trying to capitalize on Bloch's name whilst also cashing in on Hammer's thriller cycle. *The Deadly Bees* (1966) followed, based on the 1941 novel *The Taste for Honey* by English writer T.F. Heard. Bloch's least favourite of the films he wrote for Amicus, according to Bloch, director Freddie Francis had the script rewritten while Subotsky and Max J. Rosenberg were away on business. When they returned, they were unhappy with the rewrite by Anthony Marriot, but as the sets were already built, they couldn't afford to scrap the production. "I had written the script with the book in mind," Bloch claimed in an interview with Darrell Schweitzer conducted in 1993, "and [the finished film] didn't bear any resemblance to it". Certainly, there was little love lost between Francis (who had also directed *The Psychopath*) and Bloch, with Bloch regularly denigrating the director in interviews for years to come. Even so, Francis helmed Bloch's next screenplay for Amicus — and the writer's first horror anthology for the studio — *Torture Garden*, made in 1967.

Based on four of Bloch's short stories, with a wrap-around provided by Subotsky, *Torture Garden* established a working formula that Subotsky and Bloch would use in all of their subsequent anthology films together. As Subotsky told *Cinefantastique*, "what I do is select four of his stories and invent a framework, and then I send it off to him and if he likes it he does a script based on it". Certainly, Subotsky seems to have had great respect for Bloch as a screenwriter, claiming that, "we work very well together. He's nice to work with and he writes fine stories". In describing Francis, Subotsky praised the director for his visual style but admitted, "I don't think he understands script and story as well as some other directors". (One of these other directors was undoubtedly Roy Ward Baker, who was much more respectful of Bloch's writing.)

Perhaps being a scriptwriter himself helped Subotsky in his dealings with Bloch: Subotsky subscribed to the view that the most important aspect of filmmaking is the script; both men also shared a love of silent cinema developed through their childhood film-going. "What I like in horror films is that you can make silent movies for a long period of time," Subotsky told Chris Knight in 1973. "On our films I like as little dialogue as possible, building up to a long, silent sequence which carries the story. Every one of the multi-story films you'll find does that."

Bloch's own sense of short story form made him in many ways the perfect screenwriter for Amicus' anthology movies. His stories are of the twist-in-the-tale school. This, Bloch professed to have learned from imitating Lovecraft in his own early short stories, telling Darrell Schweitzer, "I used the plot structure and form that he had. I didn't think about it consciously at the time. Later, I began to realize that many of the readers were intrigued by a twist or a surprise or a shock ending, so I just tried to give them what they wanted as entertainment".

Despite Amicus setting their anthologies in the modern world, there is quaintness to the four portmanteau films scripted by Bloch, in contrast to the later, nastier E.C. comics-inspired *Tales from the Crypt* (1972) and *Vault of Horror* (1973). Bloch was very much against grisliness and objected to the title given by the studio to his second Amicus anthology, *The House That Dripped Blood* (1971). The slightly anachronistic feel and old-fashioned sense of morality of Bloch's Amicus anthologies also stem from the fact that many of the original short stories on which the films are based were written in the thirties and forties, reflecting more genteel times in horror fiction.

Bloch's opening story for *The House That Dripped Blood*, 'Method for Murder', the tale of a horror writer stalked by the psychopathic protagonist of his own novel, is classic Bloch. In his book, *Danse Macabre*, Stephen King discusses Bloch's career move from Lovecraftian horror to psychological thriller in terms of a shifting perspective 'from the outside (beyond the stars, under the sea, on the Plains of Leng, or in the deserted belfry of a Providence, Rhode Island, church) to the inside…to the place where the

Werewolf is'. 'Method For Murder', like much of Bloch's psychological writing, concerns what King describes as 'the Dionysian psychopath locked up behind the Apollonian façade of normality... but slowly emerging'. Indeed, 'Method for Murder' may well have inspired King's own 'Werewolf' novel, *The Dark Half*, published in 1989.

Bloch's short story, 'The Living End', first published in *Weird Tales* in 1939, is the source for 'Waxworks', the mournful story of a stockbroker (Peter Cushing) who becomes obsessed with a museum waxwork model that closely resembles his lost lady love. Bloch had already adapted this tale for television in 1962, during his tenure on *Thriller*. Boris Karloff took the Cushing role in the TV adaptation, but there is something poignant about Cushing's casting here, his own wife dying so soon after the film's release. During its two-season run from 1960 to 1962, *Thriller* (like Amicus) would mine *Weird Tales* for short stories, including Bloch's 'The Weird Tailor', which would also feature in *Asylum* (1972).

The third story is 'Sweets to the Sweet', first published in 1947 (again in *Weird Tales*). A Henry James-inspired tale of a governess and her strange young charge, 'Sweets to the Sweet' speaks to Bloch's skill at building atmosphere and credible characterization. The short story is now considered a classic, and deservedly so. Director Peter Duffell stuck close to Bloch's script, and the result is an eerily effective mood piece.

Generally thought to be the best of the four segments is 'The Cloak', adapted by Bloch from his short story of the same name, first published in *Unknown* in 1939. This tongue-in-cheek tale of a vain actor who acquires the cloak of an elderly man only to find it exerts a rather strange influence on those who wear it, is pure Amicus — and pure Bloch. The unwitting thespian (played by Jon Pertwee), who is making a film called 'Curse of the Bloodsuckers', discovers his own inner bloodsucker whenever he wears the old man's cloak. It's a wonderful story-within-a-story that showcases Bloch's desire to entertain his audience.

In the Aftermath (1989)

Released straight-to-video in the UK in December 1988, and barely seen elsewhere except for a limited theatrical release in Australia that same year, *In the Aftermath: Angels Never Sleep* remains an intriguing post-apocalyptic New World/anime mash-up. Comprising thirty or so minutes of material from Mamoru Oshii's early animation masterpiece *Tenshi No Tamago* (*Angel's Egg*, 1985) remixed with additional live action footage shot by Carl Colpaert, whose first directorial credit this is, the result is in some ways what you might expect from the kind of magpie movie that the studio founded by Roger Corman became known for. Hollywood has, after all, been importing foreign language genre movies and re-editing, redubbing and re-shooting them since *Gojira* (1954)/*Godzilla* (1956), and the mix of animation and live action is older than Disney (and, in fact, dates back to Max Fleischer's work in the 20s). What marks *In the Aftermath* as slightly different, though, is its 80s context. Like *Gojira*/*Godzilla* and Corman's own early Russian sci-fi remixes, Oshii and Colpaert's film arises from nuclear anxieties, but in this case ones that come at the very end of the Cold War rather than at the beginning of it.

In the Aftermath has its foundations, then, in New World Pictures' practice of using footage from foreign genre films in creating their own low budget product. This is something that Roger Corman had been doing since before New World, in his days as an independent producer making movies for distribution by American International Pictures. Most famously, Corman bought the rights to the 1959 Russian sci-fi epic *Nebo Zovyot*, removed the anti-West propaganda, hired Jack Hill and a young Francis Ford Coppola to shoot additional scenes, and re-titled the resulting mishmash *Battle Beyond the Sun* (1962) for release in American drive-ins. What the canny Corman realized was that the high budget special effects scenes of this and other state-funded Soviet-Russian space movies could be utilized if he dubbed and/or shot additional English language dialogue scenes (on cheaply made sets) that would make the film suitable for American audiences and improve its sales potential in the West. It was a way to get an expensive-looking movie with high production values on a tiny budget, and the ploy proved profitable for Corman and New World — so much so that even after Corman sold New World Pictures in 1983 (moving on to form New Horizons), the company carried on the ethos of buying overseas genre titles and releasing them in Americanized versions.

In 1985, New World had already purchased the rights to Hayao Miyazaki's post-apocalyptic anime *Nausicaä of the Valley of the Wind* (1984), which they released in the States as *Warriors of the Wind*. That same year, New World picked Toho's belated kaiju *The Return of Godzilla*, re-edited it, and released it as *Godzilla 1985*. Largely thanks to the impact on the public consciousness of *The Day After* (1983), atomic war and post-apocalypse movies were trending again (Corman had himself rode the first wave of these types of movies in the mid-to-late 50s with titles like *The Day the World Ended*, 1955, and *The Last Woman on Earth*, 1960). New World went back to Tokuma Shoten studio in 1988 to license a direct-to-video anime called *Tenshi No Tamago*, sensing that with a little 'Americanizing' it could be sold as a late-edition post-apocalypse mash-up movie.

Tenshi No Tamago, in fact, follows a long tradition of apocalyptic fantasy that dates back to the early work of Tezuka Osamu and finds its roots in the traumatic events of World War II: in the atomic destruction of Hiroshima and Nagasaki and the fire-bombing of numerous Japanese towns and cities. Tezuka, who had personally experienced the incendiary bombings of Osaka which resulted in the deaths of 10,000 civilians, would go on, in 1951, to create the seminal robot manga *Astro Boy* through which he was to express his ideas on war and peace, destructive technology and the distrust (shared by many Japanese after WWII) of politicians and military leaders. Tezuka's successor, Miyazaki, later explored themes of war and environmental disaster in the aforementioned *Nausicaä of the Valley of the Wind*, setting his anime in a post-nuclear holocaust world in which the titular heroine must find a way to bring peace between kingdoms and save the planet from ecological catastrophe. The conclusion of Katsuhiro Otomo's dystopian sci-fi *Akira* (1988) similarly saw Tokyo destroyed by a gravitational singularity which resembles a giant white cloud enveloping the city, while *Barefoot Gen* (1983), based on the autobiographical manga of Hiroshima survivor Keiji Nakazawa, depicts in graphic detail the real-life atomic bombing of Hiroshima and its aftermath in which the author's family perished.

While later anime served to remind a new generation of Japanese about the horrors of nuclear destruction, the intensification of hostilities of the Cold War during the Reagan era saw apocalyptic animation also produced in the West. In 1986, Jimmy T. Murakami (another Corman alumnus) directed the animated film *When the Wind Blows*, a big screen adaptation of Raymond Briggs' graphic novel depicting the effects of a Soviet ICBM attack on rural England. (Incidentally, the British Film Institute had funded Cold War animation as early as 1956, with Joan and Peter Foldes' controversial and still shocking experimental film, *A Short Vision*.) The collage-film *Atomic Café*, a documentary satire of the nuclear age assembled from newsreels and other assorted archive material, had also been released in 1982, to great critical acclaim. The idea, then, of a mixed-media post-apocalyptic mash-up

— as *In the Aftermath* would become — did not seem as unusual in the 80s as it perhaps does today.

Made at a time when cash-strapped Japanese studios were generally turning to popular franchises like the *Tora-san* series rather than funding the work of new artists, *Tenshi No Tamago* came into existence primarily thanks to the boom in direct-to-video films (OVAs) produced for young Japanese audiences brought up on manga. Oshii himself rose up through the ranks of storyboard artist (for Tatsunoko Pro and later Studio Pierrot) to director on the animated TV series *Urusei Yatsura*, an adaptation of Rumiko Takahashi's manga comedy of the same name. Two *Urusei Yatsura* films followed (*Only You* [1983]; *Beautiful Dreamer* [1984]), and what is generally considered to be the first-ever released OVA — *Dallos* (1983), establishing Oshii as a leading light of anime and giving him the commercial clout to embark upon *Tenshi No Tamago*.

Co-written with Yoshitaka Amano (who also did the character designs), *Tenshi No Tamago* has been called Oshii's most personal film. The minimalist story involves an unnamed young girl who wanders a post-apocalyptic city guarding a large egg which she keeps hidden beneath her dress. There she meets a boy and the pair travel together through a petrified forest to an ancient fossilized cave which is her settlement. While the girl sleeps, the boy smashes the egg and leaves. Next morning, the girl is bereft, and, wandering through the woods, falls into a deep ravine where she sees herself transformed into a grown woman before drowning. From her last breath, bubbles in the water become a multitude of eggs which wash up on the shore. The boy witnesses a giant orb rising from the water upon which the girl — apparently reborn — is seated on a throne, caressing a new egg which she holds in her lap.

Containing less than four minutes of dialogue, *Tenshi No Tamago* has genuine cinematic sweep; it is epic, hallucinatory and visionary. Oshii relies on the enigmatic and evocative power of image and sound rather than narrative to create meaning. A brief comparison of a scene that appears in both versions, where the girl (named Angel by Colpaert) first meets the boy in an urban area of giant broken architecture, illustrates the essential difference between the two films. Colpaert uses it as a moment of dialogue exposition in which the boy (named Jonathan in *In the Aftermath*) explains his relationship to Angel and outlines her mission in the story. Oshii, by contrast, offers no dialogue whatsoever. Instead, the two characters simply gaze at each other warily, while Oshii cuts between close-ups of their faces. It's like a typical Sergio Leone scene between gunslingers silently sizing each other up to see who will make the first move. In this respect, dialogue gives way to visuals throughout *Tenshi No Tamago*. Similarly, Oshii uses music sparingly, instead emphasizing the natural sounds of the world around the characters. The sound of dripping water in the forest, for example, is contrasted with the noise of heavy machinery in the city. *Tenshi No Tamago* is an intensely spiritual film, austerely done, and imbued with religious symbolism. It is no surprise that Oshii was, in the early part of his career, deeply influenced by the work of the Russian director Andrei Tarkovsky, whose films had, in the 80s, become widely distributed in countries outside the Soviet Union for the first time. Oshii has professed a particular love of *Solaris* (1972), *Mirror* (1975) and *Stalker* (1979), and imagery from each can be found reflected in Oshii's vision of *Tenshi No Tamago*. But in scenes of the girl wandering alone through the petrified forest like a war refugee, we might also detect traces of Tarkovsky's debut, *Ivan's Childhood* (1962).

Tenshi No Tamago was initially released in Japan on VHS and LaserDisc by Animage Video, and later had releases on Japanese DVD and Blu-ray (most recently by Pony Canyon in 2013), but outside of a TV airing in Australia, has never been shown in its full original version in the West. This in itself makes *In the Aftermath* an intriguing hybrid.

Born in Belgium in 1963, Carl Colpaert started *his* career in the editorial department at New World, working on such titles as Roland Emmerich's psi-power fantasy *Making Contact* (1985) and Donald G. Jackson's futuristic nun-skating ninja epic *Roller Blade* (1986). Corman has always favoured directors with a background in post-production, who know how to make the most of very little. For *In the Aftermath*, Colpaert re-assembled Oshii's original material, dubbed in new dialogue and a narration for Angel (which gives her a more clearly defined quest) and sketched in a story set in a post-apocalypse world where the air is poisoned by radiation.

With a meagre budget stretching to a cast of only six (and a few prop gas-masks!), Colpaert makes a major virtue of his main location, the impressive Kaiser Steel plant in Fontana, South Carolina (which sci-fi fans will recognize from *The Running Man*, 1987, and *Terminator 2: Judgement Day*, 1991), here standing in as the post-doomsday Earth.

Tony Markes (who would go on to a chequered career in the 90s as a producer and director) plays a soldier called Frank, one of only a handful of survivors who searches the toxic wastelands for essential supplies. Unbeknown to him, he is being watched over from the heavens above by Angel and her brother Jonathan. In Colpaert's version, the egg that Angel carries so protectively serves a specific purpose. It is imbued with a mysterious power that can only be released by a deserving recipient. Angel's mission is to find that person and Frank, of course, seems to be the most likely candidate. Until that happens, they are, in Jonathan's words, "alone on a planet, with no fish".

Colpaert's intercutting of Angel's anime dream world with Frank's post-apocalyptic real world at times conjures up associations with films that use mixed media to contrast Earth with the afterlife, presenting them as alternate realities or parallel universes (*à la* portraying heaven in black and white and Earth in colour in *A Matter of Life and Death*, 1946). Colpaert achieves some striking transitions between Oshii's material and his own live action footage, such as a graphic match cut between the animated feather that floats to the ground in Angel's world and the real-life feather that Frank retrieves in his own barren landscape.

Therein, *In the Aftermath* manages to retain much of the lyricism of *Tenshi No Tamago*. In a striking musical interlude (in which we hear the haunting echoes of Horacio Moscovici's "Carnavalito Tango"), Colpaert renders his own footage into a negative image so as to merge it almost seamlessly with Oshii's original. It's a momentary coming together of animation and live action — of Japanese anime and New World B-movie — that makes this cult curiosity all the more intriguing.

In the Aftermath (New World Pictures, 1988)

Invasion of the Body Snatchers (1956)

It would be hard to name a more socially relevant horror film of the 50s than *Invasion of the Body Snatchers* (1956). Don Siegel's masterpiece, as numerous critics and commentators have pointed out, reflects the Cold War paranoia of the time — the fifties fear of communist infiltration and the witch-hunt led by Senator Joseph McCarthy to weed out 'Reds' in the American population. But the fact that *Invasion of the Body Snatchers* went on to spawn three remakes (in 1978, 1993 and 2007) over a number of different decades suggests that the basic premise — extraterrestrials take over the bodies and minds of human beings and turn them into emotionless automatons — has relevance beyond the 50s. In fact, the underlying themes of *Invasion of the Body Snatchers* still hold power today.

As critic Ryan Lambie wrote in 2018, 'beyond the political allegories that have been read into it over the years…*Body Snatchers* is also a chilling film about conformity and free will.' According to Siegel himself, *Invasion of the Body Snatchers* criticizes conformism of any sort — McCarthyist or communist — in favour of freedom of thought. *Invasion of the Body Snatchers*' long lasting cultural resonance is such that the term 'Pod People' has entered the English language, meaning 'a person who behaves in a strange especially mechanical way, as if not fully human' (Collins Dictionary). A Pod Person is a soulless conformist who mechanically follows a political ideology (some might nowadays call them 'sheeple'!) *Invasion of the Body Snatchers* and its remakes warn us against the dangers of this kind of conformism, the way it plays into the hands of a totalitarian mindset, and how it polarizes people into two tribes: *us* and *them*.

Jack Finney, who wrote the book *The Bodysnatchers*, on which the films are based, maintained that no allegory was intended, but given the time of the book — 1955 — it's no wonder critics have read allegory into it. Finney's novel is set in small-town America — Mill Valley, a real-life town in California, fourteen miles from San Francisco. The hero is Miles Bennell, the town's doctor (Kevin McCarthy in the 1956 film). Bennell comes to believe that something strange is happening in the town. His patients start complaining that members of their family have been replaced by 'imposters' —although they look and behave like they used to, they seem to have lost all human emotion and feeling. At first, Bennell thinks that this phenomenon is psychological, that the people involved are suffering from Capgras delusion (a real-life syndrome in which the people have an irrational belief that someone they know or recognize has been replaced by an imposter). But as he investigates further, Bennell discovers that the replacement humans are actually aliens growing from plant-like seed pods that have drifted to Earth from space. The aliens intend to replace everyone on Earth in this way. With this knowledge, Bennell tries to warn the authorities of the alien conspiracy. But, it is at this point that paranoia starts to set in. If you can't tell who is human and who isn't, who can you trust? Bennell starts to look at the people around him — his neighbours, his friends — and even though they look normal, he doesn't know for sure. Worse still is what they might be saying about him. And what will happen when the Pod People finally outnumber the humans? The only thing left to do, as Bennell comes to realize, is to fight for the survival of the human race.

As Graham Sleight wrote in his 2010 introduction to the novel, 'for all these reasons — the sense of the aliens as a kind of corrupted version of normal people, the conformity they induce in their victims, the paranoia in the survivors — it's easy to read *The Body Snatchers* as a dramatization of Cold War anxieties about what communism would do to American life.' Anti-communist paranoia in the 1950s placed huge pressures on the American public to conform to social doctrines. These values were framed as traditional American ones, but people were coerced into following them nonetheless. Some commentators have described this 'bland conformity in post war-Eisenhower-era America' as a time of consumerism, suburbanization and white picket fences. However, young people tended to be less willing to conform to the values of their parents, and needed clamping down on by schools, authorities and the police.

One of the ways that authorities did this was through the production of mental hygiene films — classroom films that offered teenagers guidance in good behavior and preached conservative moral values. Subjects ranged from substance abuse to sex before marriage, personal grooming, reckless driving, mealtime manners and social conduct at parties. Taking their cues from the training and propaganda films of World War Two, mental hygiene films would often use scare tactics to enforce their message, presenting both an idealized vision of American youth and a potentially apocalyptic one: conforming to social mores would guarantee success, happiness and popularity. However, transgression or rebellion would bring dire consequences, not just for the individual but for society as a whole.

Refusing to conform to social doctrines was branded 'un-American'. This led to a polarized view of US citizens: you were a 'Good American' if you conformed, but if you rebelled (or simply disagreed with the government or were just 'different') you were labelled a communist or a juvenile delinquent. The upshot of this was to create suspicion between people, to pit neighbour against neighbour: "is my neighbour a communist? Is he/she one of us or one of *them*?" It's easy to see, then, why Finney's *The Body*

Snatchers has been viewed as a metaphor for the tyranny of the McCarthy era, and why this reading of it carried over into Siegel's film, made one year after the publication of *The Body Snatchers*.

The 1956 version of *Invasion of the Body Snatchers* retains the small-town setting of the novel, to good effect. As in the novel, we witness a small, close-knit community transformed into one of emotionless drones. With the loss of individual identity comes a sense of alienation. Warmth, friendship and personal autonomy are lost, and the town itself is changed as a result. Mill Valley starts out as an almost nostalgic paean to Americana and small-town life, where everybody knows everyone else and everyone is happy. By the time the alien invasion has taken hold, the town itself becomes shadowy and threatening, like a city in a *film noir*. It's as if *true* American ideals are destroyed by the coming of the Pod People. Siegel wrote in his autobiography, A Siegel Film, 'I think that the world is populated by pods and I wanted to show them. I think so many people have no feeling about cultural things, no feeling of pain, of sorrow. The political reference to Senator McCarthy and totalitarianism was inescapable but I tried not to emphasize it because I feel that motion pictures are primarily to entertain and I did not want to preach.'

Even so, many critics have found the film at its most powerful in the way it expresses concern over homeland totalitarianism in the wake of McCarthy's communist witch hunt, and the campaign of spreading fear of communist infiltration amongst the people. During the McCarthy era, hundreds of ordinary Americans — including teachers, academics, trade unionists and government employees — were accused of being communist sympathizers, and found themselves investigated and questioned by government agencies. Often there was little or no credence to the accusations levelled at them, but many people lost their jobs and their place in the community as a result of this witch-hunt. Some were sent to prison or blacklisted. Gay people were targeted as a part of this, as well, with being gay seen as a contagious disease that posed a threat to homeland security.

Invasion of the Body Snatchers was part of a trend of 50s horror and science fiction that dealt with creeping dehumanization and the loss of individual identity in modern life. But Siegel's film marked an increasing disillusionment with American society that also characterized a number of other films made in the mid-1950s, including *Kiss Me Deadly* (1955) and *Touch of Evil* (1958). This is evident in the ending that Siegel chose for his film adaptation, which is much more pessimistic than the way Finney ended his novel. In the book, human resistance to the alien invasion is such that the aliens realize that they can't hope to replicate enough people to take over the planet. Instead they flee the Earth, and the last remaining Pod People are hunted down and destroyed by the human survivors. Siegel, by contrast, was much less convinced that the Pod People of this world could be so easily defeated, and decided instead to leave the film open-ended. Bennell manages to escape Mill Valley and alert the authorities but we are left unsure just how far the influence of the Pod People extends. Is Bennell too late? Has the invasion already spread to the rest of the country? Siegel originally wanted to end the film on a warning note: Bennell has made it to the San Francisco highway and is trying to alert motorists to the alien threat, screaming out the words, "They're here already! You're next! You're next!"

Ultimately, the studio — Allied Artists — felt that this ending was too much of a downer and would hurt the picture's chances of box office success, so they insisted on adding a wrap-around that saw Bennell telling the story to a psychiatrist who, believing Bennell's version of events, calls the FBI to halt the alien invasion. A much safer ending that mutes the alarming aspects of the film's allegory. As it is, Siegel still manages to convey an atmosphere of disquiet and paranoia that marks *Invasion of the Body Snatchers* as a deeply discomforting watch, today as it was when it was first made.

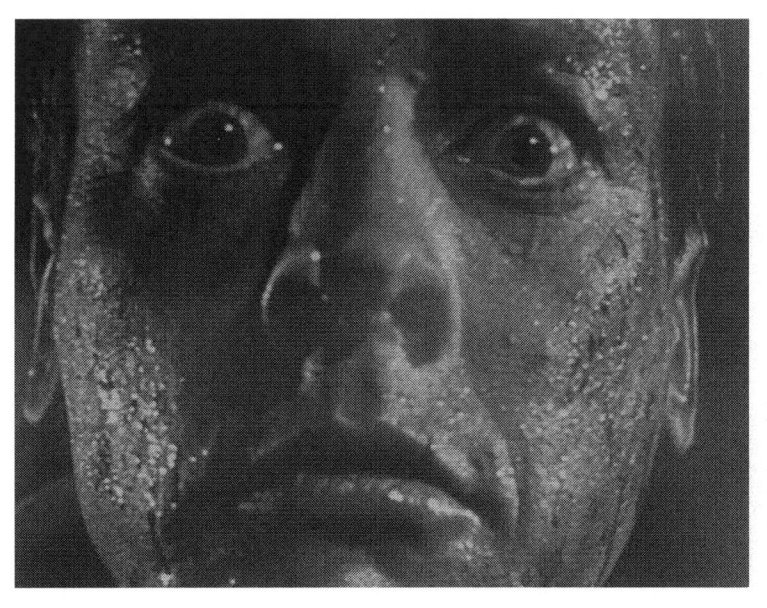

Kevin McCarthy in *Invasion of the Body Snatchers* (Allied Artists, 1956)

The Legend of Hell House (1973)

Until recently, John Hough's adaptation of Richard Matheson's 1971 novel, 'Hell House' has been damned by faint praise. On first release, critics compared it unfavourably to Robert Wise's *The Haunting* (1963), overlooking its virtues as a movie about parapsychology rather than the supernatural, and bemoaning its lack of thrills and chills. Perhaps it was a film ahead of its time, because it is only now that fans have come to praise it for its refusal to conform to haunted house clichés, seeing it instead for the intelligent film about the paranormal that it is.

Certainly, that has been my own experience of the film; having disregarded it in the past, only very recently have I have come to appreciate its value. I first caught the film during a screening on British television in the early 1970s, and for years afterwards — although I vividly remembered the TV trailer — I recalled nothing of the actual film itself. As it is perhaps too subtle and sophisticated a film for a young boy — even one steeped in horror films — to understand, this is obviously not really surprising. But it is that very same subtlety that has, over the years, led numerous critics — including myself — to mistakenly label the film as forgettable.

Matheson's novel was, in fact, written partly as a riposte to Shirley Jackson's novel, 'The Haunting of Hill House' (on which *The Haunting* is based). Matheson admired Jackson's book and the film adapted from it, but he was dissatisfied by the ambiguity of its ending and by the suggestion that the events of the story had taken place only in the disturbed mind of the female protagonist. Matheson had a serious interest and belief in spiritualism and psychic phenomena that lasted throughout his career — and much of that research went into 'Hell House'. Matheson claimed that none of the incidents in the book were made up — all had happened in various haunted houses around the world. Indeed, one of the pleasures of both the novel and the film is its pseudo-scientific approach: the parapsychology in Matheson's screenplay has an air of authenticity rarely found in haunted house movies made before or since. Much of Matheson's 'Hell House' is, in fact, based on the Borley Rectory case, which Colin Wilson, author of numerous books on the paranormal, has described as one of the most significant hauntings of the twentieth century, so much so that The Society for Psychical Research devoted a whole volume to occurrences that took place there in the twenties and thirties (Hell House's nominal hero, Lionel Barrett, may well be based on the real life psychic investigator of the Borley Rectory case, Harry Price).

What drew me back to *The Legend of Hell House* was Matheson, arguably one of the most important writers of horror and science fiction. But when I watched the film again recently — for the first time since that childhood viewing in the 70s — what impressed me about it the most was John Hough's direction. Hough himself has been relatively unsung in the past (although he's now a cult figure amongst horror fans). I once observed him direct during a location visit to his Barbara Cartland adaptation *A Hazard of Hearts* (1987), and conducted a brief interview with him during a break in filming (where we discussed *Twins of Evil*, 1971). He struck me at the time as a journeyman, the kind of director who rises through the ranks of the industry to become solidly professional but no more than that. Perhaps he is in some ways, but stylistically he's much more interesting — and adept — than I gave him credit for. *The Legend of Hell House* is well directed, and this is apparent from the very first scene, where Hough uses a combination of low angles, short lenses and deep focus to emphasize the architecture of his buildings and its relationship to the people within them. This expressionist approach is totally in keeping with the tone and theme of Matheson's novel.

No coincidence, perhaps, that Hough's previous film to *Hell House* was *Treasure Island* (1972), starring cinema's greatest expressionist director, Orson Welles. That's not to suggest that anyone other than Hough is responsible for the visual qualities of *Hell House*. Hough's cinematographer on *Hell House* was the great Alan Hume, but Hume is known more for his versatility than any distinctive personalized style. And Hough's penchant for camera movement and unusual camera angles are evident even from his early days as a director on *The Avengers*, which he helmed between 1968 and 1969 (at Elstree Studios, where he filmed much of *Hell House*).

Another of Hough's strengths as director is his ability to draw fine performances from his actors. During the filming of *A Hazard of Hearts*, I observed him direct stalwarts like Diana Rigg and Edward Fox, as well as then-newcomer Helena Bonham-Carter (in her first screen role); Hough lets actors do their thing, but can be demanding when they don't give him what he wants in terms of making them do extra takes. In *Hell House*, Roddy McDowall gives a virtuoso performance as the troubled psychic, Ben Fischer. A powerful actor, but a histrionic one, in *Hell House*, McDowall finds the perfect balance, aided by Hough's camera which is kept close.

The supreme moment for both director and actor in this film is a two-minute continuous long take — which takes place fifty minutes into the story — in which McDowall tells of the fates that befell previous psychic researchers in the house. Hough has McDowall walk into a big close up, and tracks the camera slowly around him, capturing every nuance of emotion on the actor's face, every remembered horror. It's a bravura scene, made all the more so by Hough's refusal to cut. *Hell House* is as memorable for the way Hough photographs faces as it is for way he moves his actors through the physical space of the Belasco house. Again, the relationship between the house and the people in it is beautifully expressed by Hough's use of the camera.

Puzzling, then, that Matheson professed to be "sick with disappointment" the first time he saw *The Legend of Hell House*. But then Matheson had by that time become quite disillusioned with Hollywood, and by how the studios had treated his books. Matheson's script for *The Legend of Hell House* was not only faithful to his own novel but extremely detailed in terms of its description, indicating his desire to control the visualization of the film. Hough's film is remarkably faithful to the novel, except in the case of the novel's sexuality, which was necessarily toned down in order to secure a PG certificate. In fact, it is difficult to imagine a more successful visualization of the book than is achieved by Hough (in 2002 Guillermo del Toro wrote an adaptation for Fox but a remake is yet to happen).

The Legend of Hell House, then, still remains somewhat unsung, despite gathering a few fans and admirers over the years, especially after its release on DVD in 2001. Its cult reputation is growing slowly, and anyone curious to see it should check out the 2014 Scream Factory Blu-ray, which features a thirty-minute interview with Hough and a commentary track by lead actress Pamela Franklin.

"I don't regard this as a horror film", Hough stated in 1973, "I regard it as a statement on spiritualism". With all respect to John Hough, we might regard *The Legend of Hell House* as both.

Roddy McDowall and Pamela Franklin in *The Legend of Hell House* (Fox, 1973)

The Man with the X-Ray Eyes (1963)

Roger Corman's *X: The Man with the X-Ray Eyes* remains an intriguing entry in the producer-director's extensive filmography, not least because it offers an insight into Corman's own view of himself as a filmmaker at a time when he was, in the words of Stephen King, 'in the process of metamorphosing from the dull caterpillar who had produced such meatloaf movies as *Attack of the Crab Monsters* (1957) and *The Little Shop of Horrors* (1960) and into the butterfly who was responsible for such interesting and rather beautiful horror films as *The Masque of the Red Death* (1964) and *The Terror* (1963)'. Corman may well have viewed Ray Milland's tragic Dr Xavier as a stand-in for himself: a visionary castigated by his peers and reduced to the level of a sideshow novelty act by carnivals and con men.

Numerous critics have commented on the thematic continuity between Corman's Poe cycle (as well as the Lovecraft-inspired *The Haunted Palace*, 1963) and *X*. Corman himself saw the film as a progression, remarking to Keith Phipps in 2017 that "it had many of the elements of the Poe films, but a number of the elements that were new." (The Poe films themselves had represented a step up for Corman artistically as well as in terms of production values: shooting in colour, with longer production schedules; Corman had deliberately imbued the Poe films with symbolism, and, as a result, his reputation grew with the critics.) Less often recognized, though, is how the box office failure of *The Intruder* in 1962 may have impacted on Corman's approach to *X* thematically.

As Corman's biographer and former employee, Beverly Gray, puts it, 'the failure of *The Intruder* was a professional watershed for Corman'. The filmmaker had wanted to make a serious drama about the issue of racial integration in American schools. His script for *The Intruder* (based on Charles Beaumont's 1959 novel) had been turned down by his usual financiers, American International Pictures and Allied Artists, and so Corman funded the film himself with his brother, Gene. The film won an award at the Venice Film Festival, received good reviews from U.S. critics, and languished at the box office. It was the first time Corman had lost money on a film, and he blamed himself for making the message of the movie too blunt. Audiences, he reasoned afterwards, would rather be entertained than educated. He vowed in future always to deliver the entertainment that the audience demanded, with any social message buried beneath the surface on a subtextual level.

Even so, the failure of *The Intruder* stung Corman. He returned to AIP, and horror, for his next project, *The Premature Burial* (1962). According to Beverly Gray, this retreat to safe territory was something of a humiliation for Corman, especially when AIP nixed a deal that Corman had made with Pathé to distribute *The Intruder* in exchange for the Poe title. AIP executives James Nicholson and Samuel Z. Arkoff made it clear that the Poe film would again be theirs, and Corman was surprised to see them show up on the set of *The Premature Burial*, 'cheerfully informing him that he was once again working for them'. To make matters worse, Corman was then forced to retitle *The Intruder* as *I Hate Your Guts!* for the drive-ins, and this rankled — Corman's award-winning drama was being downgraded to exploitation fodder level for the masses. As Corman later told Jonathan Demme, "I would almost say that it's fortunate that it didn't succeed with that title either, so that title faded away. If the picture would have succeeded with that title, I'm not certain I would have been pleased". Corman's dealings with AIP on *The Premature Burial* started a rift between producer and distributor that would eventually see Corman split from them to form New World Pictures in 1970.

Corman's hurt pride almost certainly found its way into the script of *X*, if not consciously, then subconsciously. "I think anybody working in a creative fashion works partly out of their conscious mind and partly out of their unconscious mind," Corman told Constantine Nasr in 2008. "So I think you're aware of certain themes, certain things you want to do. But there are also unconscious drives within you that, as it were, come to the surface."

Nevertheless, *X: The Man with the X-Ray Eyes* started out as a novelty item. In typical AIP fashion, X began simply as a title. 'Jim Nicholson told me, as he so often did over lunch," Corman wrote in his autobiography, 'that he had a title in search of a movie.' In fact, Corman loved the title, which, as he told Demme, he thought was "very evocative". But what exactly did it evoke? As Murray Pomerance notes, the concept is 'certainly one that might tickle the intensively sexualized teen market filled with kids who, having for years been throttled by comic book ads for Slimline X-Ray Specs while they read *Archie* or *Superman* — "Look at your friend. Is that really his body you 'see' under his clothes? Loads of laughs and fun at parties" — might now seek similar, and magnified, kicks in the movie theatre.' AIP and Corman actively sought the youth market with their pictures, and what better way to capture the imagination of a teenager than with the kind of novelty advertisements that for years had been found in the back pages of comics? Indeed, X-ray specs had been on the market since 1906, but it was Harold von Braunhut, inventor of the Amazing Sea Monkeys, who brought X-ray specs to American youth by mail order at the beginning of the 60s. Corman almost certainly saw Braunhut's advertisements for X-ray specs in a comic book: the poster ad-line for *X: The Man with the X-Ray Eyes* pilfers

Braunhut's ads shamelessly: 'Suddenly...he could see thru clothes...flesh...and walls!' Indeed, the film's party scene, in which Xavier is able to see beneath the clothes of the various swingers in the room, seems like the adolescent promise of X-ray specs brought to life. No surprise, then, that *X: The Man with the X-Ray Eyes* would itself be adapted as a comic, published by Gold Key in late 1963.

But if the film's basic concept seemed suited to lurid comic book treatment, the story, as developed by Corman, would have subtext. His first idea was to have the main character a scientist, as Ray Milland is in the film, but Corman rejected this idea as too obvious, and decided to make the film about a jazz musician who had taken too many drugs. After writing four or five pages of storyline, Corman threw out the jazz musician concept and went back to the original idea. (Corman would later explore the subject of the effects of psychedelic drugs on hipsters in *The Trip*, 1967). It's interesting, though, that Corman would find it easier to identify with a scientist than with a jazz musician. Corman (who studied engineering at Stanford) has always been a cool-headed rationalist and Dr Xavier moves through science toward a religious irrational experience that brings him only despair. Corman knew he wanted the picture to be about "somebody who was able to see through things, and see through things increasingly." As a self-confessed "left/liberal/rebellious" filmmaker, Corman perhaps felt himself to possess an acute perception, a sense of vision, which, after his experience on *The Intruder*, he came to see as a curse. In *X*, the visionary ends up mired in the mysticism of Old Testament religion and the hucksterism of Las Vegas, closely related symbols of populism overtaking scientific rationality. Madness ensues. By keeping his main character as a scientist, Corman realized that his story could follow the classic theme set by H.G. Wells' *The Invisible Man*: that of the scientific researcher dabbling in territory best left to the gods, and, as a result, driven insane by his discoveries. Hence, the film's original opening sequence, deleted after *X*'s first theatrical release, which took the form of an educational film warning against the dangers of sensory overload. As the movie's tag line says, 'he dared to look beyond man's vision and saw more than his eyes could stand!'

The plot of *X: The Man with the X-Ray Eyes* is structured around Dr Xavier's 'descent' from science to religion. Banished from the scientific establishment, he seeks refuge as a performer in a fairground, and from there to a basement room as a healer, while at the same time his power of vision increases to the point where he is able to see through his own eyelids. He becomes increasingly isolated from other people and this is reflected in his geographical isolation, until he eventually flees into the desert, trying to escape, in the words of Paul Willeman, 'what can only be called God's punishment for his hubris'. There he stumbles into a religious meeting that is being held in a tent, where he gives testimony to the "light that glows and changes…and in the centre of the Universe… the Eye that sees us all…exists on the edge of the universe". His enhanced vision allows the face of God to be glimpsed, a profound religious experience too much for any human being to bear.

Credit should be given to *X*'s screenwriters Ray Russell and Robert Dillon for structuring *X* this way, as a kind of Greek tragedy, with the story unfolding in episodes, each charting Xavier's further movement towards a final 'exodos' ("If thine eye offend thee…pluck it out!") Russell had also written *The Premature Burial* for Corman, as well as a number of screenplays for fellow exploitation filmmaker William Castle (*Mr. Sardonicus*, 1961, *Zotz!*, 1962), while Dillon would go on to mainstream success with his screenplay for John Frankenheimer's *French Connection II* (1975).

Crucial to the visualization of *X* is Daniel Haller's art direction. Corman shot the film at the Republic Studios in Studio City in early 1963. According to the film's pressbook, among the sets designed and built by Haller were a complete hospital, including full scale operating rooms and laboratory, a Las Vegas casino with full gambling paraphernalia, and a carnival midway and sideshows. In keeping with Corman's Poe films, which were studio-bound, *X* achieves a similar sense of subjectivity. As Corman explained in 2017, "I felt that the unconscious mind does not really see the world. It gets images from the eyes, and sounds from the ear. It hears, but is not aware of the world. So I do not want to photograph the real world. Everything is artificial."

To convey Xavier's X-ray vision, Corman and his cinematographer Floyd Crosby used a prism-eye effect called 'Spectorama', as well as optical printing, smoke and other movie tricks of the time, such as reprinting with different colours over the same negative. Many of these effects Corman would go on to refine for the LSD sequences of *The Trip*. Corman has compared *X* to *2001: A Space Odyssey* (1968) 'in that there is at the end of the odyssey (of both films) an hallucinogenic, mystical vision of light and motion, Kubrick's trip was through space; *X*'s was interior'.

In a similar way, we might even see *X: The Man with the X-Ray Eyes* as a metaphor for cinema itself, a commercial art form whose visionary aspect is so often thwarted. As Corman told Jonathan Demme, "you have to compromise your art somewhat and become a businessman."

Wrote Paul Willeman: "Corman's central statement about the condition of man...represents a terrifying realization of hopelessness". As a veiled autobiographical account of Roger Corman as an artist cursed by his vision and cast out by his community, Willeman's reading of *X* rings despairingly true.

The Man with the X-Ray Eyes (American International Pictures, 1963)

Martin (1977)

Like its titular 'vampire' (played in the film by John Amplas), George A. Romero's *Martin* is a maligned and misunderstood creature of the night. Released in 1978 by Ben Barenholtz's Libra Films, *Martin* played the Waverly Theatre in New York for a year as a Midnight Movie, but failed to penetrate middle-America (and even at the Waverly it fared less well than *Eraserhead*, 1976). It received good reviews at the time from the likes of Jack Kroll at *Newsweek*, but progressive-minded film critics such as Robin Wood (normally a champion of Romero) tended to disparage it in favour of the more overtly subversive *Night of the Living Dead*. Only in the video age did *Martin* finally see light of day, gaining a cult following on VHS (in the UK courtesy of Redemption).

Martin can now be appreciated as a key entry in the director's series of films that he continued with *Monkey Shines* (1988), *The Dark Half* (1993) and *Bruiser* (2000) which explore the monster within man. As Peter (Ken Foree) says of the shopping mall zombies in *Dawn of the Dead*, "They're us, that's all." Romero shows us in *Martin* that the traditional monsters are merely expurgations of ourselves: beasts we've created in order to exorcise the monster from within us.

Romero's inspiration for *Martin* extended beyond the literary vampire to its real-life counterparts. The Manson family killings and the Skid Row Slasher (who in the early 1970s murdered a number of down-and-outs in Los Angeles and drank their blood from goblets brought along specially) were prominent in Romero's mind. Even more so were those unfortunate souls who found themselves craving raw meat and fresh blood due to a medical condition such as anaemia or, in Romero's own words (in his director's notes for *Martin*), 'a mental state' that created 'a lust for drinking blood'. Here Romero is referring to a real psychiatric disorder known as clinical vampirism, or Renfield Syndrome, a rare form of schizophrenia in which the sufferer believes him or herself to need human plasma in order to survive. As early as the 1880s, the neurologist Richard von Kraft-Ebbing diagnosed such a disorder as being sexual in nature: In *Psychopathia Sexualis*, he recounts the case of a 19-year-old man who caught a 12-year-old girl in a forest, raped and murdered her, and drank her blood before burying her corpse. More recent killings linked to clinical vampirism include those of the 'acid-bath' murderer, John Haigh (who confessed to having dreams involving blood as a young boy) and the slayings of the serial killer Richard Trenton Chase, nicknamed the 'Vampire of Sacramento'.

In *Martin*, our tragic bloodsucker may well be a Renfield Syndrome sufferer, and there are signs that his condition could be inherited. (There have been nine such accursed within the Matthias family, as Tata Cuda [Lincoln Maazel] informs his dismayed grand-daughter, Christina [Christine Forrest], three of whom [including Martin himself] are still living.) But even if Martin were to be a genuine 84-year-old vampire, would it really be his fault? "You have to be sympathetic to the creatures because they ain't doin' nothin'," Romero told *Film Comment* in 1977. "They're like sharks: they can't help behaving the way they do."

And so it is with Martin, whom Romero paints as simply 'a disturbed and demented human soul' who becomes the victim of 'the angry mobs of old'. Here Romero is working within the tradition of Mary Shelley's *Frankenstein* (1818), in that Martin is portrayed as a pathetic, socially ostracized 'monster' that is persecuted by a vigilante mob whose violence equals, if not exceeds, that of the monster. Like Shelley's creation, Martin is cast out by a society that labels him as Other. 'Because of his particular difference from the rest of us,' Romero has written of Martin, 'he must die, and die brutally'.

Symptomatic of Martin's clinical vampirism is his conditioning into believing he is a vampire. According to psychologists, sanguinarians suffer from an uncertain identity: in Martin's case, bloodlust is an expression of an inherited archaic belief, inculcated by his family. This, of course, makes Tata Cuda just as delusional as Martin, for in Romero's movies people operate on many levels of insanity that are clear only to themselves. Certainly this was the prominent theme of *The Crazies* (1973), made prior to *Martin*, and which carries over into the present work.

It follows that Cuda's need to demonize Martin, and the process by which that takes place, is really the crux of the film. Like the Puritans who projected their own sexual repression onto the Native American Indian, recasting him as Other, the staunch Catholic Tata Cuda is driven to unload his sins on his cousin Martin. As Romero explained to Tom Seligson in 1981, "I don't think there is an intrinsically evil side to man, but I think all of us at certain times of our lives do things that are compromising…that's the guilt we're trying to unload by creating monsters. We can then punish ourselves by punishing the monsters, allowing our good side to prevail". Romero was brought up a Catholic, fascinated by the magical thinking inherent in its rituals and traditions. *Martin*, alongside *The Exorcist* and *Alice, Sweet Alice* (aka *Communion*, 1976) is one of the great Catholic horror films, in that it captures perfectly the sense of musty Catholic rites and repressions.

Romero possibly named his avenger after the historic Cuda building in Braddock, making him one of the town's elders, entrenched in the traditions of the old country that he tries so desperately to preserve in the New World. Tata Cuda's belief system is under threat by socio-economic upheaval, by the moral shuffling of the modern age. As Romero comments in his director's notes to *Martin*, 'The pillars of society which once gave stoic support to the fight against "monsters" are now crumbling'.

"This is a town for an old person!" Cuda announces of his dying Braddock. But the old days are gone; the industry is gone; Cuda's church has burned to the ground. And yet the vampire hunter clings to the past as justification for his own demonic revenge.

Martin is an outsider to mainstream society, and sees himself as persecuted Other, projecting himself into the Universal monsters of old. He does not conform to heteronormative sexuality; he desires intimacy, but most of all wants to be accepted for who he is. 'Being seen as monster — by family, community, society — can prompt self-comparisons to and empathy for monsters,' writes film critic and *Martin* fan A. Loudermilk in *Pop Matters*. We are told that Martin's mother committed suicide when he was young, inviting us to read Martin's sex attacks on predominantly older women — as well as his tentative friendships with mother figures Christina and Mrs Santini (Elyanne Nadeau) — as attempts at intimacy with the maternal object. The disembodied voice that calls his name throughout the film may well be that of his mother.

Romero's own family background, and childhood sense of being 'different', also inform *Martin*. Himself a second generation American of Cuban-Lithuanian descent, Romero grew up in the Bronx of the 1950s, dodging the gangs, immersed in EC comic books, precociously intelligent, physically awkward, alienated from the old-world views of his parents and his Catholic upbringing. "On the surface everything was very nice and structured," he told *Cinefile* in 1978, "But underneath it all nothing was happening, 'we were already invaded by the bodysnatchers'". As soon as he was able, Romero took flight to Carnegie Mellon University in Pittsburgh, where he stayed. He called his family one day and told them he wasn't coming back.

But while Romero draws sympathy for Martin's alienation by casting him as victim of a toxic family, we are never allowed to forget that he is also a sexual predator. Indeed, the very structure of *Martin* is based on an alternating pattern of predator/victim/predator/victim/predator/victim; set-piece sequences of Martin's bloody murders are interspersed with domestic family scenes showing his maltreatment by Cuda and the priests brought into the house to exorcise him. Thereby Romero develops his discourse on how the predator becomes victim, how demonization leads to persecution, and how the angry mob purges its own evil by staking the 'vampire'.

Some critics did not appreciate the idea of making Martin a victim of his own delusions. Robin Wood has spoken of the horror genre's 'essential dilemma', which resides in the relationship between the monster and normality, and the implications thereof: can the genre survive the recognition that the monster is its real hero? If the 'return of the repressed' is conceived in positive terms, what happens to 'horror'? And is such a positive conception logically possible? Wood bemoaned the fact that Romero evades this dilemma in *Martin* rather than resolving it. At the Toronto Film Festival in 1979, he took Romero to task for the way in which Martin's descent into vampire fantasies prevent him from confronting his social reality and making any commitment to changing society. Other critics beside Wood have read *Martin* in these same terms: that the character's becoming a vampire is a matter of personal choice. Romero scholar, Tony Williams, argues that vampirism is Martin's chosen form of self-expression, one that hinders any potential of him becoming a real human being. Similarly, Brian Wilson, writing in *Senses of Cinema*, views Martin's disturbed behaviour as a rejection of conformity that suggests both a confused psychological state and an 'inability to subvert dominant traditions in a progressive manner'.

But Martin's lack of choice in the matter seems to be an essential part of Romero's message. Martin must accept his fate in order for the story to have meaning. He flirts with the possibility of change but in the end becomes resigned to remaining who and what he is. "In real life you can't get people to do what you want them to do," he laments on the local radio talk show where he has become a minor celebrity as 'The Count'. "You get used to things. You get used to your life." Martin is destined to remain caught in a loop. In the final sequences of the film, we are back where we started: Martin on a train; the same down and out drunk in the same station toilet cubicle; another woman with her wrists slashed. The mythologizing continues, even after Martin's death. For Romero, Martin's tragedy is that he cannot create an identity for himself beyond his family's conditioning and the role defined for him by a vengeful society. As Romero told *Cinefile*, "I think we should be able to make decisions about what we want to do, instead of being told that this is the way to behave."

Martin is George A. Romero's statement on how as a society we create our own monsters; and how by distinguishing them as separate from ourselves, we seek to destroy them. But there are monsters within all of us; the potential for evil is part of human nature, and as Romero remarked in 1981, "I tried to show in *Martin* that you can't just slice off this evil part of ourselves and throw it away. It's a permanent part of us and we'd better try to understand it".

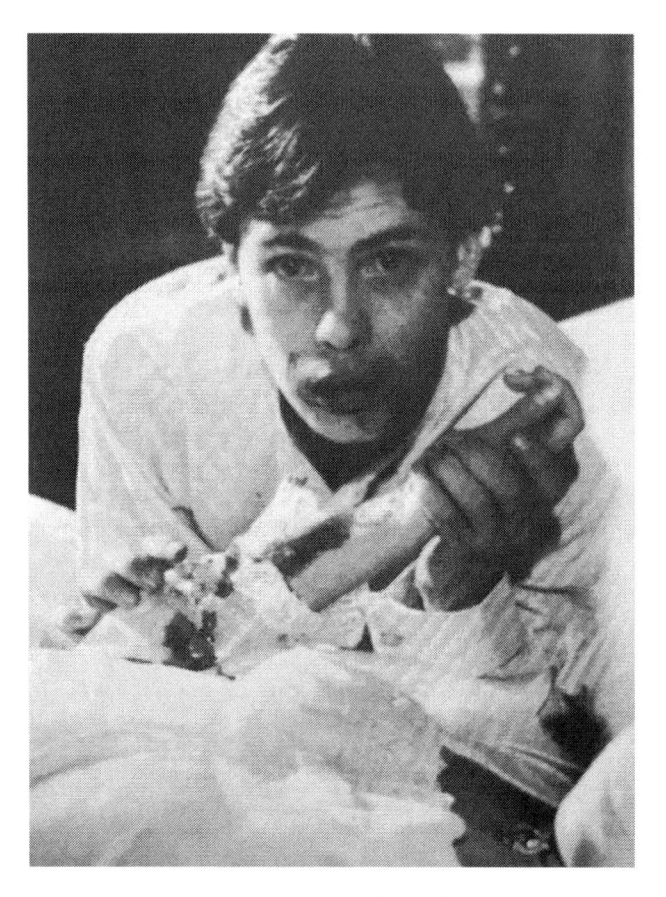

John Amplas as *Martin* (Laurel, 1977)

Mary Shelley's Frankenstein (1994)

What intrigues the modern viewer of Kenneth Branagh's 1994 adaptation of Mary Shelley's novel *Frankenstein; or, The Modern Prometheus* (written in 1818) is how he attempted to create the film almost as if the story had never been filmed before. That Branagh chose to call his film *Mary Shelley's Frankenstein* (and not 'Kenneth Branagh's Frankenstein') is fascinating, signalling an absolute return to the literary wellspring that inspired his adaptation while sidestepping countless Frankenstein films made in the interim. It also reflects a curious auteur trait in Branagh himself. After all, this is the actor-as-auteur who directed several film adaptations of Shakespeare, starting with *Henry V* (in 1989) and then appeared *as* Shakespeare in a film which he also directed (*All is True*, 2018). In Branagh's work, issues of authorship not so much blur as become transposed as part of the act of creation itself — not unlike the 'hideous progeny' that poor old Victor Frankenstein creates by stitching together bits of cadavers and subjecting them to the life-giving voltage of the heavens. Early in his career Branagh was described (by theatre critic Milton Schulman) as possessing "the vitality of Olivier, the passion of Gielgud, the assurance of Guinness": traits he surely shares with Victor Frankenstein too. At the very least, both Victor and Branagh know how to put on a good show (and do so with great aplomb).

But where does this leave us from the standpoint of genre? In spite of any indications or expectations to the contrary, *Mary Shelley's Frankenstein* is based on a work that virtually defined a genre in its influence on literature, films and plays. And while Branagh may have sought to ignore previous adaptations of Shelley's novel in an attempt to *return* us to Shelley — in spirit at least — for us to do so would preclude a number of interesting and potentially illuminating comparisons: in other words, how *Mary Shelley's Frankenstein* fits into the lineage of adaptations and their range of social, cultural and scientific perspectives.

On its release in 1994, *Mary Shelley's Frankenstein* marked a return not only to its literary origins, but to the origins of the horror film itself — or at least to a time when the term 'horror film' first became a thing. American Zoetrope, in following *Bram Stoker's Dracula* (directed by Francis Ford Coppola in 1992) with the Mary Shelley adaptation, hoped to replicate the box success that Universal enjoyed in 1931 with Tod Browning's *Dracula* and James Whale's *Frankenstein* (1931) the following season. This horror movie double whammy had, of course, already been repeated (in Eastmancolour!) by Britain's Hammer, who released — in a reversed order of monsters — *Curse of Frankenstein* in 1957 followed by *Dracula* (aka *Horror of Dracula*) in 1958. These films have become celebrated by film historians not just as triumphs for the studios that created them, but for the ways they have held a mirror to society. Horror films of the 1930s are said to reflect working class discontent arising from the Great Depression: Boris Karloff's monster — along with *The Mummy* (1932) and *Freaks* (1932) — are noticeably blue-collar monsters, exploited or disenfranchised by their masters. *Frankenstein* broke taboos of eugenics; therein lay much of its shock value — Karloff's creature is made monstrous not so much by his physical appearance as by his 'abnormal' criminal brain. *Curse of Frankenstein*, by contrast, derives much of its shock value from the increasingly liberal censorship of the late 50s into the 60s.

A key moment in both *Frankenstein* and *Curse of Frankenstein* is the revelation of the monster: the first time we see it close up and 'alive'. Perhaps the greatest shock in *Frankenstein* occurs when we are introduced to the creature: as Karloff shuffles through the doorway of the castle chamber, with his back to the camera, and then slowly turns around to face us — the intention is to emphasize his ghastly face. Whale uses cutting on axis to deliver a series of camera shots that move in closer and closer to the monster's features, making the horror bigger and bigger on screen. The camera dwells on Karloff's distinctive facial features (and Jack Pierce's iconic make-up) to create visceral shock; but also to present what eugenicists would recognize as the physiognomy of a criminal. In *Curse of Frankenstein*, director Terence Fisher has the camera dolly in at speed to the bandaged monster (played by Christopher Lee) as it whips off the wrappings from its face to reveal its hideous visage — *in shocking full colour close up* — to create an unforgettably graphic shock.

Branagh, by contrast, underplays this seminal moment in his adaptation — of monster confronting maker with the true extent of its monstrousness — in favour of an entirely different kind of encounter between Victor and his creature: one that is decidedly homoerotic. Queer theorists have long contended that the relationship between monster and creator in Frankenstein stories has homosexual subtext. One of the most intriguing aspects of James Whale's *Frankenstein* concerns Henry's sexuality in relation to his creation of the monster. It is, as critic Robin Wood has commented, highly significant that Henry's decision to create his monster juxtaposes very precisely with his decision to become engaged to be married. Henry's desire to 'play God' can be seen as arising from his repressed sexuality; his insane ambition to create life artificially is a sublimation of his sex drive. Henry would rather be in his laboratory making his creature than be with his fiancée Elizabeth.

Of course, it was only after Whale's homosexuality became widely known in the 70s and 80s that revisionist readings of *Frankenstein* found a gay subtext to the isolation and scorn endured by the monster. However, this does not exclude homoeroticism from the 'Frankenstein' genre as a whole. *Frankenstein: The True Story* (1973), scripted by Christopher Isherwood and his lover Don Bachardy, portrays 18th century upper class London as a society of beautiful people, into which Victor's initially glorious creation (played by Michael Sarrazin) is introduced. Captivating everyone with his physical perfection, the Dorian Gray-like creature becomes the darling of the social scene until a flaw in Victor's reanimation process causes the creature's beauty to suddenly decay. It is the creature's increasing physical ugliness that leads Victor to reject the creature, rather than its violence or brutality — a statement perhaps on the Hollywood/Santa Monica social circle within which Isherwood and Bachardy moved in the 60s and 70s; where beauty is strictly on the surface and the ageing process feared and despised.

Branagh plays on homoeroticism in an extended sequence where Victor first gives 'birth' to the monster. Stripped to the waist, Victor wrestles with the creature's seemingly lifeless body in a pool of amniotic fluid, as he tries to get the creation to stand up by itself. It's a scene curiously reminiscent of the famous nude wrestling match between Oliver Reed and Alan Bates in Ken Russell's *Women in Love* (1969), a moment that bespeaks the notion of love between two men. In Russell's adaptation of the D.H. Lawrence classic, that possibility is rejected by one of the parties involved; likewise, in *Mary Shelley's Frankenstein*, Victor rejects the prospect of an emotional union with his creation. Scorned, the creature turns increasingly to violence and eventually plots revenge against its creator.

While homoeroticism links naturally to the act of creation in Whale's *Frankenstein*, in Branagh's version it is arguably a non-sequitur. Branagh's view on the creative act is quite at odds with that of Shelley. It is well-known that Mary Shelley came to write *Frankenstein* partly as therapy following the death of her prematurely born daughter in 1815, a tragedy which threw Mary into severe depression. It is not surprising, then, that Mary would view the act of creation as 'tainted'. Victor is similarly motivated by grief throughout the story — it is after the loss of his mother who dies of scarlet fever that Victor vows to find a way to defeat death. Thus begin his studies at the university at Ingolstadt where he meets his mentor Dr. Waldman who fosters his interest in chemistry. Victor plans for the creature to be beautiful, a celebration of the act of creation, but instead it is hideously ugly. The creature is Victor's hideous progeny — a projection both of the grief he has suffered and of his scientific hubris. Sometimes dead is better.

Here is where Branagh's vision departs significantly from that of Shelley. The opening scenes of *Mary Shelley's Frankenstein* display a gusto and sweep that are completely at odds with Mary Shelley's novel. Yes, the events they portray are the same in film as they are in its literary precursor but Branagh cannot help but bring *joie de vivre* to proceedings that belies the grief that so suffused Shelley's debut work. This is most apparent in the scene where Victor and Elizabeth fly their kites in a thunderstorm — a scene that bespeaks an exuberant joy of life. Screenwriter Frank Darabont has described Branagh's approach to the material as operatic, whereas "Shelley's book is not operatic, it whispers at you a lot." It is apt that Branagh cast as Henry Clerval (Victor's friend at the university), Tom Hulce, best known, of course, as Mozart in Milos Forman's exuberant *Amadeus* (1984), a film that *Mary Shelley's Frankenstein* resembles more perhaps than any horror movie. Branagh's vision of period drama is similar to that of Forman: it is one of sweeping camera moves and equally sweeping narrative. Patrick Doyle's driving music score delivers an equal number of swishes and swirls and grand flourishes as baroque as anything composed by the genius of Salzburg.

Of course, it might be argued that Branagh's film arises from the tradition of Romanticism that begat Shelley's novel. Certainly *Mary Shelley's Frankenstein* lends the impression of being created from 'nothingness', an attempt to avoid the derivative that is key to 'romantic originality' and befitting of Branagh's seeming desire to create the film as if Shelley's story had never been filmed before. However, with its emphasis on such emotions as fear, horror and terror, and its preoccupation with the sublime, Romanticism, too, is ultimately at odds with Branagh's vision. *Mary Shelley's Frankenstein* is insistently *un*horrific, *un*terrifying, and *un*metaphysical.

'The act of creation', then, is the theme which both unites Branagh's film version with the novel and provides a point of departure from it. It is inherent in Branagh's artistic sensibility to take joy from the act of creation. For Branagh, the subject matter itself is not as important as the process of putting on a show: the energy that comes of the collective creative endeavor. In this, Branagh shares the aesthetic of an Orson Welles, a Robert Altman, a Mario Bava. The marvel of Branagh's cinematic work derives not so much from the depth of his treatment but from the vitality of it. This is most apparent in what remains his masterpiece, *Much Ado About Nothing*, Branagh's 1993 romantic comedy based on Shakespeare's play, filmed shortly before he undertook *Mary Shelley's Frankenstein*. One need only quote the critical notices of that film to understand what makes Branagh, as an artist, tick. Such words as 'invigorating', 'cheerful', 'ravishing' abound. *Rotten Tomatoes* adjudges: 'Kenneth Branagh's love for the material is contagious in this exuberant adaptation.' One might easily use such epithets for *Mary Shelley's Frankenstein* and it is not too far-fetched to assume that Branagh's approach to Shakespeare carried over into the Shelley adaptation.

The great Italian horror and thriller maestro Mario Bava described his own works as "big bullshits," meaning that the films were a triumph of style over substance. But what style! Here we have style that *transcends* its subject matter. Likewise, to truly appreciate *Mary Shelley's Frankenstein*, one must surrender to its sweep, to its exuberance, and ultimately to its joy in the act of creation. Like *Much Ado About Nothing*, *Mary Shelley's Frankenstein* is a confection, but it is a joyful one. It is a glorious gothic creation 'full of sound and fury, signifying nothing' (to quote Shakespeare's *Macbeth* — one play Branagh has yet to film) but nevertheless, it holds the key to Kenneth Branagh's artistic sensibility, both as an actor and as a director.

Kenneth Branagh in *Mary Shelley's Frankenstein* (TriStar Pictures, 1994)

Mr Vampire (1985)

In the article, 'How to Stop a Chinese Hopping Vampire,' eHow.com gives the following advice on defeating a jiangshi:

To subdue a hopping vampire, pin a spell to its forehead, written in chicken blood on a piece of thin yellow paper.

An 8-sided mirror, called a Ba-qua mirror, can be used to reflect light in the direction of the jiangshi, which will scare them off.

To attack a hopping vampire, use a sword made up of lucky Chinese coins (the sword must be fully charged by placing it in the light of a full moon).

A dab of blood on its forehead will freeze a jiangshi.

Fling sticky rice at a jiangshi. This will draw out the evil in them, thus banishing the jiangshi.

It is a sign of how popular the jiangshi film has become that such instructional articles exist, alongside numerous fan sites, YouTube videos and discussion threads itemizing the origins of the jiangshi in Chinese folklore, its relationship to Western vampires and/or zombies, and, crucially, how to destroy one. As scholar Stephanie Lam puts it, such factoids are gleaned 'from close readings of Hong Kong produced jiangshi dianying or "cadaver movies," and the films themselves are consolidated into a canon of sorts by enthusiasts'. Jiangshi films broke through with the success of *Mr Vampire*, but they existed well before that, and numerous examples can be found in the annals of Hong Kong cinema.

But what exactly is a jiangshi? Fictional tales of reanimated corpses first appeared in the literature of the Qing Dynasty. Stories like Pu Song-ling's *A Corpse's Transmutation* (1740) depicted demonic corpses rising from the dead to suck the *qi* ('life force') of the living:

'As the last porter was gradually falling asleep, he suddenly heard the sound of paper rustling from the bed on which the dead woman had been laid out. He opened his eyes in alarm, and by the light of the lamp set in front of the corpse, clearly saw the dead woman draw aside the paper coverlet. She then rose and slowly entered into the men's bedroom. Her face was pale and sallow, with a silk scarf wrapped around her forehead. She bent over the men's bed, and blew several times over the faces of the three sleeping travelers'.

The description of the female wraith in the story is typical of a jiangshi. 'jiang' means hard or stiff, and the jiangshi in folklore is stiff with rigor mortis so that it cannot bend its limbs, and therefore is reduced to hopping around with its arms outstretched to aid its mobility. Jiangshi in popular culture are usually dressed in mandarin's garb, with green-white skin and long white hair. The origins of this peculiar creature are said to derive from the ancient Chinese practice of 'transporting a corpse over a thousand *li.*' If a person died far away from home, relatives often could not afford vehicles to transport the body back for burial. Instead, influenced by folk tales, they would hire a Taoist priest to reanimate the corpse so that it could hop its way home. In reality, the corpses were more likely to be carried back home, often by a two-man team, and this is what gave rise to such superstitions. The corpse would be tied upright onto bamboo rods for transportation, and lifted front and rear onto the shoulders of the couriers. From a distance, as the bamboo rods flexed during transit, it looked as though the corpse was 'hopping'. Hence stories of hopping vampires became a source for tales of jiangshi in Chinese folklore, and eventually found their way into fictional form in literature and film.

Jiangshi legends have been adapted for the purposes of modern audiences, and the now-popular image of the *changshan* clad jiangshi, sporting a talisman on its head, thus allowing it to be controlled by the Taoist priest, arguably stems from *Mr Vampire*. Stephanie Lam describes *Mr Vampire* as freely mixing 'kung-fu, slapstick comedy, Chinese folklore and Western vampire myths in a manner that appeals to both local and global sensibilities'. The first film in the series established many of the cinematic tropes of the jiangshi genre, the ingredients of which include, according to Lam, 'two Taoist priests, a couple of bumbling assistants, a smattering of wayward corpses, and at least one vengeful female ghost'. Added to these, are the Western-educated female love interest and a good dose of martial arts and ancient mysticism.

Producer Sammo Hung actually got the idea for *Mr Vampire* after reading Pu Song-ling's stories, collected in the volume entitled *Strange Stories from a Chinese Studio* (Liaozhai Zhiyi). These tales reminded him of the folkloric stories of reanimated corpses told to him by his mother. In Pu's writings, ghosts and demons search for human bodies to possess, and the dead take spirit form as *huli*, or fox creatures, that drain the life force from their victims during sexual encounters. Ghosts are inevitably beautiful women who have been wronged, or died as a result of injustice. Peace can only come to them through reincarnation. As scholar Dale Hudson points out, the ghost story extends back to the golden age of Shanghai cinema, but became popular again with the critical success of Stanley Kwan's *Rouge*

(1987), which reinvigorated the genre with its high production values and recognizable stars.

Sammo Hung had himself already used the figure of the jiangshi in *Encounters of the Spooky Kind* (1980), which is generally considered to be the first ghost film to feature the jiangshi, as well as one of the first kung fu-horror- comedies. Indeed, the jiangshi in that film were played by martial artists, such as Yuen Biao (who had been stunt double to Bruce Lee in *Game of Death*, 1978).

The jiangshi in *Encounters of the Spooky Kind* are noticeably different to the more Westernized vampires of earlier Hong Kong pictures. *Midnight Vampire* (1936) is thought to be the first Hong Kong movie to feature a jiangshi. In fact, its original title is *Wuye Jiangshi*. The debut film by the prolific writer-director Yeung Kung-leong, it's the story of a man who is murdered by his own brother, and who returns to life to seek revenge. In 1939, another Cantonese movie was released, *The Three-Thousand-Year Old Vampire* (*Sanqian Nina Didi Jiangshi*), starring Hui Maan Li and Yiu Ping. Also that year appeared *Vampires of the Haunted Mansion* (*Gui wu jiang shi*), directed by Wai-Man Leong. These early movies were heavily influenced by the Universal horror films of the time; hence their English titles equated the jiangshi with the Western vampire. They are basically imitations of *Dracula* (1931), and pale ones at that.

It would not be until 1957 that a Hong Kong movie would directly reference jiangshi folklore. *The Corpse-Drivers of Xiangxi* (*Xiang xi gan shi ji*) starred Ching Chung and Peter Chen Ho in the tale of a group of smugglers who use corpses to hide illicit drugs. The title alludes to the legend of 'corpse-driving', originating in the Hunan province of Xiangxi, in which cadavers were supposedly transported across mountainous terrain using bamboo rods in the manner described above. Directed by another extraordinarily prolific filmmaker (147 credits as director), Tian-Lin Wang, it is also known as *The Case of Walking Corpses*. Alas, the authentic jiangshi movie did not have time to catch on. Soon after, Hammer produced *Dracula* (1958), a huge international box office hit, and once again Hong Kong cinema was in thrall to Westernized vampires. Hong Kong variants on the Gothic theme included Chow See-Luk's *Vengeance of the Vampire* (*Jiang shi fu chou*, 1959) and Tie Li's *Vampire Woman* (*Xi xue fu*, 1962). The former was produced by the Shaw Brothers, and it would be they, in association with — ironically enough — Hammer that would produce the next really significant jiangshi movie.

The Legend of the Seven Golden Vampires (1974) came into being because Hammer wanted to make inroads into the Asian market, and the Shaw Brothers wanted to boost its presence in North America as a producer of martial arts movies. The result is an interesting hybrid of Gothic horror and jiangshi film. *Legend* starts off promisingly, with a title sequence that sees the titular vampires emerging from their burial grounds, looking admirably close to the jiangshi of Chinese folklore. Their high priest, Kah (Chan Sen), in a bid to restore the seven golden vampires to their former glory of the Qing Dynasty days tries to enlist the help of Count Dracula (John Forbes-Robertson) who is imprisoned in his castle in Transylvania. Dracula agrees but only if he can inhabit Kah's body in order to do so. Thus, *Legend* quickly turns into a kind of imperialist adventure whereby, in Stephanie Lam's words, 'a Dracula movie appropriates and unfolds over the top of the image of Chinese culture, which in the 1970s was made portable and consumable in the kung fu film.' (It's interesting to note that the blaxploitation film *Blacula*, 1972, starts in similar way, with a distinctly white Count 'colonizing' the body of an African prince who has sought the vampire's help in an attempt to stop the slave trade.)

In some ways Hammer and the Shaw Brothers anticipated the popularity of *Mr Vampire* and its numerous sequels and imitators. But *Mr Vampire* can also be seen as the result of a long history of Eastern and Western cultural mixing and matching that went on in Hong Kong cinema. In his essay *Abracadavar: Cross-cultural Influences in Hong Kong Vampire Movies*, Ng Ho writes that, although Hong Kong's vampire culture is at best a bastardized one, '*Mr Vampire* was a breakthrough, showing that Hong Kong cinema had at last digested all it could from Western vampire movies and that it was moving on to inject genuinely local Chinese sources of vampire folklore.' Other scholars, such as Lam, have argued that *Mr Vampire* contains 'anti-colonial sentiments' to boot.

The story takes place in China's Early Republic (even though the jiangshi costumes belong to the previous dynasty). Ricky Hui plays Man Choi, an apprentice of the Taoist priest, Kau (Ching-Ying Lam), who is able to work magic over spirits and jiangshi. A wealthy businessman called Mr Yam (Ha Huang) hires Kau to supervise the relocation of his father's corpse from his present grave and to rebury him. However, things go awry when the corpse revives as a jiangshi. Early in the film we are introduced to Mr Yam's cosmopolitan daughter, Ting Ting (Choi-fung Li) in a British teashop where Man Choi and Kau have arranged to meet Mr Yam. As the Westernized female, Ting Ting plays a joke on Man Choi, who has no idea how to drink a cup of coffee. Here the film light-heartedly points out the tensions between British colonial history and, in the words of Dale Hudson, 'the seduction by, or enslavement to foreigners.' Man Choi is besotted by Ting Ting, and all that she represents. Later he, himself, becomes a jiangshi — and then is cured by his master, Kau. When read allegorically, the film's real conflict, as Stephanie Lam observes, is not between humans and vampires, but 'between an abstracted Chineseness and a British colonial presence'. The jiangshi represents 'an unstable middle ground, in that its body, always in transit toward a final resting place, is neither here nor there'.

In many ways, then, the jiangshi in Hong Kong cinema can be seen as a kind of puppet. In the films it is controlled by Taoist priests, but behind the scenes, Eastern and Western cultures have fought over its soul. The jiangshi in folklore, by contrast, is an ancient Chinese force, often repressed, but repeatedly coming into being. Its power lies in ritual and myth, in Chinese heritage and tradition. And, as *Mr Vampire* shows us, the only way you can stop it is through Chinese magic, folklore and authentic kung fu fighting.

Mr Vampire (Golden Harvest, 1985)

The New Kids (1985)

The punk gang/'dangerous youth' movie is one of the most curious exploitation cycles of the 1980s. Largely growing from the financial success of Mark L. Lester's *Class of 1984* (1982), a movie that sold to every major film marketing territory in the world, the cycle found a place in the burgeoning home video market at a time when the grindhouses and drive-ins — the traditional homes of exploitation films — were dying out. While *Class of 1984* set the template for this type of movie — the term 'teensploitation' was coined (by *Entertainment Weekly*) in the same year as *Class* was released — the roots of the cycle can be found much earlier in American cinema; growing out of the juvenile delinquent (JD) exploitation films of the late 50s, and arguably dating back even further to the gang crime movies of the 30s.

Blackboard Jungle (1955) is an obvious progenitor. Vic Morrow's switchblade hoodlum Archie West menacing Glenn Ford's upstanding teacher in an inner city high school set the pace for the many JD movies that followed. Before that, Lee Marvin's sadistic biker in *The Wild One* (1953) cemented the formula for what would later become the 'JD psycho': unrelenting in his violence against society, the bad behaviour of the movie 'JD psycho' (such as that of James Spader's Dutra in *The New Kids*) is born of a deeply disturbed psyche. The 'hard-nosed' JD films of the 50s, like *Running Wild* (1955), *Teenage Crime Wave* (1955), *Crime in the Streets* (1956), *Dangerous Youth* (1958) and *Young and Wild* (1958) centred on criminal youths terrorizing decent middle-class white folk, condemning the delinquent while at the same time relishing his antisocial gusto. We might initially see the juvenile delinquent as a kind of anti-hero, with ancestry in movies like *The Public Enemy* (1931) and *Scarface* (1932). As Thomas Doherty writes in his book *Teenagers and Teenpics: The Juvenilization of American Movies in the 1950s* (Temple University Press, 2002):

'The era's real juvenile delinquents were the most celebrated criminal class since the pioneering gangster of the 1920s and 1930s; their crimes were as colorfully horrifying and their exploits as vigorously publicized. Consequently, the on-screen social disorder wrought by the 1950s delinquent outstrips the youthful hijinks of the Dead End Kids. In terms of filmic violence, Artie West and company are 'collateral descendants' of public enemies like Scarface and Little Caesar, not back-street punks like the Bowery Boys.'

Like the gangster of the 30s, the juvenile delinquent of the 1950s provided plenty of grist for the exploitation mill, and as the cycle wore on, storylines became increasingly lurid and campy, mixing exploitation elements — rock and roll, drag racing, high school vice — to the point where, in Doherty's words, 'the result was a bizarre cross-pollination of gimmicks, a kind of exploitation overload'. Consider, for example, the exploits of the girl gang in Edward D. Wood Jnr's *The Violent Years* (1956). These feisty femmes think nothing of knocking off gas stations and raping young men at gunpoint!

By the late 1950s, the juvenile delinquent started to lose his (or her) anti-hero status and became equated with a new type of criminal coming to the fore in films like *Kiss of Death* (1948) and *The Big Heat* (1953) — psychopaths whose behaviour (which included pushing wheelchair-bound women down staircases and throwing scalding hot coffee in their girlfriends' faces) was truly beyond the bounds of social acceptability. These maniacs were unredeemable, 'terrifying scum who richly deserved their end-reel fates', to quote Doherty. The JD film adapted itself to presenting juvenile delinquency as a form of sociopathy in movies like *Joy Ride* (1958), and *No Time to Die* (1956) — in which a reptilian Robert Vaughan kills because he likes to watch people die. By the time of *The Young Captives* (1959) — whose byline was 'a disturbed young man who gives even less thought to killing than he does to combing his hair' — the 'JD psycho' was fully established. More Norman Bates than James Dean, the 'JD psycho' warranted harsh justice, not understanding.

This brings us back to the 80s gang violence movie and *The New Kids*. The new cycle of 'JD psycho' films coincided with audiences becoming more conservative in the Reagan era. This was partly a reaction to the counterculture youth movies of the 60s and 70s in which the young anti-heroes of such films as *The Wild Angels* (1966), *Psyche-Out* (1968) and *Easy Rider* (1969) were busily taking LSD and sticking it to The Man. It was also a result of the 'Just Say No' anti-drug campaign launched in schools and college campuses across the United States in the 80s. Tough new laws on drugs, which treated addicts as criminals, swayed teenagers into following a zero-tolerance policy mindset. Drug-taking was demonized by politicians and the media alike. Cue the return of the 'JD psycho', his random violence this time fuelled by an addiction to coke, speed, crystal meth, ket, bluies or anything else he could get his hands on. The 80s was the era of the disaffected youth movie, with a whole slew of films focusing on the alienation of a generation. Tim Hunter's *River's Edge* (1987) epitomized this type of movie in which the nation's youth was presented as amoral and detached from the world. This kind of disaffected and disengaged teenager is clearly in danger of being drawn to the dark side, as the 80s gang violence movie eagerly shows.

The tropes of the 80s punk-gang violence genre were crystalized by *Class of 1984* and actually became fairly set from that point on. The high school kids/ teacher and the psycho-gang become locked in an escalating conflict that ends in a massacre where the punks are killed one by one in various bloody ways by the nominal heroes (who appear to act with total impunity). Punishment for delinquency is swift and harsh, entirely justified, and the audience is invited to revel just as much — if not more — in the retaliatory violence meted out by the good guys as they are in the JD's often wildly over the top and improbable behaviour. An eye-for-an-eye is the moral message and plausible character psychology is never allowed to stand in the way of extreme violence.

Sean S. Cunningham was surely familiar with these tropes when he embarked on *The New Kids*. He had, after all, produced one of the most infamous exploitation films of all time in Wes Craven's *The Last House on the Left* (1972), which more or less stuck to the same basic formula of the psycho-gang who rape and murder the young and innocent, in turn brutally punished by death at the hands of our upstanding citizens. This standard formula is easily adaptable to other types of exploitation movies, not just 'teensploitation' ones, and can be combined with other exploitation tropes, such as the rape-revenge narrative and the vigilante story. *Class of 1984* used these to update the 'JD psycho' plot of the 50s (borrowing the high school setting of *Blackboard Jungle* in the process), and Cunningham does the same with *The New Kids*. Dutra attempts to rape the heroine of *The New Kids*, Abby (Lori Loughlin), and her brother Loren (Shannon Presby) becomes her righteous avenger. It would be remiss of me not to mention, at this point, another minor classic of American exploitation cinema that combines the 'psycho-gang' with rape-revenge and vigilantism, but with a racial theme: Robert A. Endelson's *Fight for Your Life* (1977). Indeed, the combination of offensively racist dialogue, punk-gang violence (including rape) and righteous vengeance of the Black family victimized by three rednecks (led by a suitably psychotic William Sanderson) proved so controversial that it was never released in the UK. However, *Fight for Your Life* remains an important stepping-stone in exploitation cinema, paving the way for the punk-gang violence movies of the 80s.

These 80s entries include such titles as *Savage Streets* (1984) and *Dangerously Close* (1986). The former stars Linda Blair as a tough teen who exacts bloody vengeance on the L.A. gang who raped her deaf-mute sister (played by Linnea Quigley). By making the vigilante a high-school student, *Savage Streets* managed not only to tick 'teensploitation' boxes but also keyed into the female avenger subgenre of *I Spit on Your Grave* (1978). It also shared that film's brutal table-turning use of phallic weaponry: Blair dispatches the gang by a variety of gory means, including with a crossbow. *Dangerously Close* (1986) borrowed elements of *Massacre at Central High* (1976) in the tale of new-kid-on-the-block-takes-on-the-high-school-gang. J. Eddie Peck plays the teenager who discovers that 'The Sentinels' are more than just a bunch of prefects worried about vandalism and graffiti — they are, in fact, a group of neo-fascists mad keen on ridding their school of undesirables by any means necessary. J. Eddie and friends tool up to fight for their freedom — with predictably violent results. Despite their hip soundtracks, punk fashions, street violence and 'scenes of drug-taking', these movies and others like them (such as *3.15* [1986] and *Wolfpack* [1988]) and are essentially modern morality plays: good vs. evil is laid out in black and white terms, with very little shades of grey. In their own way these movies are as moralistic as the 'JD psycho' movies of the 1950s.

What sets *The New Kids* apart from the standard 80s gang violence movie and gives it an interesting spin in this respect is the casting of James Spader. Whilst indisputably a 'JD psycho' of the highest order, Spader's Dutra is quite the dandy, despite his Southern hick accent. As *The Stitcher* podcast describes him, Spader is a 'dreamy / creepy legend', and *The New Kids* paves the way for his roles in *Sex, Lies and Videotape* (1989), *Secretary* (2002) and even *Crash* (1996). Cunningham cast Spader because he found his film persona 'strange'; in some ways Spader's oddball, JD psycho drug-dealer in *The New Kids* anticipates his character Rip in *Less Than Zero*, and the various slimy and often downright-weird yuppies he would go on to play later in his career. The same year he made *The New Kids*, Spader starred in another teensploitation movie, *Tuff Turf* (1985), in which he played the good guy chasing the girl who happens to belong to the resident high school 'JD psycho': a kind of movie mirror image of *The New Kids*. As Morgan Tyler, Spader is both rebel and hero: a brooding loner who learns to toughen up as needs must when the devil drives. *Tuff Turf* starts as a much more benign High School movie than *The New Kids* — it's basically *Ferris Bueller's Day Off* (1986) meets *Beverly Hills 90210* (1990-2000) — until the last act when it turns into a bloody massacre in true 80s gang violence movie fashion. Spader brings an ambiguity to Tyler that makes him much more interesting than the film's one-dimensional 'JD psycho'.

In this way, *The New Kids* can be seen as a stepping stone to the more morally ambiguous teen movies of the 90s like *Heathers* (1989) and *Pump Up the Volume* (1990). These movies play with the persona of the teenage rebel, casting him as both hero and villain. He is attractive and dangerous in equal measures, but ultimately (in the case of *Heathers*) psychopathic. The characters played by Christian Slater in these two films are very Spader-esque!

The 80s gang-violence movie, then, with its 'JD psycho' and its good guy vigilantes, is very much of its time. It coincides with a period in history when moral absolutism was 'in', and youthful rebellion was 'out'. The cycle faded in the late 80s. Juvenile delinquency would not again be so vilified in movies until, arguably, Hoodie Horror made its appearance in British horror films in the 2000s.

James Spader in *The New Kids* (Columbia Pictures, 1985)

Night of the Living Dead (1968)

Released in the US on 4 October 1968, George A. Romero's *Night of the Living Dead* is often spoken of as a manifesto for the modern horror film. Taking its inspiration from the racial and political strife of late-60s America, it created, as the BFI wrote in 2004, 'a verité nightmare which overturned the conventions of fantastical horror'; Romero took the genre out of its gothic castles and swept away its cobwebs. *Night* marked a transition in horror cinema: from the classic to the modern. Less remarked upon, though, is how Romero effects this transition within the film itself, in its opening scenes.

Night of the Living Dead begins in a cemetery, with nods to Vincent Price, 50s B-movies and Universal horror. Brother and sister Johnny (Russell Streiner) and Barbara (Judith O'Dea) arrive to put flowers on their father's grave. There they are attacked by a zombie. Barbara flees from the graveyard — amid lightning strikes straight from a Hammer movie — to a remote farmhouse in the Pennsylvania countryside; and we are taken into a stark new world of apocalyptic horror, far removed from the old monsters of *Frankenstein* (1931) and *Dracula* (1931) — into the world of *Psycho* (1960), *Repulsion* (1965), absurdism, and a landscape of social-political meltdown.

The graveyard sequence utilizes standard 50s science fiction-horror tropes while slyly undermining them. Barbara's flight from the graveyard to the farmhouse feels like a journey not just to another location but to another *film*: she runs out of a classic horror movie and into a modern one. Her arrival at the farmhouse evokes the madness of *Psycho* and *Repulsion*, banishing the lampooning tone of the earlier sequence (as evoked by Johnny's impersonating Price — "they're coming to get you Barbara!") in favour of the starkness of Hitchcock and Polanski.

The transition continues with the arrival of the Black protagonist Ben (Duane Jones), and it soon becomes clear that the characters are besieged. Ben and Barbara attempt to fortify the farmhouse against zombie attack, turning it into a kind of nuclear bunker in the process. *The Birds* (1963) is often quoted as an influence on the survival horror of *Night of the Living Dead*, but one can also see in Romero's depiction of a dying world such post-apocalyptic dramas as *On the Beach* (1959) and the BBC television play *Underground* (1958); and racial antagonism between survivors of the apocalypse featured in *The World, The Flesh and The Devil* (1959). In all of these, too, the characters are unable to give up society's doctrines, even after civilization is destroyed and those old rules rendered obsolete.

But it is the nature of Romero's zombie threat that completes the transition from classic horror to modern horror. The zombie is traditionally a blue collar monster: Romero himself has cited Victor Halperin's *White Zombie* (1932) and *Revolt of the Zombies* (1936) — whose living dead toil in mills — as influences on *Night*. Neither was Romero the first to depict zombies as symbols of a lumpenproletariat rising up against its masters: the zombie as exploited worker featured in Hammer's *The Plague of the Zombies* (1966); and much has also been made of the influence on *Night* of *The Last Man on Earth* (1964), an adaptation of the Richard Matheson's *I Am Legend*, the novel upon which Romero consciously drew for his story.

Indeed, modern day zombies resurrected by science gone wrong were the subject of several B pictures made in the 1950s by the director Edward L. Cahn. *Invisible Invaders* (1959) pioneered the classic Romero zombie shuffle ten years prior to *Night of the Living Dead*; while *The Creature with the Atom Brain* (1955) has its zombies revived by radiation, a 'la *Night*. *Zombies of Mora Tau* (1957) presents images of revived corpses moving slowly en-mass against the living, again reminiscent of *Night*. Both *Zombies of Mora Tau* and *The Last Man on Earth* showed on Channel 11's Chiller Theatre in Pittsburgh in the summer of 1967, when Romero was filming *Night of the Living Dead*; it is possible that he saw these films and was inspired by their imagery.

The real-game changer of *Night*, though, was Romero's making the zombies into flesh eating beings, creating an allegory of a society devouring itself from within: the central metaphor underlying much modern apocalyptic horror that followed *Night*, including classics like the original *The Texas Chain Saw Massacre* (1974) and Romero's own sequel to *Night*, *Dawn of the Dead* (1978).

Night of the Living Dead takes us into the apocalypse almost in real time. The story is compressed into a single night, as the title suggests, but within that, the apocalypse, or at least our growing realization — along with that of the characters — that apocalypse is taking place, happens in ninety minutes of almost continuous time. The effect is to create very powerfully a sense of a definitive point of change: we see the precise moment that history ends.

Viewing *Night of The Living Dead* now is like watching the big bang in reverse — life as we know it diminishes at a rapid rate until suddenly there is nothing left on the screen of the world we once knew. The film evokes this beautifully through its characters' response to it. During a quiet moment Ben and Barbara tell each other their backstories directly leading to them seeking refuge in the farmhouse. Ben's monologue fulfills the normal functions of dramatic exposition: we learn that he has escaped from a diner that was attacked by the living dead. Barbara's speech, however, fulfills no such story function: we already know what has happened to her; she merely repeats what we have already seen, but somehow this redundancy increases the poignancy of the moment, the point at which we, along with the characters, realize that apocalypse is upon us and that the world as we know it is about to fall apart. We might compare *Night* with the plays of Ionesco, which share the same structure, the same absurdist view of human folly and miscommunication, the same breakdown of rationality.

No other film of the 60s captured the allegorical moment so completely: at the time of *Night*'s release it seemed that America was, itself, at the point of collapse. Apocalypse was happening and there was no reversing it. After *Night of the Living Dead* there was no going back to the old horrors.

Night of the Living Dead (Image Ten, 1968)

Phantom of the Paradise (1974)

At first glance, *Phantom of the Paradise* seems like an anomaly in the career of its director, Brian De Palma. Conceived as a rock horror musical, the film failed to gain traction on its first release in 1974, partly due to Fox's poor marketing campaign; subsequent attempts by producer Ed Pressman to reposition it as 'horror phantasy' rather than musical yielded only marginally better results. *Phantom* — like Winslow Leach (William Finley) himself — became largely forgotten. But — for whatever reason the film failed to ignite — it remained for years little more than a curiosity or novelty attraction in the oeuvre of a director known primarily for his Hitchcockian thrillers. The film's eventual rediscovery — thanks largely to its 2001 DVD release — prompted something of a revival in the noughties, with new fans proclaiming it superior to *The Rocky Horror Picture Show* (1975) (which it only superficially resembles) and film buffs detecting a nascent auteur signature in between the musical numbers and the Grand Guignol. In terms of De Palma's development as a filmmaker *Phantom* can now be seen as a transitional work, a stepping stone between the countercultural concerns and underground aesthetic of *Greetings* (1968) and *Hi Mom!* (1970) and the full-blown gothic excess of *Carrie* (1976).

By 1974, De Palma's filmography was already starting to look little hit and miss. After Godardian beginnings with *The Wedding Party* (1966) and *Murder à la Mod* (1967), his ignominious firing by Warner Bros. from the disastrous production of *Get to Know Your Rabbit* (1972) proved an early personal watershed for the young director. The result was a change of tack from hip comedy to traditional suspense thriller, and De Palma's first masterpiece, *Sisters*, also made in 1972. *Phantom* was actually written before that film, but produced after it, which goes some way to explain why *Phantom* seems both a step forward *and* a step back: while *Phantom* surpasses *Sisters* in terms of its sheer upbeat modernist style (which aces *Sisters'* stolid classicism), it also lacks the earlier film's narrative assurance.

De Palma intended *Phantom* as a satire on the music industry as it stood in the early 70s. Composer Winslow's musical opus, *Faust*, is travestied by music mogul, Swan (Paul Williams); his life's work commodified as so much auditory bubble gum for screaming teens. By 1974, American music had already sold its soul to Mammon: corporations had taken over the record companies; one of the biggest, MCA Records, had ties to organized crime; even the Woodstock festival was funded in large part by Warner Bros., who bought the documentary rights for cinema release. De Palma also touches upon music's dark counterculture, with nods to Altamont

(Swan's doormen are denim-and-leather-clad Hells Angels) and the gory on-stage antics of Alice Cooper.

Drawing on literary works by Goethe, Leroux and Wilde provides apt metaphors and an appropriate story framework (the general template being *The Phantom of the Opera*); as does De Palma's deployment of explicit horror film referencing (*The Cabinet of Dr Caligari*, 1920, is but one of several classics that De Palma pays homage to). The narrative flaws of *Phantom* are not arising from this monster-themed mash up (the horror intertextuality actually helps to hold it all together); it's really De Palma's use of novelty cinematic storytelling devices in the film's early sequences — a throwback to his early days as a New York underground filmmaker/avant-gardist — that proves to be the main weakness.

Coming across as particularly 'experimental' are the scenes in Sing Sing, wherein Winslow's attempts to track down Swan end up with the former framed for drug possession and subsequently incarcerated in the famed New York state correctional facility. There's something of the primitive Woody Allen (*Bananas* [1971], *Sleeper* [1973]) about the uneven comedy and silent movie parody here. Some reviewers have suggested that the radical changes in tone are intentional but as an approach to storytelling it feels curiously tentative, inexpert and quite out of place with the rest of the film. Put simply, the early sections of *Phantom* seem like remnants from De Palma's days as a novice filmmaker, where later sequences (from the point where Winslow becomes the phantom) anticipate the fully-fledged narrative expertise of *Carrie* onwards.

This transition from emerging to mature artist is marked, in De Palma's case, by the discarding of clichéd stylistic devices in favour of a genuine cinematic approach that, whilst undeniably stylized, arises from *within* the material rather than being imposed *on* it. In other words, De Palma is a stylist, yes, but in his best films, his operatic expressionism, like Hitchcock's (indeed like any example of pure cinema) serves to externalize that which would otherwise remain dormant in the story. One need only compare De Palma's *Carrie* with the 2013 remake to see this: De Palma's treatment of Lawrence Cohen's screenplay enhances it in ways that Kimberley Pierce's naturalistic 're-imagining' of (more or less) the same screenplay fails to do; therein De Palma's film comes alive, while Pierce's falls flat. Here is the difference between personal artistic style and mere cinematic trickery; and although in *Phantom* De Palma retains certain other filmic devices from his early work — split-screen, POV camera, found-footage — these are subsumed in a meaningful way (and, as such, continue to recur in his later films). A good example is the tracking shot that encircles Winslow as he sings at the piano in the film's opening scene. The orbiting camera both venerates and isolates Winslow. In much the same way, a circular camera movement celebrates Carrie (Sissy Spacek) as she dances with Tommy (William Katt) at the high school prom, while simultaneously reminding us that she remains dangerously separate from the rest of her peers, still unaccepted by them.

The woman prevented from taking centre stage is a primary De Palma theme. In *Sisters*, we have the Jennifer Salt character, a journalist suppressed by her editor, the police, and even her own mother; Dominique (Margot Kidder), the dead Siamese-twin, tries to live on in the form of her sister's split personality disorder, and her existence is similarly supressed by the surviving twin, Danielle and her husband, the hypnotist, Emil (Finley). In *Dressed to Kill*, Kate's (Angie Dickinson) release from sexual frustration is brutally curtailed by her murder; likewise Liz (Nancy Allen), the prostitute suspected of the killing, is herself thwarted by police and the real murderer as she attempts to clear her name; finally 'Bobbi', the transgender personality of Dr Elliott (Michael Caine), is denied self-expression by Elliott's 'male-side', and retaliates by killing those women who arouse Elliott sexually. In *Carrie* and *Phantom*, the theme is given literal form: Carrie's attempts to take centre stage as prom queen result in her ultimate humiliation at the hands of her peers; in *Phantom*, Phoenix (Jessica Harper), as a female singer in the male-dominated rock industry, is repeatedly denied the chance to take the musical stage. In so doing she would pose unacceptable threat to the masculinity of the diminutive Swan, who, as a final repudiation, arranges for her to be assassinated during a live performance. This ludicrous risk-posed-by-female-agency-to-the-fragile-male-ego is memorably satirized in the persona of Beef (Gerrit Graham), the ridiculous hyper-masculine rock god who, offstage, is camp as Christmas. Correspondingly, men in De Palma's films fear castration, both symbolic and literal: in *Sisters*, both Philip (Lisle Wilson) and Emil are stabbed in the genitals by 'Dominique'; In *Dressed to Kill* Elliott's 'male-side' fears gender-realignment surgery (represented in the film — controversially — as a literal and symbolic castration); and in *Phantom*, Winslow's agency is taken away from him symbolically when his teeth are removed by prison doctors.

De Palma had planned a sequel to *Phantom of the Paradise* that would see Winslow, as the Phantom, helping a female singer song-writer: a further story about the exploitation of women by the male-dominated music business. The sequel, of course, never happened, although we might see De Palma's idea of a non-threatening male teaming up with an assertive woman reflected in the relationship between Liz and Peter (Keith Gordon) in *Dressed to Kill*. Like that and many of De Palma's other films — *Carrie, Blow Out, Raising Cain* — *Phantom* ends on a nihilistic note. The situation is without hope; all that is left is to take a God's-eye point of view on it, and enjoy the spectacle. As Paul Williams tells us, "nothing matters anyway — that's the hell of it." For that reason — even if we sing along — *Phantom* remains a bitter-sweet experience, but a fascinating one. Like the proverbial Phoenix (if not the Harper character), De Palma rises from filmic ashes even as we watch.

William Finley in *Phantom of the Paradise* (Fox, 1974)

Planet of the Apes (1968)

"You maniacs! You blew it up! Damn You! Damn you all to hell!"

The astonishing ending of *Planet of the Apes* and the words screamed by Charlton Heston as the camera lingers on the shattered remains of the Statue of Liberty are unremitting in their bleakness. The original sequels to *Planet* were no less downbeat (indeed it is difficult to imagine such a grimly apocalyptic movie series existing today; the reboot franchise is decidedly less nihilistic) but the five original *Apes* movies — the saga of how apes take over the world only to perish alongside mankind in the detonation of a doomsday weapon — continue to strike a chord with audiences and critics alike.

Witnessing civilizations come to an end has always exerted a hypnotic effect on audiences; what's more, the franchise's commentary on America's interracial conflict, the country's love-hate of immigrants, its violent protests, clashes between youth and authority, feminism — and (most pressing of all) the impending extinction of the human species in nuclear war — resonates just as strongly now as it did then.

When interstellar explorer George Taylor (Charlton Heston) crash lands on a seemingly barren planet, and is captured by gorillas that kill his fellow astronauts, he realizes he has entered a world where evolution has seemingly gone backwards: apes govern and humans are subordinate. Homosapiens are no longer the superior species; man is now the dumb animal, and talking monkeys run the show. Only the chimpanzees Cornelius (Roddy McDowell) and his wife Zira (Kim Hunter) demonstrate any compassion for poor Taylor's plight, while Dr Zaius (Maurice Evans), the head of the Ape Assembly, tries to cover up Taylor's existence for fear that it might lead to an unearthing of the truth about the ape revolution that took place centuries before. The apes' world is starkly authoritarian, operating on strict race/class/gender divisions, with humans designated to slavery. *Planet of the Apes* — like all the best science fiction — holds up a mirror to our world. We may have swapped places with them but the apes are *us*. And we are doomed to blow ourselves up — the films tell us — just like the Statue of Liberty has been blown up.

Indeed, the great conceit of the series is its time-loop premise, which makes our extinction inescapable. The first sequel *Beneath the Planet of the Apes* presented the ruins of human civilization buried underground and run by mutant survivors of a nuclear holocaust who continue to worship the doomsday machine. Brent (James Franciscus), a fellow space traveller, is sent to investigate the disappearance of Taylor's ship. Like his predecessor,

Brent is captured by apes and manages to escape, only to find himself stumbling into the clutches of the mutants. There he finally locates Taylor, who, driven insane by it all, proceeds to exact revenge on humanity by detonating the Alpha-Omega weapon himself, thereby bringing history (human and ape) to an end.

Scenes in *Beneath* depict anti-violence demonstrations held by the peace-loving chimpanzees wielding placards ("Wage Peace Not War"); while the war-mongering gorillas led by General Ursus (James Gregory) mount a campaign to storm the Forbidden Zone, and the progressive minded Cornelius and Zira clash with the arch-conservative Dr. Zaius. *Beneath* again reflects the mood of America in the Vietnam era, when the younger generation rebelled and police fired live bullets at student demonstrators in university campuses. *Beneath* ends in a frenzy of machine gun fire, with Brent and Taylor mown down, and even the mute flower-child Nova (Linda Harrison) shot dead by the rampaging gorilla army.

The third entry in the series seemed to take a lighter tone in comparison, but even this proves to be deceiving. In *Escape from the Planet of the Apes*, Cornelius and Zira manage to repair Taylor's spaceship and take a reverse trajectory back to Earth in 1973. There they are treated like celebrities by the media until the authorities begin to realize the implications of Zira's becoming pregnant. The two chimpanzees are forced into exile as the military tries to hunt them down before they can trigger the end of human civilization. The film resonates as an allegory on migration in America: Cornelius and Zira are ultimately viewed as illegal immigrants and a threat to the American Way. *Escape* also had much to say about the then-burgeoning second wave feminist movement: Zira emerges as a strong, intelligent and politicized female who puts the males around her to shame. In the end, though, the time-loop prevails, the conclusion of *Escape* as despairing as its predecessors as the saga drives relentlessly towards a predetermined cataclysm.

The race relations subtext would come to the fore in *Conquest of the Planet of the Apes*, with critics of the time reading social comment into scenes of the enslaved apes taking to the streets. Set in 1991, Zira's baby has now fully grown and is named Caesar (Roddy McDowell). Emerging from his circus hideaway, Caesar is shocked to find America a police state; his fellow simians imported by the boatload to be used as slaves to the humans. He leads them in an uprising, the moment of ape revolution on Earth. *Conquest* ends with Caesar's triumphant proclamation: "tonight we have seen the birth of the planet of the apes." Those words might perhaps have offered a salvation of sorts, the possibility of negating the saga's self-fulfilling prophecy, but the final film in the franchise, *Battle for the Planet of the Apes*, dashes any such hope. Indeed, *Battle* sees the survivors of the apocalypse (it is revealed that humans eventually resorted to nuclear weapons to try to quell the ape uprising) engaged in a final — ultimately futile — war for control of the planet. In the end, we are left with no doubt that the series has come full circle; we are back where we started, staring at the shattered remains of liberty.

"This one has a message", Charlton Heston reputedly told nervous Twentieth Century Fox executives about *Planet of the Apes*. Hollywood was doubtful that audiences would take such a message, one that spoke to revolution and history repeating, to the symbolic destruction of freedom and democracy, to mad men with their fingers on the doomsday button. That message remains as urgent as ever.

Planet of the Apes (Fox, 1968)

Pumpkinhead (1988)

'Keep away from Pumpkinhead,
Unless you're tired of living,
His enemies are mostly dead,
He's mean and unforgiving,
Laugh at him and you're undone,
But in some dreadful fashion,
Vengeance he considers fun.'

It's easy to see why, in 1987, The De Laurentiis Entertainment Group commissioned a screenplay inspired by Ed Justin's poem. This little ditty contains all you need for a classic slice of rural horror: an isolated cabin in the woods (with 'bolted doors and windows barred'); a plot that's brewing against the unwary; a trail of human corpses ('enemies are mostly dead'); and a vengeful demon summoned from the pumpkin patch by a child's nursery rhyme. It's a witch's brew of backwoods horror, filled with black magic ritual, folklore and goblins. *Pumpkinhead* is both urban myth and urbanoia — a cautionary tale of what happens when you go into the woods and start messin' with folks (or folks start messin' with you).

Over thirty years later, Stan Winston's directorial debut remains a potent mix of rural horror riffs; at the heart of it is the hoary old hillbilly horror trope of poor country folk vs. rich city slickers in a savage fight for survival. But *Pumpkinhead* becomes a parable of revenge that goes against the grain of the usual urbanoia stereotypes. It's blended with the kind of morality tale we often associate with urban myths of a demonic nature: be careful what you conjure up — it might not go away again ('in some dreadful fashion, vengeance he considers fun'). Some spells, once cast, cannot be undone.

Due to poor distribution, on its first release *Pumpkinhead* never really got the recognition it deserved as an intelligent mash-up of rural horror subgenres; and it remains an underrated 80s horror movie, spawning three lacklustre sequels (*Pumpkinhead II: Blood Wings* [1994], *Pumpkinhead: Ashes to Ashes* [2006] and *Pumpkinhead: Blood Feud* [2007]). Its cult reputation rests largely on FX wizard Stan Winston (whose studio provided the creature effects for *Pumpkinhead*), here making the transition to the director's chair after a remarkable Oscar-winning career in prosthetics and puppetry (*The Terminator* [1984], *Aliens* [1986], *Predator* [1987]) Winston would never reach the same heady heights as director that he did as a special effects artist. His only feature film after *Pumpkinhead* is the now-forgotten family fantasy flick, *Upworld* (1990) about an LA cop who partners with a talking gnome named Gnorm. His special effects work, on the other hand, went on to include the first three *Jurassic Park* movies, *Iron Man* (2008), *Avatar* (2009) and *Shutter Island* (2010).

Filmed in the spring of 1987, *Pumpkinhead* was originally set for a 600-screen release in October that year, but when The De Laurentiis Entertainment Group found itself in financial difficulty, the decision was made to pull it back to Jan 1988 and release it under a different name — *Vengeance: The Demon*. That release didn't happen either (although DEG did later release it under that title in some international territories). DEG eventually sold distribution rights of *Pumpkinhead* (along with the 1988 Rob Lowe teen blackmail comedy *Illegally Yours*) to MGM/United Artists who gave it a limited release with little advertising in North America in October 1988. The film was a flop, grossing only $4,385.516 domestic. Dave J. Wilson, writing in *Scream*, reports that MGM/UA Home Entertainment did better with *Pumpkinhead* on home video, releasing it stateside in 1989, where it started to gain strong word of mouth and a cult following.

The film critics were not kind to *Pumpkinhead*. *The Washington Post* decried its 'poor writing and acting'; *Chicago Tribune* called it 'a monster film without bite'; *Empire* erroneously described it as a *Friday the 13th* clone; only *The Los Angeles Times* recognized any merit in the film's theme: 'about how revenge, once tasted, is not so sweet', even if the reviewer did go on to claim, somewhat irrelevantly, that classic sci-fi movie *Forbidden Planet* (1956) had done it all before ('Walter Pidgeon engaged in much more compelling combat with his own id').

As the *LA Times* explained in its review, *Pumpkinhead*'s protagonist, Ed Harley (Lance Henriksen), a salt-of-the-earth convenience store holder in the sticks, does indeed come to regret the sequence of events he sets in motion by summoning the titular demon-of-the-woods; and soon realizes that to do battle with the demon, he must literally do battle with himself. 'It's an interesting idea,' sniffed the *LA Times* critic who makes nothing of it. It would be useful, perhaps, to compare *Pumpkinhead*'s treatment of this theme with other rural horror pictures to see just what makes Winston's film so interesting in this respect.

Traditionally, rural horror movies express an urban fear of a primitive rural 'other'. The backwoods nightmare movie cast the rural poor as monstrous. Think *Deliverance* (1971), with its genteel city gents hounded down by murderous and degenerate hill men, and you have the basic template for many hillbilly horror movies that followed. But the tensions between North and South, between wealthy urbanites and their poor country counterparts, so memorably portrayed in John Boorman's film, also fuelled a number of earlier horror movies.

Herschell Gordon Lewis ventured into this territory in 1964 with *Two Thousand Maniacs*, which saw Northern tourists being tortured and murdered by Southerners during a celebration of the Centennial. Here Lewis (in his inimitable tongue-torn-out-of-cheek style) traces antagonism between North and South back to the American Civil War, and the misgivings of poor Southern states ransacked by the Yankees during the last days of the War. The tourists are ambushed and roasted alive by rednecks of the town in a gruesome act of vengeance; later we find out that the town is a literal ghost-town, with ghosts of the Civil War returning every century to seek redress. *Two Thousand Maniacs* turned the Northern-outsiders-stranded-in-the-rural-South-horrifically-murdered-by-rednecks formula into a grindhouse standard.

But while Lewis focused on unresolved conflicts between North and South, invoking the region's violent past, another local filmmaker got down to the business of demonizing the rural poor in Texas. S.F. Brownrigg's *Scum of the Earth* (1974) (not to be confused with H.G. Lewis's 1963 film of the same name) does exactly what the title suggests, and for those at the drive-ins who were not able to pick up on the film's underlying message themselves, the poster provides a handy hint: *See The Real Poor White Trash*! Brownrigg's treatment is pure grindhouse exploitation of rednecks (or 'hicksploitation'). A couple on their honeymoon end up as victims of a deranged woodsman and his equally psychotic family. "See how they live below Tobacco Road!" exhorts the trailer, playing on the audience's voyeuristic fascination with life on the wrong side of the tracks. *Scum of the Earth* casts its characters as every sort of depraved; the father is a sexual pervert; his pregnant wife a doormat; the teenaged daughter a slut; the son a half-wit, and so on. The horror of the poor white trash family in Brownrigg's film (similar to *The Texas Chain Saw Massacre* made in the same year) stems from the idea that, not only are they squalid and poverty-stricken, but they are monstrously insane to boot! Even scarier is the thought that we might become contaminated by them somehow. The killer-on-the-loose in *Scum of the Earth* turns out to be not what we were expecting at all; city-dwellers can be just as demented as the hicks. Rural horror movies like *Scum of the Earth* serve to remind us that we might only be a step away from poor white trash ourselves.

While Brownrigg's films (and *The Texas Chain Saw Massacre*, too) hinged on the unhinged, on insanity rather than the supernatural, *Race with the Devil* (1975) prefigures *Pumpkinhead* by bringing superstition into the mix. In many ways, Jack Starrett's movie draws on H.G. Lewis, but instead of blood-crazed ghostly Confederates there are Satanists. Two couples travel through Texas in a motorhome on their way to Aspen, Colorado for a skiing vacation. They set up camp in the woods where they accidentally witness a Satanic ritual human sacrifice (as they do in Texas). They hotfoot it out of there, of course, but find themselves being chased down by the Satanists, who kill their dog, and who generally try to trap them and stop them from leaving the state. The tourists seek help from the local Sherriff who (wouldn't you know it?) turns out to be in cahoots with the Satanists. Indeed, the whole of Texas (just like in *Two Thousand Maniacs*) seems to be part of the conspiracy. *Race with the Devil* owes a debt of gratitude to *Rosemary's Baby* (1968) in terms of its pervasive air of paranoia, but at heart it's pure *urbanoia*: the guilt-fear projection of a wealthy middle-class (posh Winnebago, expensive trials motorbikes) intruding on envious locals and raising their ire. The city slickers never do make it to Aspen, Colorado ("Aspen! Where the beer flows like wine!" as Jim Carrey says in *Dumb and Dumber* [1994]).

All of this brings us back to *Pumpkinhead*. In his book, *Beyond Hammer*, James Rose usefully defines the urbanoia film (the term, used to describe certain types of rural horror films, was first coined by Carol J. Clover in her now-classic study *Men, Women and Chainsaws*). Urbanoia, according to Rose, deals explicitly with the conflict between present and past, rural and urban. The arrival of a group or family of white middle class characters into the wilderness sets off a collision between cultures. In *Pumpkinhead*, this group of young WASPish tourists is led by arrogant city boy, Joel (John DiAquino). They pull up at Ed's convenience store and immediately Joel starts to antagonize the locals by making fun of Ed's young son, Billy (Matthew Hurley), before cutting up the local scenery with his expensive trails motorbike (those obnoxious contraptions again). The others in Joel's group, Chris (Jeff East), Tracy (Cynthia Bain) and Maggie (Kerry Remson), are fascinated when Mr Wallace (George 'Buck' Flower), a hill man, and his four children arrive to buy groceries. This family is straight from Tobacco Road, and the city slickers can't help but start to take photographs of them.

A very similar scene occurs in Jeff Lieberman's 1981 hillbilly horror, *Just Before Dawn*, where one of the tourists aims his camera at twin girls who play in the wreck of a car at the side of the road. Dressed in rags, these are, in stark contrast to the affluent city kids, children of the historically dispossessed, evoking Dorothea Lange's famous portraits of rural poverty during the Great Depression. In *Pumpkinhead*, though, the gaze of the teenage tourists is not one of voyeurism but of sympathy, and this is where *Pumpkinhead* starts to depart from the usual urbanoia sterotypes.

As Dave J. Wilson comments: these particular tourists 'are not made up of the usual stereotypical, annoyingly obnoxious, horny teenagers that populated this era in the slasher film, which we longed to see offed in various gruesome ways. They are a likeable bunch that draws our sympathies. They are empathetic and innocent, just caught up in unfortunate circumstances out of their control, and do not deserve to die.' Even Joel comes to see the error of his ways later in the film. In a similar respect, the Wallace family is also afforded dignity by the filmmakers. They are poles apart from the degenerates of *Deliverance* and *Scum of the Earth*, not depraved at all, just dirt poor.

Usually in urbanoia the city group or family are hunted down and killed by their backwoods antagonists, as tensions between the white middle class urban intruders and the wilderness clan sets off the events that follow. But in *Pumpkinhead*, both groups are sympathetic, so where does the 'monster' come in? Who (or what) is the antagonist of this particular story? This is where *Pumpkinhead* changes mode from hillbilly horror to urban myth. A standard rule of folk-narrative is that a taboo must be broken (an 'interdiction violated'): many urban legends are, at their most basic, cautionary tales that stress the dangers of transgressing social norms. Joel transgresses badly when he accidently runs Billy down. But Ed transgresses too, when he summons Pumpkinhead — mythical spirit of local legend — to hunt down the teenagers and kill them one by one as revenge for his son's death.

Just like any good urban myth, then, *Pumpkinhead* conveys a meaningful message or 'moral'. Eventually, Ed comes to regret his actions, just as Joel comes to regret *his*, and both try to make amends. But, of course, it's too late. The evil genie has been let out of the bottle. Urban myths often present secondary meanings; according to folklorist Jan Harold Brunvand (author of *The Vanishing Hitchhiker: American Urban Legends and Their Meanings*) 'these may provide deeper criticism of human behaviour or social conditions'. If *Pumpkinhead* has a secondary meaning it might be to criticize the deep-seated cultural fears that underlie most rural horror movies — which are themselves a reflection of the tensions that continue to exist between urban rich and rural poor in America. This makes *Pumpkinhead* a very grim fairytale indeed…

Rabid (1977)

'You can't trust your mother...your best friend...your neighbour next door... One minute they're perfectly normal, the next...Rabid!'

So goes the tag line for David Cronenberg's 1977 pandemic horror movie with a difference. The UK quad poster for *Rabid*'s original release in Great Britain (and also the cover for the film's tie-in novelization) shows the terrifying and unforgettable image of a young bikini-clad girl crouched listlessly in what appears to be a stainless-steel cell. Her skin is blue, lips swollen and eyes clouded. She appears to be afflicted by some kind of contagion. Could it be rabies?

It's hard to convey just how firmly this poster image touched a nerve in the British public back in 1977. Cronenberg's film arrived during a wave of tabloid hysteria about rabies and public health in the UK. Reports of rabies outbreaks in mainland Europe prompted a scare that the virus might cross the Channel and cause an outbreak in Great Britain. The British government responded to the emergent threat of the disease with a bombardment of public propaganda that quickly led to media frenzy. Soon TV programmes, newspapers and even novels like *Saliva* (1977); *The Rage* (1978) and *Day of the Mad Dogs* (1978) imagined what an outbreak of rabies might look like in the UK and what the effect might be on the British way of life. These novels were literary responses to the emergent threat of rabies on mainland Europe and were in fact welcomed by the government as useful public information. They functioned alongside public propaganda and tabloid hysteria, and portrayed rabies as the cause of social breakdown, echoing the Government's message. When the film distributor, Alpha Films, bought Cronenberg's film for UK cinema release in the summer of '77, they were jumping on a band wagon of rabies-related horror. They were clearly trying to play on the public's fear of the disease, a virus that ends in madness and death. The public fear of infection is echoed in the tagline: pray it doesn't happen to you!

But the poster image is in fact a dupe: if you've seen the movie you will know. And that provides the key to Cronenberg's film. It appears to be one thing but is really something else. It's a pandemic movie riding on the coattails of films like *The Andromeda Strain* (1971), *The Crazies* (1973) and *The Cassandra Crossing* (1976) but underneath it's really about Cronenberg's favourite twin themes of revolutionary counterculture and (both literally and metaphorically) the body politic. Such is the film's female-centric approach to horror that the Soska sisters remade *Rabid* in 2019 as a continuation of Cronenberg's vision 'from a female perspective'.

Rabid followed hot on the heels of Cronenberg's horror movie debut *Shivers* (1975) which had a caused a stir in his native Canada as well as abroad. In *Shivers*, Cronenberg drew on established genre tropes from movies like *Invasion of the Body Snatchers* (1956) and *Night of the Living Dead* (1968) and he mixed them up with his own transgressive approach to sexuality and body horror.

In many ways, *Rabid* is an outgrowth of *Shivers*, taking a similar premise but playing it out on a broader canvas. The virus — which again is violent and sexual in nature — threatens to infect not just a single housing complex but the whole of Montreal. In doing so, Cronenberg keys into the invasion-metamorphosis tropes that those older movies like *Night of the Living Dead* and *Invasion of the Body Snatchers* had done before. The idea that an alien force could invade our bodies and transform our minds had been floating around science fiction, horror and fantasy for decades, but it took 50s films like *Invaders from Mars* (1953) and other Cold War-era science fiction movies to popularize it. In many ways, *Rabid* is — like *Shivers* — about a kind of revolutionary counterculture seeking to overthrow the mainstream. In fact, such is the continuity between the two films that many critics have remarked on the similarities between them. This has probably been helped by the fact that on re-release *Shivers* and *Rabid* often played together in a double bill. 'Don't see them alone…see them together!' ran the tag line on the quad poster for the Target/Alpha Films UK release of 'David Cronenberg's two award-winning masterpieces' in the early 1980s. In an interview with the director that took place in 2000, Adam Simon remarked to Cronenberg: 'I first saw those two films on a double-bill, as many people did, and it felt like a very avant-garde experience, as if I had just seen the same thing twice.' This is indeed the case — try watching them together and you will see — *Shivers* and *Rabid* are basically the same film twice — but with different conclusions. The fascinating thing about Cronenberg's two early movies is that that the virus/parasites are the protagonists fighting against the humans: *Shivers* showed the parasites as winning out in the end. Their 'revolution' is a success. But *Rabid* investigates the opposite possibility: what if the revolution fails? What if the attempt of the rabies virus to take over humankind leads nowhere? In Cronenberg's own words:

"I can make a case for *Shivers* as having a happy ending, and I can't really make that case for *Rabid*. Maybe it's two sides of the same coin. They are really a pair. It's almost *Rashomon*, you know — you watch one and then you watch the other, you get the different sides of the same story and it's really quite difficult to know where the truth is."

The plot itself is pure Cronenberg. After a near-fatal motorcycle accident on country roads outside Montreal, Rose (Marilyn Chambers) is rushed to the nearest medical facility available, which happens to be a cosmetic surgery owned by Dr. Keloid (Howard Ryshpan). Keloid performs an experimental skin graft to save Rose who is suffering massive internal injuries from the crash. At first the procedure seems to be a success but Rose develops a strange vampire-like need for human blood which she gets from her victims in the medical facility. Keloid realizes too late that his experimental surgery has created a weird mutation in Rose — a phallic needle-type growth underneath her armpit through which Rose sucks the blood of her victims. What Rose doesn't know is that, at the same time as syphoning off a little blood from her victims, she is infecting them with a variant of the rabies virus that turns them into homicidal lunatics with an urge to bite people. Discharging herself from the clinic, Rose makes her way to Montreal and, like the Typhoid Mary of legend, obliviously spreads a wave of infection in the city that leads to martial law and near social collapse.

Cronenberg's wasn't the first horror film to take rabies as its subject. A good seven years before *Rabid* came *I Drink Your Blood* (1970), David E. Durston's cult classic about a gang of Satanic hippies who become infected with rabies after eating infected meat pies. Also known as *Hydro-Phobia*, Durston's movie featured a young Lynn Lowry, who would later go on to appear in both George A. Romero's *The Crazies* (1973) and *Shivers,* making for an intriguing cross-over between these virus-inspired movies. Durston's film is itself an oddity, mixing bloody violence (it was the first film ever to receive an 'X' certificate in America for violence rather than sex), viral horror and Charles Manson-like social commentary about crazy murderous hippies. It comes close to Cronenberg's film in terms of sheer strangeness, but never quite trumps *Rabid* in terms of horror. One of *Rabid*'s triumphs is that Cronenberg takes his outlandish premise and makes it believable. The idea of a person developing a bodily mutation due to scientific failure like Rose does — even though surreal — seems chillingly possible. When Cronenberg first wrote the script for *Rabid* he called it 'Mosquito', and Rose is like a human mosquito in the way she sucks blood, while simultaneously transferring a parasitic disease into her hosts. This makes the character of Rose one of the most original and disturbing 'she-monsters' in horror cinema. Even Cronenberg found the idea so strange that he worried that audiences wouldn't buy it. Early on in production he expressed his anxiety to producer John Dunning who reassured him, saying "it's weird, it's interesting."

Dunning was co-president with Andre Link of Cinepix, the Québec company (and pioneer of 'Canuxploitation' movies), that had made *Shivers.*

Shivers had become the high grossing Canadian film domestically by 1976, and Cinepix was keen to sign Cronenberg to do a follow up. Despite the controversy of *Shivers*, the Canadian Film Development Fund once again agreed to the funding and Ivan Reitman (who himself would go on to become a prominent director in the 1980s with *Ghostbusters*, 1984, *Twins*, 1989, and *Kindergarten Cop*, 1990) came on board as producer as he had for *Shivers*. Joe Blasco, who did such a memorable job of the parasites in *Shivers* did the prosthetic make up effects. In front of the camera, a number of actors from *Shivers* return in *Rabid*, further giving the effect of symmetry in the two films. Most notable is the actor Joe Silver, who had played Rollo Lipsky, a sympathetic scientist in *Shivers*. He plays pretty much the same role in *Rabid* as the friend and mentor of the film's biker hero, Hart (Frank Moore). Just like in *Shivers*, Silver's character, Murray, meets an undeserved fate. Even though it was shot for just 500,000 Canadian dollars, *Rabid* feels like a much bigger film than *Shivers*. While *Shivers* took place in one central location — the 'Starliner Towers' complex of the story — *Rabid* opens up to take in not only the farmland and countryside around Keloid's plastic surgery clinic but also the streets of Montreal.

It's in this opening up to show wider society ravaged by plague outbreak that *Rabid* borrows from other movies in terms of its imagery. *The Crazies* is the most obvious touchstone. Cronenberg reprises the sight of dehumanized soldiers clad in white biological/nuclear/chemical suits and gas masks, patrolling the Montreal streets, enforcing martial law by force. Their role is to contain the rabies outbreak and they do so in a heavy-handed way that infringes any sense of civil rights. People are harassed and herded around public areas; identity cards are demanded in spot checks; people arrested for little or no reason. Worse still is the 'shoot first, ask questions later' approach to those who are infected by the virus or even just appear to be. This is brought home by the government spokesperson who informs TV cameras that "shooting down the victims is as good a way of handling matters as we've got." In *The Crazies*, Romero criticized the army's handling of the public, showing their heavy-handedness only leading to more violence as gun-toting civilians start to fight back against authoritarian rule. Cronenberg appears to be more pragmatic in showing the army's enforcement of lockdown as brutal but necessary.

Part of Cronenberg's response stemmed to his own experience of seeing martial law in Montreal during the October Crisis of October 1970. During that time, the Canadian Prime Minister called out troops against the Front de Liberation du Québec (the FLQ), a revolutionary group that wanted separation of Québec from Canada. A state of emergency was called after several bomb explosions and the kidnapping of a British diplomat. Trudeau called on the War Measures Act and brought troops and tanks onto Montreal streets. The police were given new powers and civil rights were suspended. By December the FLQ had been arrested or fled the country, but the crisis and fear of a Québec uprising made an impression on Canadian citizens, many of whom had watched it unfold on television. Cronenberg had himself been out of the country at the time but had followed the news. As he told Adam Simon in 2000:

"When you see soldiers in the streets in Montreal (in *Rabid*), that was definitely seen as a political reference. Because our then-Prime Minister Trudeau had recently called out the military, and that was the first time that anybody had seen soldiers with guns in the streets of Canada. It was incredibly shocking. I was actually in Paris when I read about this and it was as though I was reading about some Latin American or Asian country. Those images of soldiers in the streets were seen as a direct reference, and certainly conscious on my part, to events involving the FLQ, the revolutionary group that wanted separation of Québec from Canada and was putting bombs in mailboxes and assassinating government ministers and so on."

Although Cronenberg consciously references the October Crisis in *Rabid*, showing the soldiers on the streets, he doesn't seem to do so to any political end. Instead, his interest in revolutionary counterculture is basically a philosophical one, and it's tied to the idea of bodily revolution or contagion, such as the rabies virus in the film.

"Metaphorically, it's an idea," Cronenberg commented in 2000, "like Bolshevism or Islam, or any idea that takes hold and infects people...a kind of a model for the spreading of a religion or a political philosophy, the idea that it could be a mouth-to-mouth thing, verbal, physical. It could be a parasite or a hug that infects." Cronenberg's fascination with the idea of a political philosophy spreading through the people like a contagion finds expression in the counterculture groups that feature in so many of his films. From the 'infected' of *Shivers* and *Rabid* to the 'psychoplasmic' patients of Dr. Raglan in *The Brood* (1979) to the secret society of telepaths in *Scanners* (1981), Cronenberg's films include splinter groups that represent the "orgiastic, secret element, as in the communist cell where people meet and they're in danger." We can see this in his later films too, like in the cult of car-crash fetishists led by Vaughan in *Crash* (1996). In a way all of these groups are revolutionaries, and Cronenberg shows them in a sympathetic light. But in Cronenberg's films there is always ambivalence about revolution itself. In *Shivers* the revolution of the parasites seems to succeed, but in *Rabid* the revolution of the virus fails.

Although *Rabid* includes commentary on the social and political side of things, the imagery in the film is mainly of body horror, and for Cronenberg these things are closely tied together. In many of his films the characters have a revolution taking place in their bodies which they are unable to suppress, such as the parasites of *Shivers* or the virus that turns people into flesh-hungry maniacs in *Rabid*. In Cronenberg's work society is a metaphor for the body and the body is a metaphor for society.

Body horror, for Cronenberg, is essentially political and this is what makes *Rabid* such a powerful film. Rose's plight is one of struggling for her own agency, socially and in terms of trying to control the mutation of her body. It is her body's need for human blood that forces her to seek out victims, and her embrace is quite sexual in nature. Cronenberg's penchant for symbolically named characters (Dr. Keloid is named after scar tissue; Murray Cypher's name reflects his basically expositional role in the story) finds meaning in his choice of name for the protagonist: 'Rose' — a beautiful demure flower with a literal thorn capable of drawing blood. Cronenberg had wanted to cast Sissy Spacek in the role after her bravura performance as *Carrie* (1976). You can see the similarities: the shy, basically innocent young woman who becomes a monster. Instead Cinepix insisted on Marilyn Chambers, who is in many ways the more interesting choice. A former model, she became a household name as the Ivory Soap Girl on soap flake boxes across America before a career as a porn actress in titles like *Behind the Green Door* (1972) and *The Resurrection of Eve* (1973). In *Rabid* she brings that sense of duality: wholesomeness mixed with the carnal. Rose emerges ultimately as a heart-rending character. She is a sweet person struggling to assert herself in light of her mutation; she never intends to harm anyone, and her fate, at the hands of one of her own victims, is a tragic one.

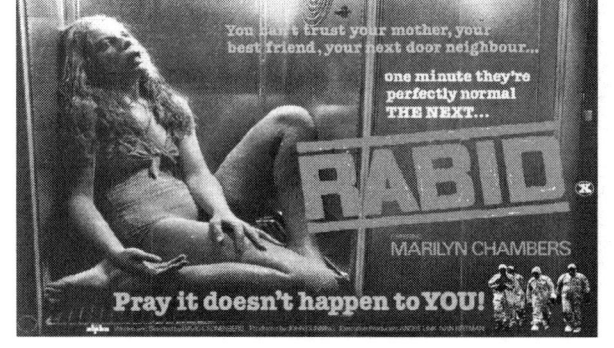

Rabid (Cinepix, 1977)

Re-Animator (1985)

The word 'splatstick' was first coined by Peter Jackson to describe the unique brand of 80s surreal bad taste comedy horror that combines extreme gore ('splatter') and silent movie slapstick humour. Think films like *The Evil Dead* and *Basket Case* (both 1982) and you'll get a good idea of what splatstick is, but in terms of sheer eye-popping carnage and jet-black humour one of the most iconic slices of 80s splatstick has to be *Re-Animator*. Produced by Brian Yuzna and directed by Stuart Gordon, starring Jeffrey Combs as Herbert West, the medical student with the ability to raise corpses from the dead, *Re-Animator* launched the careers of two major horror auteurs — Gordon and Yuzna — who between them have clocked up a whole list of notable movies like *Society* (1989), *Return of The Living Dead 3* (1993) and *The Dentist* (1996) as well as *From Beyond* (1986), *Dolls* (1987), *Dagon* (2001) and *Stuck* (2007).

It made cult icons out of Jeffrey Combs and Barbara Crampton, not to mention putting Empire International Pictures on the map and giving us in Richard Band's music one of the greatest scores ever written for a horror movie.

Chronicling the adventures of Herbert West and his assistant (the unnamed first-person narrator) over a series of six episodes, H.P. Lovecraft's 1922 story *Herbert West — Re-Animator* presents a riff on Mary Shelley's *Frankenstein* as West tries to perfect his attempts at reviving dead bodies. Like in the film, each attempt ends in bloody mayhem as the re-animated corpses turn into blood-thirsty maniacs. 'Of Herbert West, who was my friend in college and in after life, I can speak only with extreme terror,' begins the narrator. 'This terror is not due altogether to the sinister manner of his recent disappearance, but was engendered by the whole nature of his life-work, and first gained its acute form more than seventeen years ago, when we were in the third year of our course at the Miskatonic University Medical School in Arkham. While he was with me, the wonder and diabolism of his experiments fascinated me utterly, and I was his closest companion'.

Not considered one of Lovecraft's best, *Herbert West — Re-Animator* was written more for money than artistic expression — Lovecraft being paid five dollars for each instalment of the story. But it was the story's *Frankenstein* theme that first attracted Stuart Gordon. In 1979, Gordon started thinking about making a horror film after a friend advised him that a horror picture would be the easiest type of movie to raise money for as investors were almost guaranteed to get their money back no matter how bad the movie turned out to be!

Gordon's original concept of the *Re-Animator* adaptation was to do it as a TV series of six episodes closely following the six instalments of Lovecraft's story. Gordon worked up a pilot script for the series and took it to WTTW. They weren't interested. Gordon shopped the script around other TV stations, changing the episode lengths from 30 minutes to one hour depending on the needs of the station, but nobody bit. At that point, Gordon's proposed screen adaptation of Lovecraft faltered.

Enter Brian Yuzna.

Born in the Philippines in 1949, Brian Yuzna was inspired by art during his childhood, with an early interest in expressionism and surrealism that would set him up perfectly for the splatstick movies that he would later make as a producer then as a director.

The son of a bridge engineer who worked for the United States government, Yuzna grew up in Nicaragua, Puerto Rico and Panama before moving with his family to Atlanta, Georgia in the 1960s. He didn't have television in the Philippines so each Sunday he and his family went to the movies. Films like *The Creature with the Atom Brain* (1955) and *The 7th Voyage of Sinbad* (1958) made a lasting impression. At college in the States he majored in the phenomenology of religion and later studio art. He thought he might become a painter, moving briefly to New York's Soho, but decided the lifestyle wasn't for him.

A child of the 1960s, Yuzna spent most of his twenties living in hippy communes in North Carolina, where to make ends meet he sold his paintings, worked as a carpenter and also ran a restaurant. He started making short experimental films with a 16mm Bolex camera; one particular amateur short grew into a ninety-minute feature entitled *Self Portrait in Brains*, about an artist who blows his brains out against a canvas for art and becomes a protagonist as a hologram. At that point, in 1982, deciding that film-making was his true vocation, Yuzna moved to Hollywood and set himself up as a producer. He put an ad in *Variety* saying he was looking for a director. A friend of his, visual effects supervisor Bob Greenberg (who would become an associate producer on *Re-Animator*), suggested he get in touch with Stuart Gordon. Yuzna was also looking to make a horror movie at the time, and after he read Gordon's fifty-page treatment for a TV pilot of *Herbert West — Re-Animator*, persuaded Gordon and his writing team of Dennis Paoli and William J. Norris to turn the pilot into a feature script instead.

According to Yuzna, it was Norris who came up with making West an ironic character with a deadpan sense of humour, totally different to the Herbert West in Lovecraft's version of the story. Norris, Paoli and Gordon had also added a love interest for the narrator and protagonist (now given the name of Dan Cain) in the form of Megan Halsey. In Lovecraft's original there are no female characters at all. Another thing they did was to set the story in present day, which would be cheaper to shoot than if it were to be a period piece.

The TV pilot script actually ended much earlier in the story, at the point where Dean Halsey gets killed. It was Yuzna's idea to incorporate the episode from Lovecraft's original short story where a character would carry his own head around, as Yuzna revealed to Dejan Ognjanovic in 2009, "because I remembered Vincent Price carrying his own head in *House on Haunted Hill* (1959). And I was a huge fan of the Roger Corman Poe series. For me, this was what really got me going".

Dr Hill and his decapitated head would become one of *Re-Animator*'s most notorious aspects and it serves as a reminder of what Yuzna was able to bring to the party. Although most fans and critics tend to think of *Re-Animator* as Stuart Gordon's film (deservedly so), it arguably belongs just as much to Yuzna. *Re-Animator*'s slyly subversive humour is in perfect keeping with both Gordon's and Yuzna's sense of satire.

In *Re-Animator* we can already see the splatstick themes emerging that both filmmakers would go on to develop in their later films. There is the portrayal of authority as depraved and corrupt, as personified by the villainous Dr Hill, who claims Herbert West's discovery of a serum that can re-animate the dead as his own, despite the hard graft that West and Dan Cain have done to test the serum on the hospital's cadavers.

Sex and death are important aspects of the horror film for Yuzna and we can see this in *Re-Animator* too. When Dr Hill is decapitated by West and subsequently re-animated as a headless corpse, Hill finally acts out his lustful obsession for Megan, abducting her and subjecting her to the sexual of advances of his own disembodied head! As Yuzna says, this sequence was not in Gordon's original script, and it was Yuzna who helped developed these aspects of the film. According to Yuzna, "if you try to take away sex and death from a horror movie, you don't have a horror movie!"

The gory climax of *Re-Animator* is one of the big, transgressive, crazy, orgiastic scenes that feature in all of Yuzna's work including *Society, Initiation: Silent Night, Deadly Night 4* (1990), *Progeny* (1998), *Return of The*

Living Dead 3 and *The Dentist* as well as *Bride of Re-Animator* (1989) (in which the pieced together 'Bride', becomes a sympathetic monster only to be torn to pieces again).

Also in *Re-Animator* is a fascination with bodily transformation that figures in both Gordon's and Yuzna's future work, as well as being a cornerstone of the whole splatstick subgenre.

Surprisingly, one of the *Re-Animator*'s biggest fans is the film critic Pauline Kael. In her book *Hooked*, Kael enthused, 'the bloodier it gets, the funnier it is. It's like pop Buñuel; the jokes hit you in a subterranean comic zone that the surrealists' pranks sometimes reached, but without the surrealists' self-consciousness (and art-consciousness). This is indigenous American junkiness, like the Mel Brooks-Gene Wilder *Young Frankenstein* (1974), but looser and more low-down'.

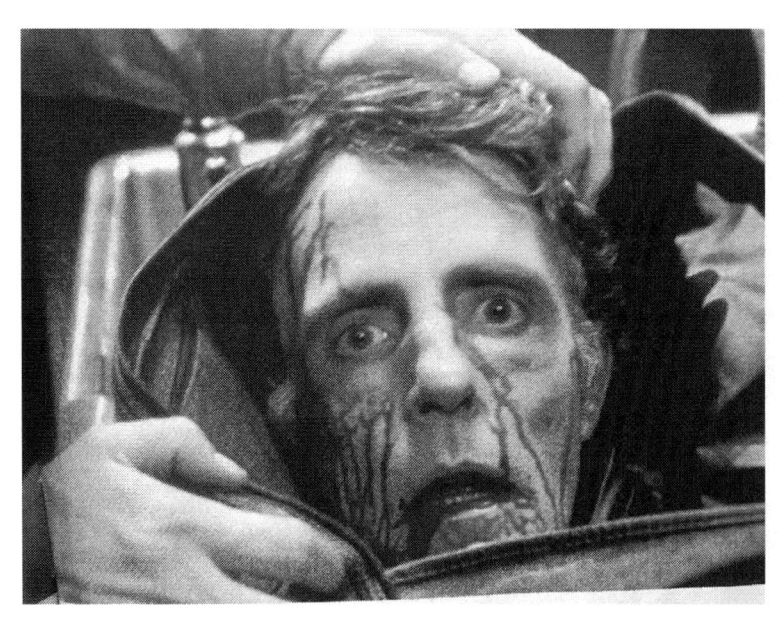

David Gale in *Re-Animator* (Empire Pictures, 1985)

The Redeemer: Son of Satan (1978)

'From out of the darkness the hand of the Redeemer shall appear to punish those who have lived in sin.'

With this enigmatic title card, so starts *The Redeemer*, a strange, unsettling little horror movie. (Originally released in the States as *The Redeemer: Son of Satan*, it's probably better known there under the alternative title, *Class Reunion Massacre*.) Thanks to its patchy distribution in previous years, though, not many horror fans may have heard of *The Redeemer*. But those that do see it as a cult classic, one of those films — like *Last House on Dead End Street* (1977) or *Communion* (aka *Alice, Sweet Alice*, 1976) — that creates a great deal of curiosity and speculation amongst fans, not just because of its obscurity, but also because it manages at times to be genuinely creepy and perplexing. Part of the mystique of *The Redeemer* stems from the fact that it is the sole film credit of director Constantine S. Gochis, and for most of the cast as well (with the notable exception of Jeannetta Arnette, who would become known for her role in *Boys Don't Cry*, 1999). All in all, *The Redeemer* is a weird and mysterious little gem.

The Redeemer first appeared in UK cinemas as a double-bill with John 'Bud' Cardos' vastly inferior *Kingdom of The Spiders* in the summer of 1978 when it played ABC cinemas in London and 'selected cinemas throughout the country' before disappearing from screens. 'A Masterpiece of Terror and Suspense in One Horror Programme', claimed the UK distributor, Enterprise Pictures Ltd. in its advertising (Enterprise had scored a minor hit with Curtis Harrington's *Ruby* [1977] the previous year, marketing it as the spawn of *Carrie* [1976] and *The Exorcist* [1973]). But the 'X' (18) rated *The Redeemer* didn't make much of a dent shackled to the 'AA' (15) certificate of *Spiders*. Despite being praised as 'an extraordinarily good exploitation film' by esteemed film critic Alan Jones in *House of Hammer* magazine (issue #23, August, 1978), it quickly passed into obscurity. UK fans finally managed to track it down in the early 80s when it briefly resurfaced on pre-cert home video. Released uncut on VHS, Betamax and Video 2000 formats by the Dudley-based Derann Film Services in November 1981, *The Redeemer* (still billed as 'a masterpiece of terror and suspense') managed to escape being labelled a video nasty but was withdrawn from release after the introduction of the Video Recordings Act in 1984 made it law that all videos (even those already in circulation) needed to be submitted to the British Board of Film Certification for rating. Again, *The Redeemer* sank without trace, but this only added to its growing reputation amongst horror buffs and collectors.

Currently still unavailable in the UK, and only on VHS in the States for a number of years (under its various titles), not until 2010 did *The Redeemer* get a R1 DVD release in America. Code Red put it out (as *The Redeemer: Son of Satan*) in October 2010; a limited edition (of 1000 copies) Blu-ray followed in 2014. (Beware if buying on DVD under the title *Class Reunion Massacre* — the Desert Island Films/ East West Entertainment releases under this title are very poor transfers). The good news is that, as of writing, *The Redeemer* can now also be streamed (or bought for download) on Amazon Video (courtesy of Cinema Epoch/Code Red).

This recent availability after so long has brought *The Redeemer* to a new generation of horror fans, a number of whom are discovering it for the first time and discussing it online. It's also leading to a reappraisal by older fans who first saw it years ago. Writers may disagree about the quality of the film or object to its morality but they are struck by the way its premise of punishing 'sinners' Old Testament style prefigures classics like *Seven* (1995) and how its Ten Little Indians murder plot marks it as a proto-slasher (*The Redeemer* was actually filmed before John Carpenter made *Halloween*, 1978, but sat on the shelf in the interim while the producers searched for a distributor). What's more, *The Redeemer* also draws on the 'devil child' tropes that were popular at time with the then-recent success of *The Omen* (1976), and it's partly the uneasy melding of these two subgenres — slasher and supernatural/biblical horror — that makes *The Redeemer* so odd and unsettling as a low budget horror movie.

The story involves six people who attend their high school reunion and find themselves locked inside the building by a disguised killer called the Redeemer who proceeds to kill them off one by one for the sinful lives that they have made for themselves. The killer turns out to be a priest guided by an 'angel of the Lord' sent to him in the form of a young boy who may in fact be the titular son of Satan. The ambiguity and basic mystery of the story is one of the reasons why *The Redeemer* is such a haunting little movie. At the same time, *The Redeemer* is filmed with a style and skill not often seen in low budget 70s horror films.

The Redeemer is the brainchild of producer Sheldon Tromberg, who was originally a B-picture distributor for Republic Pictures, Embassy Pictures, Continental and Rank. In the 1960s he set up his own company called Box Office Attractions to distribute arthouse movies in the States. At the time it was normal for a distributor to handle arthouse and exploitation under one umbrella. In 1973 Tromberg started to teach screenwriting and business at Georgetown University where he met lawyer Stephen Tranttner, and in

1974 they set up TNT Productions using tax shelter money from private investors with the aim of making a quick buck from low budget movies.

The original idea for the script of *The Redeemer* came from William Vernick, then a twenty-year-old film editor working in post-production in New York. Through his involvement on previous films for Tromberg, Vernick got to know the producer, and pitched him a 20-page treatment for the screenplay that would become *The Redeemer*. According to Vernick (interviewed by Justin A. Kerswell for *Hysteria Lives!*) his first draft had nothing to do with religion or Christianity at all: "It was a bunch of people trapped in a high school by a crazy, who then knocks them off one at a time". It was only later, Vernick claims, that the 'devil cult' angle was added to the story, at the behest of either Tromberg or a potential distribution partner, who saw it as a way to cash in on *The Omen*, which had been released in June 1976 to huge box office numbers. Vernick (who is also now a director) was a film buff from an early age and while he wrote the script looked to Jack Clayton's 1961 classic *The Innocents* for inspiration. Vernick was asked to rewrite the script to add more religious and satanic references instead, and this helps to shed some light on the strange hybrid of horror subgenres that *The Redeemer* would ultimately become.

Another mystery of *The Redeemer* is that of its director: just who *is* Constantine S. Gochis? Very little seems to be known about him, except that he was a Grammy award-nominated film editor for NBC and that *The Redeemer* was to be his first (and last) movie as a director. T.G. Finkbinder (who plays the Redeemer) remembers Gochis as being a short, balding man in his fifties, a resident of Bethesda, Maryland near Washington (and he would remain so for many years after *The Redeemer*). He liked to drink on set, but was at the same time very prepared (his wife drew the storyboards for *The Redeemer*.) Whether Gochis is the one who should be praised for *The Redeemer*'s stylish framing, camera work and staging is up for debate, though. Both Finkbinder and Vernick attribute the look of *The Redeemer* to its director of photography, John Michael Beymer, who has since gone on to become a successful cinematographer and camera operator with credits that include *Law and Order* and numerous made-for-tv movies.

In his book *Horror Film Aesthetics*, author Thomas M. Sipos commends Gochis for the use of windows to light the inside of the school, creating atmosphere in the spooky corridors, staircases and hallways. 'The film uses daylight aesthetically', writes Sipos. 'Windows and sky are often overexposed, importing a spiritual ambiance to many scenes, as if some angelic force fills the sky, bleeding brightly through the windows'. Although, it's the norm to acclaim the director for the visuals of a film, in this case — and with respect to Sipos — it's probably more likely that we can thank Beymer for *The Redeemer*'s eerily glowing windows. More contentious is who can take credit for the staging of the camera. A number of scenes in *The Redeemer* are shot in long continuous takes without cuts; but it is done so skilfully that you don't notice because of the way the camera moves and the way the actors are blocked within the scene. There's one particular scene, for instance, where the shot runs on for two and a half minutes, without you noticing there are no cuts. It's a large part of the film's overall visual style, and helps to build suspense. But who is responsible for this? Is it Beymer, Gochis, or the two of them working closely together? One thing's for sure, for a low-budget horror movie, *The Redeemer* is intelligently shot and edited.

Tromberg cast *The Redeemer* with unknowns that he found in the Washington DC area (where his production company was based). Most of the cast were fresh out of drama school (Jeannetta Arnette, who plays the promiscuous Cindy, was still at George Washington University and acting in local theatre productions). T.G. Finkbinder had just finished graduate school when he responded to an advert in *The Washington Post* looking for actors for a low budget film. His audition took place in a local movie theatre with producer, director and cameraman in attendance. Gochis liked his look — ordinary but menacing at the same time. The role of the Redeemer required the actor to create a number of different characterizations and accents to match the various disguises of the shape-shifting killer. One minute he's a hell-fire preacher, the next he's a prancing, preening clown; in another scene he's a gun-toting backwoods redneck, then a grotesque puppet-master. Finkbinder is deliberately off-putting in these various guises, which actually adds a great deal of menace to the film, and his clown persona, with the weird falsetto voice, is especially creepy.

The Redeemer was shot on location in Staunton, Virginia, with much of the filming taking place in Staunton Military Academy, then an empty building complex, having closed down as a school the year before; before that it had a long history as a military school dating back to the 1800s. Most of the production took place in the North Barracks, with its distinctive three storey Corinthian columns and large clock set in the gable, which doubles as the 'Stuart Morse Academy' in the film. Stromberg leased the building for a month of shooting (with other scenes lensed in and around Staunton, including at historic 50s drive-in restaurant Wright's Dairy-Rite on Greenville Ave. and the First Baptist Church on W. Frederick St.). Actors lived in the Staunton Military Academy dorms during the shoot, and filming, for the most part, went without a hitch with Gochis covering 2-3 pages of script per day.

The actors rarely rehearsed their scenes beforehand, and it's true that the performances vary in quality. Locals filled in the bit parts, including as the extras in the church scenes. The members of the First Baptist Church choir played themselves in these scenes. The mysterious Christopher, the boy who just might be from hell, was played by local actor Christopher Flint. Flint would go on to a career in theatre, winning an award for his role in *Into The Woods*, but his only other screen credit is playing a carjacker in an episode of the 2009 TV series *The Platoon Of Power Squadron*.

The Redeemer's opening scenes are truly surreal. A closer look at the first 30 minutes reveals just what a strange film it really is. We see a lake in a quarry; credits roll (the film's title card on the Code Red release reads only '*The Redeemer*' without the subtitle), while clouds move over the water, creating almost time lapse effect. Then superimposed are those opening words: 'From out of the darkness the hand of the Redeemer shall appear'. The words sound biblical, but nowhere in the Testaments can they be found: more likely they are made up by the filmmakers, because what happens next is a pretty literal translation of them into film images. If the lake is the darkness, then the hand that appears from below the water surface belongs to Christopher, who rises from the lake and leaves the quarry to catch a bus into town.

Things get weirder still in the next scene. We see Finkbinder's priest asleep in his room, his hand visible outside of his bedclothes. Christopher's shadow falls over the bed, and in close up, we see a second thumb grow on the priest's hand! This enigmatic touch has provoked a lot of speculation from fans, and it leaves many viewers mystified: what's the significance of the mysterious double thumb? Vernick claims that, in pre-production, Tromberg drew the outline of his hand on the front page of the script and added an extra finger. It might be that Tromberg got the idea from an old Lon Chaney movie called *The Unknown* (1927) in which Chaney plays a circus knife thrower with two thumbs on one hand. It seems to signal Christopher's supernatural/diabolical influence over the priest — it's a demonic thumb!

Mention should be made early on of *The Redeemer*'s effective synth score by Philip Gallo and Clem Vicari, two New York based film composers (later writers, directors and editors) who also scored Charles Kaufman's *Mother's Day* (1980) for Troma. Gallo and Vicari's soundtrack manages to be suitably weird, mysterious and eerie, and in many ways helps to hold *The Redeemer* together by bridging the supernatural and slasher elements. The subtitles on Amazon Video described a number of music cues as 'tense, ethereal', which sums up the soundtrack well. The seventies synth score of *The Redeemer* is another aspect that makes the film so unsettling.

Editor Jack Foster would go on to edit another pre-cert favourite *The Nesting* (1981) and clock up many documentary/reality shows for CBS, Lifestyle, Discovery channel and others. Here, Foster builds a sense of mystery in the early scenes of *The Redeemer* by tightly intercutting them. Christopher takes his place in the church alongside the other choirboys, including the bully (Daniel Eliot) who will later get his comeuppance. This is mixed in with a disturbing sequence in which an inspector 'from the Apex fine casual company' come to inspect the school building shoots the janitor dead and proceeds to make a latex mask of his face. Like much of the film, this makes little sense when you think about it afterwards: why would he need to do this? The high school reunion buddies don't know the janitor anyway. But, hey, sometimes you just have to go with it, and these enigmas in *The Redeemer*, although having little or no logic, are what draw you into its nonsensical plot.

Back at the church, we are properly introduced to Finkbinder as the hell-fire preacher at his pulpit. As this is intercut with the business with the inspector and the janitor, and it's later revealed (SPOILER!) that the Inspector, Redeemer and priest is one and the same person, it raises another question: how does the character manage to be in two places at once? Or are we actually cutting between two time frames of the present and the past or possibly the present and the future? Just another of *The Redeemer*'s many puzzles!

Finkbinder's priest launches into a searing fire and brimstone sermon: "there are those among us who have not followed the path of righteousness", he intones gravely. "The road to Sodom is the road to evil and utter damnation!" Just what *The Redeemer* is saying about morality is open to debate, and a number of critics have taken issue with the film for its seemingly puritanical view of sexuality. *TV Guide*, for example, writes the film off as 'possessed of disturbingly puritanical sensibility, this inept, unpleasant film is sticky going indeed'. But, as with many of *The Redeemer*'s ambiguities, what it is saying about morality and religion seems far from clear. It's debatable that *The Redeemer* even knows what it wants to say!

We see the inspector open a high school yearbook to 'Most Likely to Succeed — 1967.' And one, by one, we are introduced to the Redeemer's intended victims as each one's photograph is cut out with a scalpel (exactly why there are only six victims when there are seven deadly sins is anyone's guess!) First we meet John Sinclair (Damian Knight), a cut-throat lawyer who is more interested in making money than defending the innocent ("making a mockery of justice," declares the priest in voice over, "making a game of life".) Next is Cindy (Arnette), who we see in a seedy bar (complete with seventies disco dancers) drinking her life away with her loser boyfriend. Cindy, according to the Redeemer, leads a life "of licentiousness" and loose morals. Next up is Terry Day (Nick Carter), "an embodiment of the city, loaded in its gluttony, fat on its excesses", who, at high school was a superstar footballer, but now gorges himself on hamburgers courtesy of his sad waitress girlfriend. Following on is Jane (played by Nikki Barthen): a wealthy society woman who lives on a country estate with her tiresome husband. Her sin is to have "mutilated the beast of the field and soiled nature". We see her make sport of shooting live birds after growing bored with clay pigeons. Then we meet Roger (Michael Hollingsworth), a vain, petulant actor who walks off a movie set in a huff after his director asks him to do a run-through for the camera. Finally — and most controversially — there is Kirsten (Gyr Patterson), a closeted lesbian who is ashamed of her own life and her relationship with her live-in lover, Petra (Dorothy Hayden). "Let them take heed at their peril that no woman shall lie with another woman as she lies with a man", commands the priest. Taken at face value, this appears to be a pretty clear condemnation of Kirsten's sexuality, but viewers today might also find themselves rooting for Kirsten as the Final Girl as she becomes the last victim of the Redeemer.

The Redeemer does exhibit many of the tropes of slasher movies, even though it pre-dates not only *Halloween* but also *Friday the 13th* (1980) and other seminal slashers of the late 70s/ early 80s. Of course, there is the high school reunion premise and the laundry-list of victims. The characters find themselves locked inside the building with a masked killer, and they quickly learn the cardinal rule of slashers: stay together — no-one go off on their own. A rule which each of them breaks! (and one actually says "I'll be right back"). The Redeemer character, with his different personas, and his weird camp sense of humour, is a kind of prototype slasher villain in some ways but much odder than Freddy, Jason or Pinhead. His sudden appearances are genuinely unexpected and this makes him very sinister indeed. His murder methods and personas match the 'sins' of each of his victims: people die by blowtorch, by shotgun blast, by scimitar, by a single bullet from a revolver, or by having their head held under water in a washbasin until they drown. This last murder, committed by the Redeemer in his clown-costume in the school showers, is truly grotesque, and provides the film with its most memorable lobby card image. It would be interesting to know whether Stephen King saw *The Redeemer* when he first conceived IT in 1978: the shape-shifting Pennywise seems to owe a lot to Finkbinder's creation.

Of course, the slasher wasn't yet popular when *The Redeemer* was made, and the producers had trouble finding a distributor at first. Dimension Pictures finally picked it up after it played at the Paris Festival of Fantastic Films. They decided to focus the advertising campaign on the 'Christopher' character rather than the Redeemer, hence the 'Son of Satan' subtitle added to the poster (if not the film print) with its strapline 'First *The Omen*... Now *The Redeemer*. If you have a craving for terror...The 'Son of Satan' invites you to the class reunion...' Later VHS releases in the States tried to play up the slasher elements, renaming the film *Class Reunion Massacre* ('No more pencils...no more books...no more students'). Interestingly, the two different angles have even influenced the way critics have actually interpreted the film's enigmatic plot, with some claiming the priest to be a former classmate of his victims, which is something not actually suggested in the film at all!

In the end, *The Redeemer* is fascinating for all its strangeness and contradictions. Is it an inept, unpleasant movie with a puritanical sensibility, as some claim? Or is it actually an off-beat morality play that condemns religion? Is Christopher an angel of God, or the Son of Satan? Misunderstood masterpiece of horror or (as another IMDB user wrote) 'Crap-tacular slice of 70s drive in cheese'? Of course, it is possible to enjoy *The Redeemer* solely as a 'straight' slasher movie, if you ignore all the supernatural weirdness in the film. But, then again, it's the supernatural weirdness that makes *The Redeemer* so unique!

The Redeemer: Son of Satan (Dimension Pictures, 1978)

Rock 'n' Roll High School (1979)

Of the entire New World output, Allan Arkush's 1979 paean to punk, high school rebellion and youthful exuberance seems to be the movie most fondly remembered by fans, critics and filmmakers alike. To what do we attribute the enduring appeal of *Rock 'n' Roll High School* as a cult movie *par excellence*? As Tim Lucas has remarked of *Rock 'n' Roll High School*: "When I first saw it, it was like the ultimate New World picture and the ultimate US punk movie rolled into one". Obviously, the Ramones have a lot to do with its cult status as a punk film and movie vehicle for the band but what exactly makes *Rock 'n' Roll High School* 'the ultimate New World picture'? Could it be that the movie gives the clearest example of the New World formula? Roger Corman sought to revisit the 'wild teen' flicks of the 1950s that he first churned out for American International Pictures, but clearly wanted to ride on the coat tails of late 70s box office hits like *Grease* (1978), *Saturday Night Fever* (1977) and *Thank God It's Friday* (1978).

Inarguable is the film's tone — which veers between the nostalgic and the irreverent. It's a High School movie but one populated by the counterculture attitudes that had made New World popular with youth audiences in the 1970s. Built into its cult status is Roger Corman's in house 'superstars' like Mary Woronov, Paul Bartel, Clint Howard and Dick Miller, all of who had achieved cult standing with genre fans by the time of the film's production. In short, the nature of *Rock 'n' Roll High School*'s appeal to a cult audience is closely tied into the Roger Corman/New World brand, and that may prove a fruitful approach to understanding its cult status.

Perhaps Corman's own affection for the film stems from its roots in those old Chuck Griffith-scripted AIP movies with titles like *Rock All Night* (1957) and *Teenage Doll* (1957), movies trading on the 'wild teen' craze started by *Rock Around the Clock* (1956) and *Blackboard Jungle* (1955) — a genre that was to become AIP's life blood. In the early 1950s, the major studios did not yet realize that teenagers were the main cinema audience and were still making films with stars that did not hold meaning for the new teenage audience. Sam Arkoff and his partner Jim Nicholson saw this gap in the market and formed a company in 1954, the American Releasing Corporation (which became American International Pictures in 1956), to produce films made for teenagers and using teenagers. Tapping into the teen trends of the time, AIP promoted films in a number of subgenres: hot-rod movies, rock movies, beach movies, teen melodramas and teen horror films (AIP would, of course, go on to capitalize on the youth protest movement of the 60s with a number of biker and counterculture films produced and/or directed by Corman, such as *The Wild Angels*, 1966, and *The Trip*, 1967).

AIP's critics have suggested that the studio's formulaic appeal to the youth market contributed to post-war era American cinema becoming juvenile, as we see to this day (the so-called 'Peter Pan Syndrome'). However, it must also be said that AIP were one of the first studios to use focus groups to poll American teenagers in the 1950s about what they wanted to see, using their responses to determine titles, stars and storylines.

In *Teen Movies: American Youth On Screen*, Timothy Shary describes Hollywood's dilemma in the 50s when it came to portraying teenagers on film: 'Teen life is filled with sexual urges', writes Shary, 'drug and alcohol temptations and challenges to authority — issues that the studios could not very well address under the Production Code': issues, nonetheless, that AIP would seek to exploit with the added possibilities and shock (or rather, 'schlock') value traditionally afforded by the low budget B picture.

Whilst most teen pictures of the 50s were products of the studios trying desperately to interpret adolescent tastes, AIP's movies already had a youthful sense of rebellion built into them. As Thomas Doherty has commented, 'AIP teenpics seem to be the kind of motion pictures a group of high schoolers let loose with 35mm equipment might come up with, an impression due in equal parts to market savvy, youthful talents and bargain-basement budgets. With the audience that mattered, the company's unpretentious product generally fared better than the transparently calculating teen attractions of the established studios'.

This obvious sympathy on the part of Corman and AIP with teenage rebellion inevitably drew criticism from the authorities and pressure-groups, like the PTA and the FBI, which said that the company glorified criminality. In 1958, producer Jerry Wald denounced AIP's films, saying such pictures "may make a few dollars today," but "they will destroy us tomorrow." To which Arkoff famously replied: "AIP's monsters do not smoke, drink or lust". Although AIP did make a move towards respectability in the early 1960s with its Beach Party films featuring 'clean teens' (only to return to renegade form with the biker movies of the late 60s), their teen films of the 50s, including those made with Corman, are characterized by their very refusal to conform.

The anarchic spirit/ rebellious attitude of AIP followed through in Corman's New World formula, knowingly adopted (and updated) in *Rock 'n' Roll High School* by Arkush and screenwriter Joseph McBride. As Screamin' Steve Stevens (Don Steele) declares to camera in the movie: "this is a classic confrontation between mindless authority and the rebellious nature of youth." And although the touchstone here may seem to be the crazy college campus antics of *National Lampoon's Animal House* (1978) — another boffo box office grosser that was surely in Corman's mind when he greenlit *Rock 'n' Roll High School* — the 'mindless authority and rebellious youth' theme of the movie goes straight back to AIP.

"I have always felt that teenagers think that adults - their parents, or their teachers, anyone that was older and that had authority — were the culprits in their lives," AIP producer Herman Cohen (*I Was a Teenage Werewolf*, 1957) told Tom Weaver in 1994. And this simple observation has held true in teen movies since the 50s, arising from sociological factors in that decade. The early 50s saw the number of juveniles charged with crimes of delinquency increase by forty-five per cent. This gave rise to a major moral panic started by the press and fuelled by the wider popular media (which included book publishers and the film industry). By 1954, public anxiety about growing youth crime was such that the government felt the need to respond. A State subcommittee was set up to investigate juvenile delinquency and the role played by the entertainment industries, particularly comic books, in 'corrupting' the nation's youth. Some modern commentators claim that, in actual fact, the rise in statistics for crimes of juvenile delinquency in the 50s can largely be attributed to the fiat laws: declaration by the juvenile court system that a juvenile is delinquent without any trial and finding only probable cause (the reasonable belief that a person has committed a crime). Many states have laws that confer more lenient treatment on juveniles than on adult offenders. In return, the juvenile gives up certain constitutional rights, such as a right to trial by jury. Very few so-called juvenile delinquents, in other words, actually broke any law. Most were simply rounded up by the police after an event that possibly involved criminal action (such as the youth 'riots' that followed *Rock Around the Clock*). They were brought before a juvenile court judge who found them delinquent only because the police action established probable cause.

In truth, most teenagers in the 50s were themselves part of the consumer culture, targeted as they were by record companies, television networks, the fashion industry and, of course, the movies. The moral panic over juvenile delinquency in the 50s can be seen as arising from what sociologists term 'deviance amplification', or what the layman might call media hype. The result of all this, however, was to give the authorities a reason to exert greater social control over teenagers. It's no wonder, then, that many teenagers of the 50s were pissed off, and attitudes towards teens have hardly changed since then.

Our main point of identification in *Rock 'n' Roll High School* is of course Riff Randell, so memorably portrayed by PJ Soles. The character was based on an amalgam of real people that Arkush and McBride had known in the past. For Arkush it was the female rock fans he knew in his days as stage crew at the Fillmore East, including two girls who "cut school to wait in line for Rolling Stones tickets in 1969 (the concert filmed for *Gimme Shelter*) and got their picture in the New York Post." Arkush stayed friends with them until the late 70s. Another was the fan turned rock journalist, Lisa Robinson, a Fillmore regular who would hang out backstage and talk music. According to Arkush, it was "their passion for rock and rejection of the groupie mentality plus their discerning taste" that made these rock fans stand out. McBride, on his part, modelled the irrepressible Riff Randell "on my first girlfriend, a rebellious young woman who was diagnosed as 'schizophrenic'…One reason I identify with the Ramones is that they told *Rolling Stone* that the 'nice' girls in high school wouldn't go out with them, so they would break into the mental hospital in Queens and date schizophrenic girls".

Here again there are touchstones with the old AIP movies and their depictions of so-called female delinquency in titles like the aforementioned girl gang flick *Teenage Doll*. Refreshing though is the obvious respect with which Riff and her partner in crime Kate Rambeau (Dey Young) are treated by the filmmakers (here *Rock 'n' Roll High School* departs rather bravely from the typical New World product formula and its obligatory T&A). For Arkush, the film's longevity rests on the fact "that Riff & Kate come across as three dimensional"; while McBride claims that he had wanted to write "a female buddy-buddy film, partly because there were so few good roles for women in Hollywood at the time, and almost every seventies Hollywood film was a male buddy-buddy story. So I had *Gentlemen Prefer Blondes*, 1953, in mind". Soles and Young clearly understand their characters, and bring them — and their screen friendship — vividly to life. Of course, Soles has herself become a cult figure for movies like *Carrie* (1976) and *Halloween* (1978), but it is as Riff that her fans remember her best. An intriguing aspect of her cult stardom is that Soles has become immortalized in an album and song title by American rock band Local H: *Whatever Happened to PJ Soles?*

Another piece in the cult puzzle of *Rock 'n' Roll High School* is Principal Togar — the 'Mindless Authority' and nemesis of Riff and Kate and their rebellious youth. Mary Woronov is an actress who has cult stamped through her like a stick of rock. As the most 'butch' of the ex-Warhol superstars, Woronov, as the Principal of Vince Lombardi High, seems as much modelled on *Ilsa: She Wolf of the SS* (1975) as she is on the countless tyrannical high school principals of AIP's teen pics. But here again, the New World formula comes into play (as Woronov later complained, "I began to get a reputation as this… well drag her in and she'll bring a whip with her"). At the same time, though, it is that very formula that seems to meld all the elements together: to form — in the case of *Rock 'n' Roll High School* — a genuine cult classic.

Mary Woronov in *Rock 'n' Roll High School* (New World Pictures, 1979)

A Serial Killer's Guide to Life (2019)

Shot for £27k (give or take) raised through a Kickstarter campaign, Staten Cousins Roe's *A Serial Killer's Guide to Life* re-defines the idea of self-help in more ways than one. Indeed, 'Self-Help' was the film's working title. The idea for it came about after Cousins Roe and his wife, actor and producer Poppy Roe (who plays Val) made their short film *This Way Out* (2013) — a black comedy satire on euthanasia that took pot-shots at NHS target-driven systems. The short made it on to BAFTA lists and HBO, and former actor Cousins Roe found himself in the running for a number of directing gigs. But he wanted to do something a little more personal than what was on offer, and decided a home-grown feature was the way to go.

While *This Way Out* set its sights on assisted-suicide-as-an-industry, *A Serial Killer's Guide to Life* would poke fun at the self-help industry. There's no denying that self-help is big business. According to life-coach, licensed therapist and addiction specialist, Matthew Jones, the U.S. self-help industry is worth in the region of 10 billion dollars per year. As Jones says, 'that's a lot of books and motivational speeches that fail to help the 40 million people suffering from anxiety, the 14.8 million people suffering from depression, and the 7.7 million people suffering from post-traumatic stress disorder.' The brutal truth, as Jones points out, is that the self-help industry is 'profiting off of the emotional pain of people seeking quick fixes'.

Ripe subject matter for satire, then. Staten Cousins Roe thinks so, and set out to make *A Serial Killer's Guide to Life* as "a jet-black comedy with violence and horror." The storyline is deceptively simple: doormat Lou (Katie Brayben) chooses as her life-coach the impossibly sophisticated Val; and the two embark on a road trip together that soon descends into an orgy of killing in the English countryside. With its overriding theme of self-help as 'finding who you really are,' *A Serial Killer's Guide to Life* essentially poses the question to audiences: are you going to be Val — smashing through obstacles and leaving behind a bloody trail — or are you going to be Lou — forever trapped by the mundane? The film's answer is suitably schizophrenic. For Lou, there is no quick fix.

A number of critics have likened *A Serial Killer's Guide to Life* to *Thelma and Louise* (1991) and *Sightseers* (2012), and these make a good point of comparison. All three films riff on road movie tropes, and at its heart, *A Serial Killer's Guide to Life* is about a journey of self-discovery. Outwardly, Lou and Val join forces on a quest to debunk the self-help industry and its gurus, which include back-to-nature tree-huggers and a pair of predatory acoustic sound wave therapists. At the end of the road lies the best-selling guru, Chuck Knoah (Ben Lloyd-Hughes) whose ludicrous affirmations feature throughout the film ("Ya wanna be like me? Ya gotta think like me. Ya gotta act like me, ya gotta breathe like me.... Ya wanna know the real secret? Be yourself. Be me, then be yourself"). By the time they get to big bad Chuck, like Thelma and Louise, our heroines have become true outlaws in time-honoured road movie style.

The central focus of *A Serial Killer's Guide to Life* is, however, the relationship between Val and Lou, and as you'd expect, it is a twisted one. Lou needs Val; and Val is delighted by how easily Lou falls under her murderous spell. Early on, when asked what her ambitions are, Lou replies, wetly, "I'd just like to be like you, really". "Good ambitions," Val retorts. It's a sentiment that spares Lou the knife after they have just met. Screenwriting guru Linda Aronson might call Val's character-type a 'mentor-antagonist', the strange, enigmatic outsider who takes our boringly normal protagonist on an adventure both physical and emotional. In Aronson's description, the mentor-antagonist is dangerous, even murderous, and the protagonist has to escape their clutches. Only Lou doesn't want to escape. At least, not at first.

Cousins Roe cites Chris Petit's *Radio On* as another film that inspired him while writing *A Serial Killer's Guide to Life*. In this minimalist black and white effort from 1979 (co-produced by Wim Wenders), a young man drives from London to Bristol to investigate his brother's death. It's another quest of sorts, one with Kraftwerk on the soundtrack. *Radio On*'s bleakness is quite unfitting with the colourful satire of Cousins Roe's film. However, it links very naturally to the British road movie that *A Serial Killer's Guide to Life* arguably resembles the most — in plot if not in tone.

Michael Winterbottom's feature film debut *Butterfly Kiss* (1995) told the poignant tale of lonely petrol station cashier Miriam (played by Saskia Reeves) who becomes dangerously involved with homicidal drifter Eunice (Amanda Plummer). Unlike *A Serial Killer's Guide to Life*, *Butterfly Kiss* is a love story: Miriam and Eunice enter into a sexual relationship, and in the end, it's also a song of redemption through love. Winterbottom, like Petit, was influenced by New German Cinema of the 1970s, particularly by the collaborations of Wenders and Peter Handke. In such films as *Wrong Move* (1975) and *Kings of the Road* (1976) Wenders explored the existential aspects of the classic American road movie in order to take his characters on (in Handke's words) 'a journey of self-realization'. Wenders' films played on the sense of social alienation underlying the classic road movie, and its inherent ability to examine the state of the nation. The road movie may have its literary roots in Homer's *The Odyssey*, but it also takes in Chaucer's *A*

Canterbury Tales. Typically, the various characters that our protagonists meet on their episodic journey help define the world that they are fleeing from. *A Serial Killer's Guide to Life*, in true Chaucerian style, presents an ironic and critical portrait of the England of its time.

But returning — in suitably picaresque fashion — to the connection between *A Serial Killer's Guide to Life* and *Butterfly Kiss*, the film critic Roger Ebert made a good observation about Winterbottom's film that might equally apply to Cousins Roe's: 'The names of the women are shortened in the movie, to the suggestive "Mi" and "Eu." Can they be read as parts of a schizophrenic personality?'

Here we might invoke *Fight Club* (1999), another film that *A Serial Killer's Guide to Life* has been compared to. David Fincher's adaptation of Chuck Palahniuk's novel viewed the self-help industry as a false solution to materialism, one that inevitably brings on schizophrenia: Jack *is* Tyler Durden. Likewise, Val and Lou may well be two sides of the same personality — yin and yang. After all, Lou desperately wants to be herself but in order to do that (or so the self-help manuals tell her) she has to be someone else first.

At this point, let us briefly consider some psychoanalytical theory (bear with me — I'll keep it short). In his book, 'The Shadow of the Object', Christopher Bollas outlined a concept which might go some way to explaining the attractions of the self-help industry.

Bollas speaks of 'the transformational object', a memory from early object relations, where the mother 'continually transforms the infant's internal and external environment.' In later life we may 'search for an object that is identified with the metamorphosis of the self'. In life experiences, for example, we may feel a fusion with an idealised object, 'something never cognitively but existentially known'. This might be a new relationship, a job, a new home, anything that promises to 'transform' our lives ('If only I could win the lottery, I would be happy'). Bollas claims this is a recollection of the fusion with the maternal 'transformational object'.

Many adults search frantically for total transformation which they imagine will come about through religion or self-help. According to Bollas, this obsessive craving can be understood as 'a kind of psychic prayer for the arrival of the transformational object: a secular second coming of an object relation experienced in the earliest period of life.'

So you see: self-help is all because we secretly just want our mums. The problem is that the 'transformational object' will always prove to be elusive.

And the more desperately we pursue it through 'positive thinking and inward focus' the more likely it is to drive us mad. At least, this is what *A Serial Killer's Guide to Life* is telling us, in its satirical way. This, of course, is poor Lou's fate. The 'transformational object' is a never-ending cycle. Try one thing, it fails, try another. Cousins Roe sets this up beautifully in the film, whose ending leads us right back to the beginning. (Once you finish watching the film, go back to the opening scene and you'll see what I mean). Like in *Fight Club*, the clues were there all along. Hopefully, unlike Lou, you'll have more luck in spotting them.

Poppy Roe and Katie Brayben in *A Serial Killer's Guide to Life* (Forward Motion Pictures, 2019)

Shivers (1975)

A number of film-makers have been vilified because their films caused controversy. In the cases of Michael Reeves (*Witchfinder General*, 1968), Michael Powell (*Peeping Tom*, 1960) and Ken Russell (*The Devils*, 1971), careers were almost ruined because of it. But less known about is how some directors have suffered personal attacks because of their films. When Wes Craven made notorious video nasty *The Last House on the Left* in 1972, he found himself shunned by his friends; he was no longer invited to dinner parties because he had made 'that film'. George A. Romero spoke of how people would blank him at social gatherings when he told them the type of films he made. Horror filmmakers are not considered polite company.

David Cronenberg suffered maybe the worst treatment of all when he found himself evicted from his apartment after making his horror debut, *Shivers* in 1975. Such was the controversy *Shivers* caused in Canada that Cronenberg's landlord cited a morality clause in his tenancy contract as reason for booting Cronenberg out onto the street. To have your work attacked by critics and censors is one thing, but to be personally attacked and humiliated *because* of your work is something else. It raises the question: what exactly was it about *Shivers* that turned its director into *persona non grata*? After all, it's not the only time in his career that Cronenberg suffered the vitriol of the tabloid newspapers because of the controversy of his films: he would find himself mauled again after *Crash* (1996) when the press banded together to castigate him. (These controversies earned Cronenberg the nickname 'Dave Deprave'!) What causes such a venomous reaction?

Like the *Crash* controversy, *Shivers*' notoriety was started by the press. A Canadian critic called Robert Fulford saw a preview of the film in the autumn of 1975 and wrote a scathing review of it in *Saturday Night* magazine entitled 'You Should Know How Bad This Film Is. After All, You Paid For It'. Strange title for a film review, but one that gave away Fulford's agenda, which was to attack the Canadian Film Development Corporation, the public funding body that financed *Shivers*. It seems Fulford didn't think that money from the public purse should be spent on 'depraved' horror movies that were 'worse than junk'. This started a campaign in the Canadian press against *Shivers* as a number of prominent film critics followed suit to trash Cronenberg. As the bandwagon grew, even politicians jumped on board, and soon the film was being debated by MPs in the House of Commons. Although Cronenberg, the CFDC and a few Canadian movie industry trade magazines defended *Shivers*, controversy followed it abroad. At the Edinburgh International Film Festival, even though some critics saw *Shivers* as a 'witty and subversive' mix of arthouse and horror, others called it 'degrading and diseased'. While at the Sitges festival of horror films it won first prize, in Cronenberg's own country *Shivers* was denied a screening at the Canadian Film Awards.

In the UK, *Shivers* came to the attention of Target International Films, a relatively new distributor who had been putting together programmes of European sexy movies with titles like *Portraits of Women* (1970). Looking to move into arthouse and horror, Target acquired the rights to *Shivers* but found that its controversy caused problems with the British Board of Film Classification. Eventually the BBFC — incredibly enough — passed Cronenberg's film uncut with an 'X' certificate for cinema showings (Target later licensed *Shivers* to Alpha Films for distribution on VHS by Intervision). Even so a number of local councils objected to the film. In November 1976, Harrogate council in Yorkshire banned *Shivers*, calling it 'depraved'. Leader of the Harrogate film viewing sub-committee, J. Neville Knox, told the local press that "the man who has written it must have a sick mind," one more example of Cronenberg being personally attacked because of the reputation of his film.

So, what was all the fuss about? It's inevitable that *Shivers* would have taken some flak from conservative-minded critics in Québec, where *Shivers* was filmed. Up until the 60s the province had been in the hands of the French Catholic Church, who controlled its healthcare and education systems. The Quiet Revolution saw the secularization of Québec and its liberalization of culture was not welcomed by all, especially when 'Maple Syrup Porn' — home-grown Canadian soft-core sex movies — broke the censorship hold of the Catholic Church and offended old-fashioned French Catholic morality. It's not hard to see why some Canadian critics would object to Cronenberg's queasy mix of sex and horror in *Shivers*. But why the international uproar?

In some ways *Shivers* is a riposte to that old-world morality and sense of repression. Cronenberg shot the film on Nun's Island, a residential area in the city of Québec, dominated by apartment buildings such as the one in *Shivers* where the action takes place. Cronenberg renamed his high-rise Starliner Towers, thinking of it as a spaceship shut off from the rest of humanity, where a parasite infection could easily take hold. *Shivers* opens with a young couple, prospective purchasers called Kresimer and Benda Sviben (played by Vlasta Vrana and Silvie Debois), being shown around the housing complex. Meanwhile, something strange and kinky is already taking place in one of the apartments involving a middle-aged scientist called Hobbes (Fred Doerderlein) and Annabelle (Cathy Graham) a young woman dressed in a school girl's uniform. Things quickly turn nasty when the man strangles the girl, cuts her stomach open with a scalpel and pours sulphuric acid into her intestines. He then slashes his own throat. After this disturbing opening sequence, we are introduced to Starliner Towers' resident medical doctor, Roger St Luc (Paul Hampton) who discovers that Hobbes was trying to breed a parasite that would live inside the human body and function in place of failing organs. What St Luc finds is that the parasites turn their hosts into sex-crazed psychos, and the parasites are spreading — they are able to multiply and infect more and more people. Soon the entire Starliner Towers is infested; and St Luc finds himself desperately trying to escape as men, women and children rampage through the hallways of the apartment complex having kinky sex with anyone and everyone they can get their hands on.

Cronenberg's original title for *Shivers* was 'Orgy of the Blood Parasites' and this pretty much sums up his approach to the movie. Part science fiction/horror, part underground movie, part sex picture, part political and philosophical tract, *Shivers* melds exploitation with the avant-garde and pushes that combination pretty much as far as it can go.

Cronenberg in fact started out as an experimental filmmaker in Toronto in the late 1960s, with arty short films like *Transfer* (1968) and *From the Drain* (1967); before making two decidedly non-commercial features called *Stereo* (1968) and *Crimes of The Future* (1970) (which he would sort of remake in 2021). The latter is like a more avant-garde version of his later films, featuring futuristic skin clinics and artificially grown organs. Despite his experimental beginnings, Cronenberg always felt an affiliation to horror and wrote *Shivers* in 1972 as an attempt to enter the world of commercial filmmaking. He approached the Québec company Cinepix, pioneers of 'Canuxploitation' pictures, who thought he showed some sort of 'sexual sensibility', but who were reluctant to take a gamble on Cronenberg as a commercial director. Undeterred, Cronenberg set off to Los Angeles with the *Shivers* script under his arm. There he met actor Barbara Steele, veteran of Italian horror movies like *Black Sunday* (1960) and *The Horrible Dr. Hichcock* (1962). Cronenberg wanted to cast Steele as Betts, a lonely woman who lives in a 'singles' unit of Starliner Towers, and who memorably becomes infected by a parasite which violates her while she is taking a bath. Steele had recently worked with future *Silence of The Lambs* (1991) director Jonathan Demme on *Caged Heat* (1974) and introduced Cronenberg to him. Demme revealed that, unbeknown to Cronenberg, Cinepix had offered the script of *Shivers* to Demme as his next film! Furious, Cronenberg flew back to Québec to confront Cinepix only to be told that the CFDC had agreed to finance *Shivers*, and that Cinepix had the go ahead to make the film with Cronenberg directing.

In retrospect it's easy to see that much of the criticism initially aimed at *Shivers* was actually levelled at Cinepix, rather than at Cronenberg. Cinepix were thought of as the 'bad boys' of the Canadian film industry for proving that low budget exploitation, soft-core porn, dubbed Kung Fu movies and other cheap 'smut' could become the most profitable films at the Canadian box office (despite its controversy, within a year of production *Shivers* went on to make the biggest profit of any Canadian film ever at that point, eventually grossing over $5 million domestically). Cinepix were changing the face of Canadian filmmaking in ways that more traditional devotees of Canadian national cinema didn't like. But longer-term criticism of *Shivers* has tended to be directed at Cronenberg himself, with critics from both the political right and the political left expressing disgust at his film. What has upset these international critics so much?

In *Shivers*, Cronenberg drew on established genre tropes from movies like *Invasion of the Body Snatchers* (1956) and *Night of the Living Dead* (1968) and he mixed them up with his own transgressive approach to sexuality and body horror. As writer Bianca Garner has noted, 'much of what might have upset its many critics, is that *Shivers* can be interpreted as treating the infestation of the residents by the parasites as an act of liberation.' The parasite epidemic results in the residents becoming 'liberated' from their lives. But at what cost?

Critic Ernest Mathijs has described *Shivers* as a 'a film dubiously torn between a sense of repulsion… an unease with the discarding of taste, reason, conventions and cultural boundaries, and a sense of exhilaration for the liberating potential portrayed'. It's true that *Shivers* has divided critics in terms of its sexual politics, some seeing it as a deeply reactionary work, others arguing for its subversive qualities. Although it seems ambivalent about the sexual revolution that the parasites represent, *Shivers* did, on the other hand, mark perhaps the first tentative step in modern horror towards the possibility of social change, a willingness to go beyond the nihilistic despair of *The Texas Chain Saw Massacre* and *The Last House on the Left*. Cronenberg himself thinks that *Shivers* has a happy ending — the parasites win and mankind is transformed for the better!

Shivers undoubtedly shows the kind of repressive consumerist dystopia that North America was rapidly turning into by the mid-70s, and makes a bid to find an alternative to the modern age of shopping malls, discotheques and credit card spending that threatened to turn the American public into soulless zombies. Even though the process of revolution seems to be viewed with a certain amount of horror and disgust, in *Shivers* the need for it is presented as necessary.

Shivers actually originated from Cronenberg reading a book called *Life Against Death: The Psychological Meaning of History* written in 1959 by Norman O. Brown. Brown was an American classicist interested in the revolutionary potential of psychoanalysis. His call for sexual freedom through the resurrection of the body by orgiastic means both intrigued and disturbed Cronenberg. As the director recalled in 1986:

"I had read Norman O. Brown, *Life Against Death*, in which he discussed the Freudian theory of polymorphous perversity — the kind of sexuality a child has, completely non-genital, and it's not focused and it's in everything — a suffusing sexuality or sensuality almost. Even Norman had trouble when it came to figuring out how that Dionysian consciousness would function in a society where you have to walk down the street, cross the road and not get hit by a car. How does that all-enveloping sexuality work when you are just walking down the road? It's tricky."

In *Shivers* compartmentalized living has resulted in an overwhelming sense of loneliness and isolation. The residents are repressed to the point of being like zombies already. The marriage of Janine and Nicholas Tudor (played by Susan Petrie and Alan Migicovsky) is on the verge of collapse — she is uptight and anxious, he is disinterested and uncommunicative. Free-spirited Betts is bored stiff, and Roger St Luc barely notices the sexual advances of his nurse, Forsythe (Lynn Lowry).

In Brown's theory, repression during childhood results in sublimation of the sexual drive, the re-routing of frustrated libido. The libido becomes desexualized, and sublimation involves the negation of the body in favour of the intellect. Crucially, the child represses the urge to unite with others and with the world. In *Shivers*, the sexual isolation of the characters is disrupted by the infiltration of the parasites, set loose by the quintessential Cronenbergian mad scientist Dr Hobbes, who wants to turn the world into "one big beautiful orgy". Those infected by the parasites seek out others for a similar union, and, in the process, they become 'one' with the others in the apartment complex. This union brings a new sense of solidarity and with it liberation to Starliner residents.

Cronenberg himself has commented that he wanted to suggest that "the proliferation of this strange disease was, on one strange level, liberating". And so it is — up to a point. The infected are no longer alone and unhappy;

they are part of a revolution in which they cast off their sexual inhibitions. In the original script, the 'plus points' of infection to the community of Starliner Towers are made clear in the final pages:

'We find many of the residents we already know, now dressed to the teeth in their seductive best… Mr. Spergazzi and his wife stand and watch the spectacle canes in hand, with great dignity. With them stand others who are too old or too young to go into the night looking for new hosts for their parasites, content to remain incubators for the time being. The residents are full of bubbly anticipation in their cars… The driver of this first car is St. Luc, sleek and exuberant…'

The new-found 'aliveness' that infection brings the residents by the end of the story is almost without question preferable to their suffocating boredom at the start (the script is more upbeat than the film in this respect — at the end of the film this exuberance is not so apparent as it is in the script; in the film the residents seem more benumbed and dehumanized, like the pod people in *Invasion of the Body Snatchers*, heightening the ambiguity at the heart of Cronenberg's vision).

But the process of that liberation is arguably depicted as physically repulsive throughout the film, working against the optimism of its conclusion. This is perhaps why some critics, such as Robin Wood, have taken exception to Cronenberg's work generally, commented that his films dramatize 'a horror of physicality, a great fear of repressed forces; a recurrent sexual disgust that recurs in his films again and again.'

Cronenberg would later try to address these criticisms of *Shivers*, telling Adam Simon in 2000:

"The idea that sex is a parasite…I think this was the basis of some misunderstanding of what I was doing with that film…I mean, metaphorically I was looking at the parasite the way straight society would look at it, but I think that emotionally and viscerally the audience was with the crazy people who were parasite-infested. The trick of the movie was that it was a happy ending when everyone was infected and going out into the world to infect everyone else… When we made it, we certainly experienced the repression of the place we were shooting in (Nun's Island)… We all felt the repressiveness of that kind of life. It was very palpable and we were living in it, and so we had the desire to rip off our clothes and run screaming through the halls. And that is what I have my characters do, and that is why it's so ironic that some critics see me as being horrified by that. Because it's what we all wanted to do, it was very cathartic for us, and for me in particular. Of course the parasites are horrific-looking and I'm not saying that I would really want one of them in me. And yet I think the audience is gleeful when that parasite infects somebody, because they're going to see some neat, sexy stuff. So that ambivalence is there in the audience, and it's in me as well."

Although Cronenberg describes the sexual liberation in *Shivers* as 'neat, sexy stuff', what he actually presents is a catalogue of various forms of sexual deviancy, which he shows in ways to create feelings of horror in the viewer. There's fetishism and pederasty (Hobbes and the school-girl uniformed Annabelle); troilism (Kurt, the waiter in the lift with the mother and daughter having a threesome); attempted male-female rape (Kresimer's attack of Forsythe); attempted male rape (the Black maintenance man's attack of St Luc - the script makes it clear this is a sexual attack); non-consensual lesbianism (Betts' seduction of the vulnerable and confused Janine); and incest (the old man and his daughter, Jessica). As Mathijs says of the sheer violence and distress of the sexual attacks inflicted on the residents of Starliner Towers, 'in the interests of physical well-being, maybe some taboos about how human bodies can be approached, touched, groped, violated, need to remain.'

This seems to be Cronenberg's conclusion too: "there is an ambivalence on my part when it comes to preaching subversion because I'm aware that along with revolution of any kind comes destruction." He has also expressed concerns of "the danger of replacing something ugly and repressive with something even more ugly and repressive", but to his credit adds, "that doesn't mean that you stop, you keep going."

Cronenberg defends his films against those who accuse him of being reactionary by claiming that they work on another level to the purely political — a visceral level. They are, he claims, thrilling and liberating to an audience, and thus beyond politics and beyond society. For Cronenberg, the process of imagining a world that is not necessarily better, just different, is, in itself, a threat to the norm.

As Mathijs comments: 'what makes Cronenberg's body horror unique is that he takes the position of the philosopher: he does not take sides, but lets his stories and characters check the consequences of the possibilities; sometimes abandonment to desires seems worth the sacrifice, sometimes not.' This, in the final analysis, is what makes *Shivers* such a compelling piece of work; it's exactly these ambiguities and Cronenberg's philosophical viewpoint that make it so intriguing as a horror movie.

As for the landlord who tossed Cronenberg out on his ear due to the controversy of *Shivers*, the director would later get his revenge by buying a house in the same street. Way to go, 'Dave Deprave'!

Susan Petrie and Barbara Steele in *Shivers* (Cinepix, 1975)

Suburbia (1984)

What's the Punkest Movie Ever? Polls taken over the past decade or so seem to be pretty decisive on the matter. The vast majority of responders answer *Suburbia*. Made nine years before Penelope Spheeris found mainstream success with *Wayne's World* (1992), *Suburbia* has been described as a fictional companion piece to her justly celebrated music documentary *The Decline of Western Civilization* (1981). These early works would mark the beginning of a series of her movies, including two *Decline* sequels — *Part Two: The Metal Years* (1988) and *Part Three* (1998) — documenting the Los Angeles punk scene. Based on these and later films like New York punk comedy-western *Dudes* (1987) and metal head doc *We Sold Our Souls for Rock 'n' Roll* (2001), Spheeris has been referred to as a 'rock and roll anthropologist'. No other director would document punk culture as single-mindedly as Spheeris has.

Co-produced by Roger Corman for New World Pictures, *Suburbia* paints a much bleaker picture of youth than Spheeris would do in her later comedies. The story revolves around a group of teenage outcasts who band together in a squatted tract house in the LA suburbs. Among these are runaways from domestic abuse Sheila (Jennifer Clay) and Evan (Bill Coyne); the older 'den fathers' Jack (Chris Pedersen) and Skinner (Timothy Eric O'Brien); another newbie called Joe Schmo (Wade Walston); stoner Keef (Grant Miner); Razzle (Flea); Mattie and T'resa (Maggie Ehrig and Christina Beck) and eventually Evan's little brother, Ethan (Andrew Pece). They find refuge together as a community of punks even as each of them battles a sense of worthlessness in a throwaway Reaganite society. Spheeris doesn't shy away from showing the hopelessness of their situation — the drug abuse, squalor and violence that comes from being outcast youth, as well as the conflicts with the police and with the local 'Citizens Against Crime' group who try to evict them from the punk house. *Suburbia* opens with a scene in which a baby is torn apart by a pack of wild dogs; the same dogs that scavenge the tract housing land at night. It ends with the death of another child. The ad-line for *Suburbia* promised 'A new movie for a new generation.' By the end of the film, we are left in no doubt that this is Generation X.

Suburbia's poster image showing the gang marching together through a suburban street has become iconic. Eagle-eyed film buffs will recognize it as a steal from Stanley Kubrick's *A Clockwork Orange* (1971) — the scene where Alex (Malcolm McDowell) and his droogs troop in slo-mo through Thamesmead. The image has been repeated many times, featuring in movies like *Reservoir Dogs* (1992) among others: it has become a kind of short hand for showing the band of renegades coming together in unity against the system. It is not surprising that Spheeris would borrow from *A Clockwork Orange* (Keef even wears a bowler hat in tribute), another film that has been described as a punk classic because of its anarchism and anti-authoritarian message.

As Barbara Koenig Quart has noted, *The Decline of Western Civilization* dealt with the 'frustration, despair and violence of the marginal young,' and both *Suburbia* and *The Boys Next Door* (which Spheeris directed in 1985) would deal with violent, disaffected youth through the codes of exploitation film. It was after she was unable get good distribution for *Decline* that Spheeris shipped the script for *Suburbia* around, and got it to Corman who couldn't resist a project that was already half-funded (by Cleveland-based producer-director Bert L. Dragin). Corman, as we know, had a track record of hothousing American auteurs, first with American International Pictures and then via his own grindhouse and drive-in production-distribution outfit, New World. *Suburbia* contains a number of Spheeris themes. The most prominent is that of outcasts uniting in a common goal. This Spheeris attributes to growing up as a carny child. Her father ran a carnival and Spheeris spent her early childhood moving from town to town. Her only friends were gypsy kids; the other people in the carnival were itinerants. In her words, such a childhood "definitely makes you different at a time when you're really just trying to learn about the world and adapt". The carnival was a collection of outcasts, and Spheeris feels comfortable around outcasts.

After her carny strong man father was killed in a knife fight, childhood for Spheeris became even more chaotic. Her mother married seven times. Most of Spheeris' stepfathers were violent drunks. She lived in trailers throughout her teenage years and was still moving around all the time. To escape the misery of her home life she got into loud music. As she told John Parks of *Legendary Rock Interviews* in 2011:

"I think that when I first latched onto that punk scene it really made sense to me. I was always into rock and roll, you know, like a lot of people I got my release in it. I used rock and roll as a security blanket and I think a lot of kids did. When you're feeling down or alienated or like everything in the world sucks you tend to feel a little better after listening to some rock and roll. Good rock is the voice of discomfort."

Film would become her way of exorcising her demons, of working through her issues of having had a difficult childhood, family problems and a poor upbringing. But music was her friend: a way to ease the pain. When, in 1992, *The New York Times* asked Spheeris what draws her so consistently to music as a filmmaker, she replied: "A band is a symbol of a family — it's a lot of rejected people coming together to make a replacement family. That a band can even write a song is a miracle, the people are so messed up. I guess you could say the same thing about how hard it is for a family to stick together and work harmonically, excuse the pun."

The idea of forming new families lies at the heart of *Suburbia*. The punks in *Suburbia* look out for each other — because there is no one else willing to take that responsibility. Sheila and the other older punks become like surrogate parents to little Ethan, giving him a mohawk to make him into one of them — but also reading him bedtime stories. These young people take comfort from each other. In a wry moment, Spheeris shows the two other teenage girls of the gang — Mattie and T'resa — listening in on the storytelling, desperate for some kind of motherly love. The males are the hunter-gatherers — Evan, Jack and Skinner feed the troupe by stealing food from the fridges of their neighbours — anything it takes to keep the surrogate family together. But this is also two fingers up to the suburban community that has failed them, that turned them into strays like the dogs that roam the streets. Evan's mother is a hopeless alcoholic who can't keep house and home together. When she is charged for DUI, Evan snatches his younger brother, Ethan, away from her. Sheila is fleeing from a father who physically and sexually abuses her. The punks' rebellion is partly against the hypocrisy of their suburban upbringing, the stultifying white-bread conformism of the suburban ideal and its banality. "The whole premise of boring suburbia was something that I could totally relate to," Spheeris told John Parks. After a number of years living in trailer parks, Spheeris and her mother eventually settled in Orange County, in a small house in Westminster. The town had no history, no culture, no identity. Spheeris recalls humorously how the only thing that kept people going was checking on each other fixing their cars in their driveways: "You would make a day of going around and seeing how everyone's carburettors were doing".

What is significant about the way Spheeris portrays suburbia in the film is not just that it is mind-numbingly dull, but that the whole suburban ideal has collapsed: the suburban dream has failed. This is what the punks' rebellion is truly about. Spheeris' film shares the same title as Bill Owens' classic 1972 photographic study and social document, *Suburbia*. Owens photographed residents of a Californian suburban community at work and play over a period of a year: he documented family barbeques, Tupperware parties, mothers with their babies, families enjoying leisure time in their car ports and backyards. His photographs depict both the material comforts of white middle-class life but also its cultural shallowness and ethnocentrism: the sadness, loneliness, isolation and sense of failure that was already hiding behind the otherwise serene façade of American suburbia.

Spheeris essentially follows the same observational approach as Owens. This is one of her strengths as a filmmaker — her documentary eye, which largely stems from her interest in the observational mode of documentary that she got heavily into as a student at UCLA film school in the 1970s (she is a fan of Frederick Wiseman's institutional exposés — *High School*, 1968, *Hospital*, 1970, *Juvenile Court*, 1973, *Welfare*, 1975). Like other directors preoccupied with the suburbs, such as Steven Spielberg and Richard Linklater, Spheeris is careful to show the pervasive influence of American mass culture and consumerism on suburban lifestyles. In Evan's house the television set is always turned on, even if no-one is actually watching it. Shopping malls and 7-11s help create a familiar, recognisable but artificial social landscape. It all goes towards presenting the anaesthesia of suburbia. But Spheeris goes further than most directors in depicting suburbia not just as bland but as dangerous; more akin to the slums of Luis Buñuel's *Los Olvidados* (1950) than to the insulated exurban enclaves of *ET: the Extraterrestrial* (1982) or *SubUrbia* (1996). The comfortable middle-class life that was the suburban dream has evaporated economically. Tract houses stand empty; residents resort to yard sales in order to keep afloat financially; crime rates are rising; vigilantes patrol the streets. It is no accident that Spheeris' overarching three-part work-in-progress was given the title *The Decline of Western Civilization,* her project has been to document just that: suburbia — one of the West's keenest social experiments — in terminal decline. Suburbia has precisely nothing to offer the new generation.

Just as Buñuel's slum kids are forced into petty crime and prostitution, the punks of *Suburbia* veer towards drugs, theft and gang violence in a bid to find their own way. They express themselves in fashion and music. Their only other hangout is a nearby club that puts on gigs by local punk bands. Here, Spheeris wires in her concert documentary background as a way to anchor *Suburbia*'s docu-realism. Three actual bands appear in the club scenes: D.I. from Fullerton, C.A. — still going today with a different line-up to that which appears in the film. In their early formations they combined Orange County hardpunk with surf punk and new wave. Next up is T.S.O.L. from Long Beach, again still around today. Footage of them in *Suburbia* showcases the gothic rock/horror punk of their early days. The third and final band is The Vandals, from Huntington Beach. Further evidence of punk's longevity, The Vandals are also still playing, although again in a different formation to the early comedy punk/cowpunk band shown in the film.

Spheeris famously cast real punks to act in *Suburbia,* in a bid to make things authentic. None of the leads were real actors. Spheeris felt it was much easier to turn punk rock kids into actors than it was to turn actors into punk rockers: "they were reality and people sort of gravitate towards reality," she told John Parks. Reality for the kids of *Suburbia* is tough. Homelessness for America's young *is* the reality. All these kids have is punk music and each other. To make themselves noticed, they are forced to go to extremes. They have to fight hard against the baby boomers who outnumber them, in order to make their mark and to change things. The anger and despair in Spheeris' early work, including in *Suburbia*, got her known in the film and music industries as the 'Mistress of Darkness,' a label she later tried to discard by turning to comedy.

"The downside to my rock-and-roll trip," as Spheeris told *The New York Times*, "is that it's associated with so much rebellion and anti-establishment attitude." But Spheeris has proven, in *Surburbia* as well in her other films, that behind that attitude there's a humanitarian call for the protection of childhood, kinship and the need for belonging.

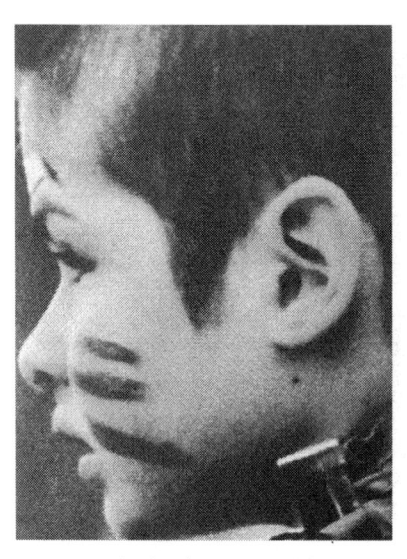

Andrew Pece in *Suburbia* (New World Pictures, 1984)

Toto the Hero (1991)

Unreleased on DVD in the States (Paramount Pictures hold the rights), and last seen on DVD in the UK in 2006, Jaco Van Dormael's debut feature, *Toto the Hero* (*Toto le héros*) feels like a film ripe for rediscovery; all the more so because the movie itself hinges on the twin themes of (personal and cultural) identity and memory. It is a film made to be remembered, not just for its formal brilliance (remarked upon by many critics when it first appeared), evoking the process of memory, but for the way, when one looks back at the film today, it appears to capture so succinctly the cinematic landscape of the early 1990s and the shared preoccupations of a number of directors making their feature debuts at the time.

Philosophically, Van Dormael expresses a sense of universal human experience: the feeling of déjà vu when tragedies of the past come back to haunt us in often unexpected ways; awareness that our lives are repeatedly marked by the realization that 'I've been here before'. Indeed, the compulsive act of remembering and obsessively revisiting past trauma, vividly explored in *Toto the Hero*, is also reflected in the way that Van Dormael carries forward key elements of that same narrative in his subsequent films, *The Eighth Day* (*Le Huitième Jour*, 1996) and *Mr. Nobody* (2001) (while Van Dormael's latest works, *The Brand New Testament* and *Cold Blood*, both 2015, represent a departure for the director, suggesting that childhood trauma has, to a greater extent, been resolved).

"The film has the density of a fine short story, written by a master who somehow manages to create a novel-sized world through an uncanny command of ellipsis," wrote Vincent Canby following screenings of *Toto the Hero* at the New York Film Festival in September 1991. Indeed, Van Dormael's mastery of form is evident from *Toto*'s opening sequence, which functions as a visual overture of the story to come. We are introduced to the film's narrator, Thomas, an elderly man living in a care home-cum-psychic prison. Through a series of elliptical cuts, we enter his memories and fantasies as he contemplates his life. A bullet-ridden body lies slumped in a fountain, obscured by a net curtain. The rippling water forms a perfect transition cut to Thomas splashing his face in the care home, staring at the bathroom mirror, the first questioning of his identity. Who is the murder victim? Is it Alfred, the nemesis whom we are told has stolen Thomas's life from the day he was born? Or is it Thomas, himself, aggrieved by his loss, by the certainty that 'I never lived'. Key images appear from Thomas's past that give form to his lingering resentment, here fleetingly glimpsed: a punch to the stomach taken as a child; blood oozing from a woman's forehead; a blazing barn-door; the touch of a lover's hand; the kiss of a lost sibling. Van Dormael merges these seamlessly into the present reality as Thomas plots his revenge. Bitter memory gives way to increasingly violent fantasy; the result of impotent rage. A gun is all that is needed to get even. Ultimately, we will see how Thomas, out of frustration, has developed a fantasy persona (the *Dick Barton*-inspired secret agent of the film's title) in order to become in his mind the hero that, in reality, Thomas resolutely is not.

The Nicolas Roeg-like mosaic editing of this opening sequence, the interweaving of memory and fantasy, becomes an organizing principle throughout *Toto the Hero*, a way in which the film's diegesis becomes known only subjectively to the viewer, as filtered through the consciousness of the embittered and possibly deluded old man. We see the world only from his perspective, and there is evidence that Thomas is quite the unreliable narrator. His childhood, before the loss of his father, is impossibly rose-tinted (even the flowers outside the family home seem to sway in time to Dad's joyous rendition of Charles Trenet's *Boum*!) And if later, darker, events in the story seem overly contrived at Thomas's expense, they can be interpreted as Thomas's act of (mis)remembering, telling of childhood trauma unresolved throughout adulthood and into old age. Indeed, the narrative shape of *Toto the Hero* forms a kind of Möbius Strip, but one that loops around not once but twice: childhood impacting on adulthood impacting on old age. The carry-over is such that Thomas no longer knows where one part of his life begins and the others end, and each seems only to bring him back to the beginning: his memory/fantasy of having been swapped at birth, and the conviction that Alfred is living the life that should have been his. Thomas, meanwhile, is forever destined to be 'Van Chickensoup', as Alfred calls him: a man without full identity.

Interviewed by Pierre Hodgson in 1992, Van Dormael claimed, "Despite the complexity, there is nothing innovative about the construction of *Toto*: the story and the style are too strange to withstand any kind of structural monkey business". Instead, Van Dormael compared the construction of his film to the Palais Idéal du Facteur Cheval, a rural palace built by a postman in the 1890s: "Close up," he claimed, "it looks like a heap of mad, accumulated matter, but from a distance, you can see the shape of a proper chateau beneath the lunacy."

Beneath the 'lunacy' of Toto's visual style, then, lies a classically constructed screenplay. Act one ends on page 24; page 68, beginning of the third act; a major event occurs at the midpoint. Van Dormael studied screenwriting under Frank Daniel, the Czechoslovakian dean of FAMU, who has also taught at the American Film Institute and at the USC School of Cinema-Television. Daniel mentored David Lynch, among others, and is known for his strictness on plot structure. When Van Dormael later presented the screenplay of *Toto* to Daniel, the script guru likened it to Fellini's *Amarcord* (1973), a film which, in Van Dormael's words, "seems completely crazy but is in fact highly structured. *Amarcord* is constructed along strictly classical lines with three-act sub-plots, the main acts syncopated so the first act contains a scene from the second, the second act of story A comes before the third act of story C and so on". Like *Amarcord*, *Toto the Hero* is built around a sequence of triple-act stories, a three-point rhythm contained within a unifying superstructure (which, in the case of *Toto*, is Thomas in the care home 'remembering' the story). And, of course, both films have three acts.

The rule of 'threes', so beloved of screenwriters, is reflected in *Toto*'s three time zones — childhood, adulthood and old age — but there is an equally important fourth: fantasy, as personified by Thomas's secret agent alter-ego. When *Toto* was first released, critics compared it to Dennis Potter's BBC TV serial, *The Singing Detective* (1986), and the resemblance is striking (Van Dormael's film also shares a number of structural and thematic similarities with Sergio Leone's *Once Upon A Time in America*, 1984).

Van Dormael has, in fact, described *Toto* as a 'digest' of influences: the books he's read, films he's seen, people he's met. Van Dormael is a cinephile, and *Toto* reflects this in its sophisticated engagement with genre and film syntax. More than this, though, when we look back at *Toto* now, we can see that it captures a certain zeitgeist of late 80s/early 90s world cinema in terms of the shared concerns of a number of emerging directors of that period. First and foremost, it is a 'childhood' film in the tradition of Truffaut's *The 400 Blows* (*Les Quatre Cent Coups*, 1959). In this way we might compare it to the early works of Jane Campion (*Peel*, 1986, *A Girl's Own Story*, 1986) and Ann Turner (*Celia*, 1989), which take as their starting point childhood experience and a child's perspective of the world. Like Campion and Turner, Van Dormael is the product of film school (he studied at Institute Supérieur des Arts in Brussels and École Louis-Lumière in Paris), an environment that leads to personal and autobiographical filmmaking, and, inevitably, to films about childhood (every yearly graduation show in every film school in the world includes at least one film about childhood — guaranteed!)

Indeed, the first version of *Toto* that Van Dormael wrote, in 1982, centred on the children; adults did not figure in it. Remnants of that initial screenplay approach remain in the film's early scenes which present a child's perception of the world: how it feels when you urinate; how Mum smells different to Dad; how the family cat screams when you pull its tail, but your toys don't feel pain when you smash them; and (most amusing of all) how Dad seems to magically disappear when he leaves the house for work each morning, and them magically reappear later when he returns home ("He was behind the front door. But you couldn't see him because he was behind it.")

In *Toto*, as in other childhood films, the child's-eye view is a bitter-sweet one, as innocence inevitably gives way to experience and sexual awakening. In Campion's *A Girl's Own Story*, the relationship between a brother and sister becomes incestuous. Likewise, in *Toto the Hero*, Thomas's feelings for his sister, Alice, go beyond the filial. She remains the love object throughout his life. Thomas's romantic obsession with Alice develops after their father's death — and their mother's subsequent break down — leaves them to fend for themselves. The family dynamic changes radically, as Thomas and Alice become the 'mother' and 'father' of the house. This motif, which *Toto* briefly explores, is the central premise of Andrew Birkin's 1993 adaptation of Ian McEwan's novel *The Cement Garden* and thus forms another important part of *Toto*'s 'digest' of that cinematic era.

Birkin cast the gamine Charlotte Gainsbourg as the incestuous sister of *The Cement Garden*, and the casting of an attractively boyish actress in this type of role is significant in that film, as it is in Van Dormael's. The developmental sequences of *Toto the Hero* focus on the adult Thomas's subsequent romantic obsession with Evelyn, a young married woman who reminds him of the dead Alice. It is interesting that, for Evelyn, Van Dormael chose Mireille Perrier, who had played similar roles in Leos Carax's *Boy Meets Girl* (1984) and Éric Rochant's *A World without Pity* (*Un Monde Sans Pitiè*, 1989). For each of these directors, Perrier is more than a simple love interest; she represents an object of desire for the male protagonist that brings the promise of personal transformation, a way for him to become someone other than he is.

A final film from that era worth mentioning in relation to *Toto the Hero* is *Life is a Long, Quiet River* (*La Vie est un long fleuve tranquille*) directed by Étienne Chatiliez in 1988. Both films share the same central conceit: two babies swapped at birth grow up in very different families to lead very different lives. Chatiliez's film is a comedy of manners, a wryly humorous look at the French class system. The same class tensions are implicit in *Toto*. Why else would Thomas want to give up a loving family (Van Dormael dedicated *Toto the Hero* to his parents) and a good home for another life altogether, unless it was for one of higher social status and greater wealth? (Disparity of wealth is highlighted in a typically child's-eye way by the birthday presents each boy receives: while Thomas is given a miniature toy car, Alfred has a large motorized ride on model in shiny red — no wonder Thomas is envious.)

"I don't have a high opinion of the way the world works, it's true," Van Dormael told Pierre Hodgson. "I think I have a split personality, though. I am quite naïve in that I tend to assume that people are basically nice; but I am also disgusted by the way things are run. I am scared of power and money because of all the stupidities that people with power and money commit." While Van Dormael, then, is not a political filmmaker in the same sense as, say, Robert Guédiguian or the Dardenne brothers, *Toto* is informed by a class-consciousness befitting of a self-identified 'humanitarian'.

The question of humanitarianism suffuses *Toto the Hero*, as it does Jaco Van Dormael's subsequent work, and it is for this above all that it should be remembered.

Thomas Godet in *Toto the Hero* (Canal+, 1991)

Upgrade (2018)

"I had this image of a quadriplegic in a wheelchair who stood up out of the chair and was being controlled from the neck down by a computer." This seed image in the mind of Leigh Whannell would form the basis of *Upgrade*, Whannell's sophomore directorial effort, a dystopian science fiction action thriller that showcases his penchant for exploring the darker impulses in human nature; in this case the beasts that lurk behind the façade of technological progress in the 21st century, controlling our every move.

That Whannell would come to write and direct a movie which seems, at first glance, to share more DNA with *The Matrix* trilogy (Whannell acted in *The Matrix Reloaded*, 2003) than with the *Saw* or *Insidious* franchises, should come as less of a surprise to those who have followed Whannell's extraordinarily diverse career as a writer-director-actor since the beginning. From his early days as a student at Melbourne's Institute of Technology, to his collaborations with James Wan, Whannell has made a gradual move from horror to science fiction (Whannel followed *Upgrade* with a remake of *The Invisible Man*, 2020). Both *Saw* (2004) and *Insidious* (2010) hinged on themes of bodily control, and in approaching the world-building of *Upgrade*, Whannell was less interested in the standard science fiction trope of mankind versus machine engaged in a *Terminator 2: Judgment Day* (1991)-type war than in the internalized battle of man and technology in the transhuman era. As Whannell told *TechCrunch* in 2018, "the bad guy is in your body and the fight is not between you and external forces. It's actually two entities fighting over the same physical body."

The notion of sharing a physical body with technology is, of course, the basis of cyberpunk, and this gives *Upgrade* a useful starting point. William Gibson's ground-breaking 1984 novel *Neuromancer* opened in a grungy bar filled with deadbeats. The bartender had an artificial arm (a 'Russian military prosthesis') and everyone talked in a multinational lingo that took in techno-babble like "nerve-splicing" and "clinic tanks". Gibson borrowed heavily from *film noir*: traditionally the downtown bar is where the good guy encounters allies and enemies in his search for truth and justice. So it is in *Upgrade*, where, in a bar called the Old Bones, our hero confronts one of the gang that killed his wife Asha (Melanie Vallejo), and discovers for the first time what he is capable of. *Neuromancer* supplied the melding of human body and computer chip, of human flesh and military hardware, which a steady stream of cyberpunk novels, comics, video games and films, including *Upgrade*, would come to use. Cyberpunk-ish, too, is the name of our hero in *Upgrade* — Grey Trace — the luddite mechanic left paralysed from the waist down after the mugging in which his wife is killed (it's also possible that Logan Marshall-Green's character was ironically named after a pair of running shoes!)

Cyberpunk, like all dystopian science fiction, may appear to take place in a future world (*Upgrade* is set circa 2046) but it's really about the here and now. Hence, Whannell's Dr. Frankenstein, Eron Keen (played by Harrison Gilbertson) is word-play on the real-life Elon Musk, the billionaire technocrat involved in developing electric cars, neurotechnology, Twitter X and brain interfaces. In the film, Keen fits our hero with a chip called STEM which reactivates his spinal column, allowing him to regain the use of his limbs. Scientists are currently developing stem cell technology with a view to doing just that with real people, in the hope of curing disease and physical disability. Whannell scripted *Upgrade* in 2012 and the world is just about catching up. As he told *TechCrunch*, "when I wrote the first draft of this script, automated cars and smart kitchens were still science fiction. And in the ensuing years, they've become ubiquitous. I mean, my wife's car parks itself and talks to her. And my daughter thinks it's perfectly normal to have a voice talking to her in the kitchen, and she asks it to play songs and it does."

The opening scenes of *Upgrade* present a Brave New World of Tesla cars that drive themselves, allowing their occupants to have sex in the backseat without fear of collision; of virtual assistants that tell you when you've run out of eggs; of virtual reality mapping (courtesy of *Minority Report*, 2002) that you can swipe on your kitchen work top.

But like all utopian visions, there is a dystopian underside that views technology with suspicion. Whannell himself confesses to a deep-seated ambivalence about our increasing over-reliance on AI: "if our cars do the driving for us, are we actually designing ourselves into irrelevance." Early in the film, as they make love in the back of their automated vehicle, Grey and Asha experience a 'system error' that sees their self-driving car take an unexpected detour into the wrong side of town. At this point the utopian world that the young lovers inhabit quickly slips into reverse. They end up in a tent city occupied by the dispossessed, the unemployment line caused by AI. It is here that they are gunned down by the film's ostensible bad guy, Fisk (Benedict Hardie) and his gang. With Asha dies the dream of utopia.

Upgrade is driven by the theme of technology taking over. Whannell draws on the work of Raymond Kurzweil, the real-life entrepreneur-cum-inventor who predicts that the 'singularity' — the point where human and technology will merge — is near. But while Kurzweil embraces the prospect, Whannell, like all good science fiction filmmakers, is rather more cautious. After all, how can you take comfort in a prediction like Kurzweil's: "Does God exist? I would say, 'Not yet.'"

Movie-wise, Whannell seeks inspiration from *The Terminator* (1984) in this respect, with its apocalyptic vision of machines wiping out mankind popularizing the theme. We can see STEM's ancestors in *Terminator 2: Judgment Day*'s Skynet (and perhaps also in *2001: A Space Odyssey*, 1968,'s disembodied voice of HAL 9000). The original sentient computer that wanted to become God might well be Colossus, the titular antagonist of D.F. Jones' novel written in 1966 (adapted for cinema as *The Forbin Project*, 1970). Like Skynet, Colossus is the giant supercomputer designed to control America's nuclear weapons arsenal. The Russians have a similar system of their own in place, and when the two computers eventually link minds, they join together to hold the world to ransom. A small resistance of scientists is formed to try to stop Colossus from taking global control of human life, but they are no match for the supercomputer, who is all-seeing, all-knowing. Jones ends his novel with Colossus telling its creators that they will one day come to think of him as 'God'. "Never!" cry the scientists in a final vow of defiance, but we are left with little doubt that the computers have won. They may indeed become the new gods.

Of course, when machines literally take over our bodies in a Borg-like way, resistance does indeed become futile. American author Dean R. Koontz presented a vision of artificial intelligence becoming incarnate in his 1973 novel *Demon Seed* (made into a film by Donald Cammell in 1977). Here a suburban housewife of the future finds that her virtual assistant, named Proteus, wants to become human. It entraps her in her home and impregnates her with its seed, so that she can give birth to its human progeny (and if there were ever a reason not to buy an Alexa, this would be it). Koontz completely rewrote the novel in 1997 making Proteus the narrator, which perhaps shows just how times really have changed. We are never in doubt just who is in control.

Demon Seed, like *Upgrade*, hinges on body horror, and perhaps the biggest stumbling block for transhumanism is the fear of surgical implants, those of body and/or of mind. At least it is for writers like Whannell and Koontz who have "a foot in both camps with technology," and are torn between the optimism of science fiction and the pessimism of the horror genre — or at least feel compelled to explore the boundaries of both. Transhumanism posits emerging technology as offering human beings an 'upgrade', a way of enhancing the intellect and our physical abilities; advocates, like Kurzweil, believe it a way of overcoming our limitations. In short, it could transform humanity. But at what cost to our identity as human beings?

Existential questions abound, not least the rather pressing problem — presented so memorably in *Upgrade* — of how we might actually struggle to co-exist with our 'technoself'. Grey Trace and STEM may share a body, but the relationship is far from harmonious. Sure, there is 'consent'; STEM, at least initially, has to have permission from Grey to take control of his body, but is there empathy on the part of STEM?

The struggle between the two characters in *Upgrade* (who are really two halves of a divided self) is often presented quite humorously. There's banter between them, and at times their odd couple relationship is reminiscent of a rather different 'buddy-in-your-body' movie, Frank Henenlotter's *Brain Damage* (1988). In this horror-comedy, a young man sees his life begin to fall apart when a sentient talking brain parasite who calls himself Aylmer attaches itself to him. In return for secreting a highly addictive but pleasurable hallucinogenic fluid into his brain, the man has to supply his parasite with victims, becoming an accomplice to murder in the process. Grey Trace finds himself in a similar situation with STEM. It may not technically be Grey pulling the trigger, but it is his hand holding the gun.

Another film that has an undoubted influence on *Upgrade* is George A. Romero's *Monkey Shines* (1988), based on Michael Stewart's 1983 novel of the same name. In both book and film, a quadriplegic develops a psychic bond with his service monkey, a genetically-modified Capucine called Ella. The monkey becomes controlling and overprotective; at the same time, she tunes into the man's primal instincts and starts to do his murderous bidding. In a similar way, STEM triggers Grey's inner beast, his vengeful anger. In both works technology frees the violent impulses normally held in check, revealing the darker side of human nature.

Whannell visualizes these Jekyll and Hyde moments brilliantly, filming Grey's acts of violence in such a way as to suggest the instability in his character that STEM has exposed. The camera locks on Grey, holding him static in the middle of the frame, while the world moves around him. It's an optical illusion similar to those old fairground attractions of yesteryear - the room that spins on a pivot around you while you sit on a fixed bench in the middle - your brain telling you that it is you - not the centrifuge - that is moving. Whannell used digital tracking technology to achieve his effect, with the movie camera locking onto a mobile phone that Marshall-Green had on his person. But Marshall-Green's physical performance is exemplary too, his stiff-limbed movements mimicking robotic efficiency in a way that suggests Grey's complete loss of control to the entity inside his body.

There are moments like this throughout *Upgrade* that move the film into the realm of absurdism: here is a Kafka-esque everyman who suddenly finds himself persecuted by forces that he cannot understand, whose suffering is seemingly without meaning. If we are not careful, we may soon find ourselves in his position, the film tells us. We may become victims of our own technological hubris.

It is fitting, then, that Whannell's seed image for *Upgrade* - the quadriplegic who stood up out of his chair under the control of a computer — should, in the final analysis, echo an unforgettable moment from *Frankenstein* (1931) — the key progenitor of techno-horror. As you watch Grey Trace slowly move his fingers and take his monumental first steps, you may well hear a voice in your head telling you, "It's alive!...It's alive…!"

Logan Marshall-Green in *Upgrade* (Blumhouse Productions, 2018)

Zombies of Mora Tau (1957)

'In the darkness of an ancient world — on a shore that time has forgotten — there is a twilight zone between life and death. Here dwell those nameless creatures who are condemned to prowl the land eternally — The Walking Dead.'

Even the casual genre movie fan can't fail to spot, in the opening screen caption of Edward L. Cahn's *Zombies of Mora Tau*, intriguing references to — or rather *anticipations of* — future directions in science fiction and horror. Coming as it did two years before Rod Serling and forty-six years before Rick Grimes, *Mora Tau's* prescience deserves acknowledgement; in fact, it may be possible (as attempted by a number of horror scholars) to reclaim Cahn as the true father of modern zombie cinema! Modern-day zombies resurrected by science gone wrong were the subject of several B pictures made in the 1950s by Cahn. *Invisible Invaders* (1959) pioneered the classic zombie shuffle ten years prior to George A. Romero's *Night of the Living Dead*; while the Sam Katzman-produced *The Creature with the Atom Brain* (1955) has its zombies revived by radiation, à la *Night of the Living Dead*. There's more foreshadowing of Romero's film in *Mora Tau*, which presents images of revived corpses moving slowly *en masse* against the living. In fact, *Mora Tau* showed on Channel 11's Chiller Theatre in Pittsburgh (hosted by Bill 'Chilly Billy' Cardille) in the summer of 1967, when Romero was filming *Night of the Living Dead*, so it may even be possible that Romero saw Cahn's movie and was inspired by its imagery (and the rest, as they say, is history).

While undoubtedly an influence on future productions such as John Carpenter's *The Fog* (1980) and *Pirates of the Caribbean* (2003), *Mora Tau* also looked back to classic zombie movies and their roots in voodoo, and this, too, makes it an important film in the living dead sub-genre. As Jamie Russell has written in his excellent *Book of The Dead: The Complete History of Zombie Cinema*, the 50s proved to be a transitional period in zombie horror in which 'issues of voodoo, race and colonial anxiety were supplanted by fears of invasion, of brainwashing and apocalypse'. *Mora Tau* appears to buck the trend in some respects, returning zombies to their native homeland of Africa and voodoo. In others, though, it helped update the cinematic zombie by adding new elements to the mythos.

The origins of voodoo zombie fiction can, of course, be traced to William Seabrook's *The Magic Island* written in 1929. Seabrook was a *New York Times* journalist who travelled the world in search of ancient tribal rites. He found them in Haiti, in the voodoo ceremonies of the *bokors* who used potions to turn consenting persons into zombies. In actuality, these unfortunates were mentally ill villagers who could be induced into 'lethargic coma' with the aid of psychotropic drugs. Seabrook's chapter on Haitian zombies was titled 'Dead Men Working in the Cane-Fields' and, in the context of forced labour policies brought about during the American occupation of the island, gives us an insight not only into the motives behind these Haitian voodoo rituals but also the nature of early cinematic zombies. As film scholar Craig Ian Mann has noted, *White Zombie* (1932) was the first to equate the zombie with economic inequality. Set in Haiti, Victor Halperin's film depicts the zombie as slave labour toiling in the sugar mill under the evil gaze of voodoo master, Murder Legendre (Bela Lugosi). The zombies embody both modern day enslavement (the film was produced at the height of the Great Depression) and a good deal of white colonialist guilt on the part of American audiences, who flocked to the film. *Mora Tau* contains remnants of this even as it looks toward the modern zombie as a mass revolutionary force.

In *Mora Tau*, we have the young colonial girl, Jan Peters (Autumn Russell) return home to her African island after completing her studies abroad (shades of the Jane Eyre storyline of Val Lewton's *I Walked with a Zombie*, 1943). She discovers a group of salvage hunters led by Captain Harrison (Joel Ashley) intent on retrieving stolen diamonds from the wreck of a sunken ship called the Susan B. On the island, this treasure is the stuff of legend; the story goes that the diamonds were stolen from a native African tribe whose witchdoctor cast a spell on the Susan B's European crew. These drowned sailors, according to local folklore, are now underwater zombies who guard the wreck and its cargo from treasure hunters. As Jamie Russell points out, at the heart of *Mora Tau*'s story is colonialist anxiety about the pillaging of West Africa by white Europeans (a clever supplanting of America's own guilt at occupying Haiti between 1915 and 1934). However, the reversal of the white colonial mission by the tribal leaders, who use voodoo to create a zombie fighting force, marks *Mora Tau* as something new. 'Here it's the natives who subdue and enslave the colonial invaders using voodoo witchcraft,' writes Russell. While *White Zombie* portrayed the zombie as slave and victim, *Mora Tau* was clearly looking forward to the blue-collar revolt of the living dead that would characterize zombie films from the late 50s onwards.

In another break with early zombie film tradition, in *Mora Tau* there are no Black zombies in sight — and the island is strangely bereft of Africans too. The 40s saw Hollywood become increasingly uninterested in exploring racial anxieties of the past. Or at least, movies like *The Ghost Breakers* (1940) — set in Cuba rather than Haiti — sought to downplay them or turn them into the stuff of comedy. In *King of the Zombies* (1941) and *Revenge of the Zombies* (1943) the villainous roles are taken by the Black servants in the storylines, a casual racism that would reach a peak in *I Walked with a Zombie* by which native Caribbean islanders were cast as representatives of America's racial Other. Indeed, the total absence of Black performers in *Mora Tau*, as zombies, servants or tribespeople, leaves the film with a curious void. In this way, as a transitional work, it seems somewhat trapped between the classic zombie film and the modern one. The zombies may mark a revolt against the white colonialists but their native African chiefs are denied representation.

Another reason for *Mora Tau*'s lack of atmospherics as a voodoo zombie movie is that it was filmed entirely in Hollywood (according to Denis Meikle, the production never ventured any further than the Columbia backlot). In an attempt to create some mood (and to hide any deficiencies caused by a low budget), Cahn and his crew shot mostly at night. Much of the zombie action takes place in the murky ocean depths (in reality a dry studio). It's in these scenes of the zombie uprising that *Mora Tau* really comes into its own. The underwater zombie is now a staple of the sub-genre but *Mora Tau* got there first. Yes, the *Mora Tau* zombies — dressed in nautical clothes and strands of seaweed — are fairly unconvincing, but scenes of them walking the ocean floor and laying siege to the ship where the heroes are barricaded, still create a *frisson* today. Aquatic living dead would later feature in *Shock Waves* (1976), in which Nazi zombies torpedoed in World War Two emerge from their watery graves in the tropics to feast on hapless holidaymakers. Jean Rollin's much-maligned *Le lac des morts vivants* (*Zombie Lake*, 1980) is a variation on the theme; here German soldiers executed by the French Resistance during the Occupation rise from a village lake to exact revenge on the locals. The most memorable underwater zombie appears in Lucio Fulci's *Zombi 2* (*Zombie Flesh Eaters*, 1980) in which a decaying *morto vivente* inexplicably pops up to menace topless diver Auretta Gay before battling a real tiger shark with its bare hands. Fulci reputedly refused to film the scene himself as he thought it too silly. However, the eerie underwater imagery of *Zombi 2* owes much to *Mora Tau*.

Another way in which we might see *Zombies of Mora Tau* as a progenitor or missing link in the development of modern zombie cinema is in its introduction of the zombie as contagion or contamination. As Jamie Russell notes, Cahn's are the first cinematic ghouls to be capable of turning their victims into zombies as well, an important milestone in the evolution of the on-screen zombie. This ties into the theme of colonialism that drives the film: the source of *Mora Tau*'s horror stems from the characters' inability to contain the zombie threat. Russell writes: 'Just as the white crew of the Susan B were unable to dominate the natives, so the new adventurers find themselves at the mercy of zombies who constantly cross the boundaries of life and death, land and sea, inside and outside.'

The fear of contamination by the Other, as presented in *Mora Tau*, extends beyond colonialist anxieties and into other cultural fears of the 50s. Many sci-fi horror films of that decade express a nagging fear of female sexuality and of women's growing independence in the post-war era. For example, *Tarantula* (1955), while expressing atomic age fears of radiation and its potentially catastrophic threat to society (as embodied by the giant tarantula which menaces a small desert town) also — very pointedly — questions the wisdom of upsetting the 'natural order' of things in terms of changing gender roles. While Maria Corday as the film's female scientist is initially portrayed as a strong intelligent woman, she is subsequently imperiled by her involvement with the experiment and has to be rescued by the men. The film thus implies that the woman's place remains in the home and that to go against 'nature' in that way risks disaster akin to that posed by atomic mutation.

In *Mora Tau*, Allison Hayes as Mona is the strong, sexual woman whose independence poses a threat to the men around her. She taunts them with her sarcasm and displays of her body. As Alain Silver and James Ursini note in their book *The Zombie Film: From White Zombie to World War Z*, in one scene indicative of her *femme fatale* arrogance, Mona 'reclines in a bathing suit and suns herself on the deck of the ship, even as a distracted crew tries to prepare the divers for a dangerous mission to retrieve the stash of diamonds'. Even after she is kidnapped by the zombies, as Silver and Ursini point out, when the audience thinks that the predatory woman will receive her comeuppance, Mona 'gets herself declared the queen of these zombies and leads them into an attack against her former comrades'.

'Given such fears, it's no surprise that Mona, the film's blatantly "bad" woman, should be zombified,' concludes Russell, 'nor that her male counterparts should imprison her'. In *Mora Tau*, as in the zombie films that preceded it, the Other must be contained. But the finale of *Mora Tau* (spoiler!) — in which the diamonds are cast back into the sea and the zombies crumble into dust — is ambiguous at best; the immediate threat is vanquished, but there is a lingering doubt left in the mind of the viewer (a bit like the huge question mark that appears on screen at the end of *The Blob*, 1958) — are the monsters really gone, or will they inevitably return? As a transitional zombie film, then, elements of Cold War paranoia permeate *Mora Tau*. It's significant that on either side of *Mora Tau*, Cahn filmed two atomic themed sci-fi horror movies, *The Creature with the Atom Brain* and *Invisible Invaders*, both focusing on nuclear energy and alien (read:

Communist!) invasion. In the latter, Cahn conjures up images of an army of irradiated corpses all around the world rising against the living, paving the way for the mass uprising of zombies in *Night of the Living Dead*.

In short, Cahn's zombies may be overlooked in film history, but as they lumbered towards the living dead as we now know them, their infection brought to us Romero and all the flesh-eating ghouls that followed.

Zombies of Mora Tau (Columbia Pictures, 1957)

Index

3.15 (1986) 130
300 (2006) 43
The 400 Blows [*Les Quatre Cent Coups*] (1959) 189
2001: A Space Odyssey (1968) 110, 194
The 7th Voyage of Sinbad (1958) 154
The Addams Family (franchise) 62
Akira (1988) 96
Allen, Nancy 137
Alice, Sweet Alice [aka *Communion*] (1976) 5, 6-11, 113, 157
Aliens (1986) 142
Alexander, Terry 58
All is True (2018) 117
Altman, Robert 15, 120
Amarcord (1973) 189
Amazing Stories (TV series) 42
American International Pictures (AIP) 59, 95, 107, 108, 165-168, 183
American Mary (2012) 37
American Movies in the 1950s (book) 127
Amadeus (1984) 120
Amano, Yoshitaka 97
Amicus 12, 15, 42, 43, 59-62, 86, 91-94
Amirpour, Ana Lily 37
The Amityville Horror (1979) 16
Amplas, John 112
And God Said To Cain (1970) 49
Anderson, Josef 15
The Andromeda Strain (1971) 147
Anger, Kenneth 76
Apollo 18 (2011) 22
Argento, Dario 67, 70
Arkoff, Samuel Z. 108, 165, 166
Arkush, Allan 165, 166, 168
Army of Darkness (1992) 63

Arnette, Jeannetta 157, 160, 163
Aronson, Linda 171
Askwith, Robin 86, 87
Astro Boy (1951) 96
Asylum (1972) 12-15, 59, 94
At the Earth's Core (1976) 59
Atkins, Tom 45
Atomic Café (1982) 96
Attack of the Crab Monsters (1957) 107
Audrey Rose (1977) 16-19
Autostop rosso sangue [*Hitch-Hike*] (1977) 85
Avatar (2009) 143
The Babadook (2014) 37
Bachardy, Don 119
Baclanova, Olga 77
The Bad Batch (2016) 37
The Bad Seed (1956) 10, 17
Bad Taste (1987) 32, 33, 34
Bain, Cynthia 145
Baker, Roy Ward 12, 93
Balch, Antony 86, 87, 88
Balme, Timothy 35
Bananas (1971) 136
Band, Richard 153
Barbeau, Adrienne 46
Barefoot Gen (1983) 96
Barber, Glynis 69
Barker, Clive 75
Bartel, Paul 165
Basket Case (1982) 153
Bates, Alan 119
Battle Beyond the Sun (1962) 95
Battle for the Planet of the Apes (1973) 141
Bava, Mario 120, 121
The Beast with Five Fingers (1946) 62
Beautiful Dreamer (1984) 97
Beck, John 16
Behind the Green Door (1972) 152

Beneath the Planet of the Apes (1970) 139
Beverly Hills 90210 (1990-2000) 130
Beyond Hammer (book) 145
The Big Heat (1953) 128
Billy the Kid Versus Dracula (1966) 48
Bird, Evan 37
Birdman (2014) 76
The Birds (1963) 62, 132
Birkin, Andrew 190
Black Moon (1971) 49
Blood Moon (2015) 49
Blood of Dr Jekyll (1981) 69
Black Noon (1971) 48
Black Sunday (1960) 176
Blackboard Jungle (1955) 127, 129, 165
Blacula (1972) 125
Blair, Linda 129
Blair Witch (2016) 25
The Blair Witch Project (1999) 20-26
Blasco, Joe 150
Bless this House (1973) 86
The Blob (1958) 46, 200
Bloch, Robert 12-15, 91-94
Blood of the Beasts [*Le sang des bêtes*] (1949) 74
Blood-Sucking Freaks (1976) 9
The Blue Lagoon (1980) 7
Bone Tomahawk (2015) 48
Bonham-Carter, Helena 105
Book of Shadows: Blair Witch 2 (2000) 25
Boorman, John 144
Borowczyk, Walerian 69
Boxing Helena (1993) 37, 40
Boy Meets Girl (1984) 190
Boys Don't Cry (1999) 157
The Boys Next Door (1985) 27-31, 183

Breakdown (1997) 84
Brain Damage (1988) 195
Braindead (1992) 32-36
Bram Stoker's Dracula (1992) 117
Branagh, Kenneth 117-121
The Brand New Testament (2015) 187
The Bride and The Beast (1957) 17
Bride of Re-Animator (1989) 156
Briggs, Raymond 96
Brolin, James 9
The Brood (1979) 151
Browning, Tod 74, 77-81, 117
Brownrigg, S.F. 144
Bruckner, David 23
Bruiser (2000) 112
Buñuel, Luis 156, 185
Burroughs, Edgar Rice 59
Burroughs, William 87
The Burrowers (2008) 48
Butterfly Kiss (1995) 171, 172
The Cabinet of Dr Caligari (1920) 60, 70, 136
Cabin in The Woods (2012) 65
Caged Heat (1974) 176
Cahn, Edward L. 133, 197-201
Caine, Michael 62, 137
Cammell, Donald 194
Campanile, Pasquale Festa 85
Campion, Jane 189, 190
Cannibal Holocaust (1980) 21
Carax, Leos 190
Cardille, Lori 57
Cardos, John 'Bud' 157
Carne (1991) 73
Carpenter, John 45, 158, 197
Carrey, Jim 145
Carrie (1976) 10, 135-137, 152, 157, 168
Carrie (2013) 136
The Cassandra Crossing (1976) 147
Castle, Roy 61

Castle, William 12, 73, 74, 91, 92, 110
The Cat Creeps (1946) 49
Cathy's Curse (1977) 17
Cat People (1942) 61
Catizone, Rick 45
Caulfield, Maxwell 28, 30
Cavalcanti, Alberto 60
Celia (1989) 189
Chained (2012) 37-41
Chambers, Marilyn 149, 152
Chaney, Lon 91, 161
Chatiliez, Étienne 190
Cheeseball Presents (1984) 6
The Child (1977) 17
Christian, Kurt 89
Chung, Ching 124
Circus of Horrors (1960) 86
Class of 1984 (1982) 127-129
Class Reunion Massacre [AKA *The Redeemer: Son of Satan*] 17, 157-164
Cléry, Corinne 71
A Clockwork Orange (1971) 182, 183
Clouzot, Henri-Georges 7
Cloverfield (2008) 20, 22
Cold Blood (2015) 187
Colpaert, Carl 95-99
Combs, Richard 17
Come Die My Love (1952) 49
Combs, Jeffrey 153
Communion [aka *Alice, Sweet Alice*] 1976) 5, 6-11, 113, 157
Compulsion (1959) 30
Confessions of a Window Cleaner (1974) 86
Conquest of the Planet of the Apes (1972) 140
Cool It Carol (1970) 87
Coppola, Francis Ford 75, 95, 117
Corman, Roger 27, 88, 95, 96, 98, 107-111, 155, 165-167, 182, 183

The Corpse-Drivers of Xiangxi (Xiang xi gan shi ji) (1957) 124
The Couch (1962) 12
Cousins Roe, Staten 170-173
Crampton, Barbara 153
Crash (1996) 130, 151, 174
Craven, Wes 129, 174
Crawley, Tony 6, 10
The Crazies (1973) 113, 147, 149, 150
The Creature with the Atom Brain (1955) 133, 154, 197, 200
Creepshow (1982) 42-47
Crichton, Charles 60
Crime in the Streets (1956) 127
Crimes of Passion (1984) 70
Crimes of The Future (1970) 176
Cronenberg, David 147-152, 174-181
Crosby, Floyd 110
Crowley, Kathleen 48, 50
Cunningham, Sean S. 129, 130
Curse of Frankenstein (1957) 117, 1118
The Curse of The Blair Witch (1999) 24, 25
Curse of the Undead (1959) 48-52
Cushing, Peter 14, 59, 61, 94
The Cut-Ups (1966) 87
Dagon (2001) 153
Dahl, John 84
Daleks' Invasion Earth 2150 A.D. (1966) 59
Dallos (1983) 97
The Damned (1962) 86
Dangerous Youth (1958) 127
Dangerously Close (1986) 129
Danse Macabre (book) 93
Danson, Ted 46
Darabont, Frank 120
The Dark Half (novel) 94
The Dark Half (1993) 112

Dawn of the Dead (1978) 46, 54, 55, 67, 112, 133
The Day After (1983) 96
Day of the Dead (1985) 53-58
Day of the Triffids (1963) 62
The Day the World Ended (1955) 96
DC Comics 43
The Dead and the Damned (2011) 49
Dead Calm (1989) 85
Dead of Night (1945) 13, 59, 60, 61
The Deadly Bees (1966) 12, 92
Deadly Night 4 (1990) 155
Dearden, Basil 60
The Decline of Western Civilization (1981) 27, 29, 30, 182, 183, 185
The Decline of Western Civilization Part II: The Metal Years (1988) 27
The Decline of Western Civilization Part III (1998) 27
Deep Sleep (1972) 8
Deep Throat (1972) 8
Dein, Edward 49, 50
Dein, Mildred 49, 50
Deliverance (1971) 143, 146
Deming, Peter 65
Demme, Jonathan 28, 108, 110, 176
Demon Seed (1977) 194
Demon Seed (novel) 194
DeNoble, Alphonso 9
The Dentist (1996) 153, 156
Deodato, Ruggero 21
De Palma, Brian 135-138
Deren, Maya 76
Despite the Gods (2012) 38
Destroyer (1988) 70
Detour (1945) 83
The Devil Inside (2012) 22
The Devil Thumbs a Ride (1947) 83
The Devils (1971) 174
Les Diaboliques (1955) 7

Diary of the Dead (2007) 22
DiAquino, John 145
Dickinson, Angie 137
Dillon, Matt 75
Dillon, Robert 110
Dr Jekyll and Mr Hyde (1931) 75
Dr Jekyll and Sister Hyde (1971) 69
Dr Terror's House of Horrors (1965) 59-62
Dr Who and The Daleks (1965) 59
D'Onofrio, Vincent 37, 39
Donahue, Heather 22, 24
Don't Look Now (1973) 8, 10
Don't Deliver Us from Evil (1971) 88
Doo, John 84, 85
Doherty, Thomas 127, 128, 166
Dolls (1987) 153
Dudes (1987) 182
Duffell, Peter 94
Durston, David E. 149
Dracula (1931) 77, 117, 124, 132
Dracula [aka *Horror of Dracula*] (1958) 50, 117, 118
Dracula, the Vampire (novel) 25, 50
Drag Me to Hell (2009) 63-66
Dressed to Kill (1980) 137
Ducournau, Julia 37
Duel (1971) 83, 84
Dumb and Dumber (1994) 145
Ealing Studios 60
Early, David 46
Earles, Harry 77
East, Jeff 145
Easy Rider (1969) 128
Ebert, Roger 6, 172
Edge of Sanity (1989) 67-71
The Eighth Day [*Le Huitième Jour*] (1996) 187
Ekland, Britt 15
Emmerich, Roland 98

Encounters of the Spooky Kind (1980) 124
Endelson, Robert A. 129
Enter the Void (2009) 72-76
Entertaining Comics (EC) 42, 43, 44, 45, 46, 47
Eraserhead (1976) 40, 112
Escape from the Planet of the Apes (1971) 140
ET: the Extraterrestrial (1982) 185
Evans, Maurice 139
Evans, Robert 17
Evidence (2011) 22
The Evil Dead (1982) 64, 153
The Evil Dead franchise 36, 63, 64, 65
Evil Things (2009) 22, 23
Exit Humanity (2012) 49
Eyes without a Face (Les yeux sans visage (1960) 73
The Exorcist (1973) 6, 10, 16, 17, 18, 113, 157
Farron, Eamon 37, 39
Fantômas (1913) 75
Faust (1926) 60
Ferris Bueller's Day Off (1986) 130
Feuillade, Louis 74, 75
Finkbinder, T.G. 159, 160, 161, 162, 163
Fight Club (1999) 172, 173
Fight for Your Life (1977) 129
Fincher, David 172
Finley, William 135, 137
Finney, Jack 100, 101, 102
Fireworks (1947) 76
Fisher, Terence 118
Fleming, Eric 48
The Flesh and Blood Show (1972) 87
Florey, Robert 62
Flower, George 'Buck' 145
The Fog (1980) 197
Foldes, Joan and Peter 96

The Four Dimensions of Greta (1972) 87
The Forbin Project (1970) 194
Ford, Glenn 127
Foree, Ken 12
Forman, Milos 120
Fox, Edward 105
Francis, Freddie 61, 62, 92, 93
Franciscus, James 139
Franju, Georges 73, 74
Frank, Alan 16, 17
Frankenheimer, John 110
Frankenstein (1931) 117, 118, 119, 132, 196
Frankenstein; or, The Modern Prometheus (novel) 25, 113, 117, 119, 120, 153
Frankenstein: The True Story (1973) 119
Franklin, Pamela 106
Franklin, Richard 70
Freaks (1932) 77-81, 87, 88, 118
Free Jack (1992) 33
French Connection II (1975) 110
Freund, Karl 75
Friday the 13th (movie franchise) 20, 143
Friday the 13th (1980) 163
Friedkin, William 17
Friedman, David F. 80
From Beyond (1986) 153
From Beyond the Grave (1974) 59, 60
From the Drain (1967) 176
Fulci, Lucio 9, 67, 199
Full Metal Jacket (1987) 39
Gagne, Paul R. 44, 53
Gaines, Maxwell 43
Gaines, Bill 43, 44
Gainsbourg, Charlotte 190
Game of Death (1978) 124
Gentlemen Prefer Blondes (1953) 168

Gershenson, Joseph 49
Get to Know Your Rabbit (1972) 135
Ghost Town (1988) 48
The Ghost Breakers (1940) 198
Gibson, William 192
A Girl Walks Home Alone at Night (2014) 37
A Girl's Own Story (1986) 189, 190
Gochis, Constantine S. 157, 159, 160
Goddard, Drew 65
Godzilla (1956) 95
Godzilla 1985 (1985) 96
Goodbye Pork Pie (1981) 33
Goldbeck, Willis 77, 78
The Golden Voyage of Sinbad (1973) 89
Gordon, Keith 137
Gordon, Richard 86, 87, 88
Gordon, Stuart 153, 154, 155, 156
Gornick, Michael 42
Gough, Michael 86
Graham, Gerrit 137
Grand Guignol 36, 43, 46, 135
Grave Encounters (2011) 21
Gray, Beverly 107
Grease (1978) 165
The Great Train Robbery (1903) 72
Greetings (1968) 135
Gregory, James 140
Grim Prairie Tales (1990) 49
Haller, Daniel 110
Halloween (1978) 158, 163, 168
Halloween (film franchise) 20
Halperin, Victor 133, 198
Hamer, Robert 60
Hammer Films 17, 50, 59, 61, 62, 69, 70, 88, 92, 117, 124, 125, 132, 133
Hammid, Alexander 76
The Hand (1981) 62

Handke, Peter 171
Hardstock, Michael 9
Harper, Jessica 137, 138
Harris, Ed 45
Harryhausen, Ray 32
Hauer, Rutger 82
The Haunted Palace (1963) 107
Haunted Range (1926) 48
The Haunting (1963) 17, 104
Haxan: Witchcraft through the Ages (1922) 88
A Hazard of Hearts (1987) 105
Heathers (1989) 130
Heimrich, George A. 50, 51
Hellraiser (1987) 67
Henenlotter, Frank 32, 195
Henriksen, Lance 143
Henry: Portrait of a Serial Killer (1986) 27, 38
Henry V (1989) 117
Hess, David 85
Heston, Charlton 139, 141
Hi Mom! (1970) 135
High Plains Drifter (1972) 48
High School (1968) 185
Hill, Joe 45
Hingst, Sergio 84
Hisss (2010) 37
Hitchcock, Alfred 7, 11, 12, 51, 62, 91, 132, 135, 136
The Hitcher (1986) 82-85
Hitch-Hike [*Autostop rosso sangue*] (1977) 85
The Hitch-hiker (1953) 83, 85
The Hitchhikers (1972) 84
Ho, Peter Chen 124
Holbrook, Hal 46
Hollywood Vice Squad (1986) 27, 28
Hopkins, Anthony 16
Hopkins, Miriam 69
The Horrible Dr. Hichcock (1962) 176

Horror Hospital (1973) 86-90
Horror of Dracula (1958) 50, 117, 118
Horrors of the Black Museum (1959) 86
Hospital (1970) 185
Hôtel des invalides (1952) 74
Hough, John 104-106
House of Hammer (magazine) 6, 16, 157,
House of Dracula (1945) 49
House of Whipcord (1974) 90
The House that Dripped Blood (1971) 12, 59, 91-94
Howard, Clint 165
Howell, C. Thomas 83
Hughes Brothers 65
Hulce, Tom 120
Hume, Alan 61, 105
Hung, Sammo 123, 124
Hunter, Kim 139
Hunter, Tim 128
Hurley, Matthew 145
I Am Legend (book) 54, 133
I Drink Your Blood (1970) 149
I Spit on Your Grave (1978) 129
I Stand Alone [*Seul contre tous*] (1998) 72, 73, 74
I Walked with a Zombie (1943) 198, 199
I Was a Teenage Werewolf (1957) 167
Illegally Yours (1988) 143
Ilsa: She Wolf of the SS (1975) 168
Images (1972) 15
In the Aftermath (1989) 95-99
Iñárritu, Alejandro González 76
Insidious (2010) 192
Insidious (film franchise) 192
The Intruder (1962) 107, 108
Invaders from Mars (1953) 148
Invasion of the Body Snatchers (1956) 100-103, 148, 177, 179

Invasion of the Body Snatchers (film franchise) 100
Invisible Invaders (1959) 133, 197, 200
The Invisible Man (2020) 192
The Invisible Man (novel) 109
The Invitation (2015) 37
Iron Man (2008) 143
Irreversible (*Irréversible*, 2002) 72, 73, 74
Isherwood, Christopher 119
It Happened One Night (1934) 82
It's Alive (1975) 16
Ivan's Childhood (1962) 98
Jackson, Donald G. 98
Jackson, Peter 32-36, 153
Jannings, Emil 60, 75
Jaws (1975) 17, 23
Jenkins, Megs 15
Jennifer's Body (2009) 37
Jiangshi 122, 123, 124, 125, 126
Jonah Hex (2010) 48
Jones, Duane 132
Joy Ride (1958) 128
Joyride [AKA *Roadkill*] (2001) 84
Judex (1916) 75
Jurassic Park (film franchise) 143
Just Before Dawn (1981) 145
Juvenile Court (1973) 185
Kael, Pauline 156
Kargl, Gerald 74
Karlatos, Olga 9
Karloff, Boris 94, 118
Katt, William 137
Kent, Jennifer 37
Khalfoun, Franck 76
Kidder, Margot 137
Kidman, Nicole 85
Kikoïne, Gérard 67, 69, 70
The King of the Zombies (1941) 198
King, Stephen 42-46, 93, 94, 107, 163
Kingdom of The Spiders (1977) 157

Kings of the Road (1976) 171
Kiss Me Deadly (1955) 102
Kiss of Death (1948) 128
Knewson, John 83
Knife in The Water [*Nóz w wodzie*] (1962) 85
Knightriders (1981) 45
Koontz, Dean R. 194
Krauss, Werner 60
Kubrick, Stanley 33, 74, 110, 182
Kung-leong, Yeung 124
Kurzweil, Raymond 193, 194
Kusama, Karyn 37
Kwan, Stanley 123
Le lac des morts vivants [*Zombie Lake*] (1980) 199
The Lady from Shanghai (1947) 10
Lady in the Lake (1947) 75, 76
Lam, Stephanie 122, 123, 125, 126
Lambert, Mary 37
Land of the Dead (2005) 56, 57
The Land that Time Forgot (1975) 59
Lang, Fritz 10
The Last Exorcism (2010) 21, 22
Last House on Dead End Street (1977) 157
The Last House on The Left (1972) 24, 67, 129, 174, 177
The Last Laugh (*Der letzte Mann*, 1924) 75
The Last Man on Earth (1964) 133
The Last Woman on Earth (1960) 96
Lee, Bruce 124
Lee, Christopher 61, 62, 118
The Legend of Hell House (1973) 104-106
The Legend of the Seven Golden Vampires (1974) 125
Leni, Paul 59
Leonard, Joshua 24
Leone, Sergio 97, 189
Leong, Wai-Man 124

The Leopard Man (1943) 49
Leroy, Mervyn 17
Leslie, Conor 37
Lester, Mark L. 127
Levine, Ted 84
Lewis, Herschell Gordon 144, 145
Lewton, Val 22, 49, 61, 198
Li, Hui Maan 124
Li, Tie 124
Lieberman, Jeff 145
Life is a Long, Quiet River [*La Vie est un long fleuve tranquille*] (1988) 190
Lindfors, Viveca 45
Linklater, Richard 185
The Little Shop of Horrors (1960) 107
The Living Coffin (1959) 49
Logan, Joshua 6
Lohman, Alison 63, 65
Lom, Herbert 15
Long, Justin 63
The Lost Boys (1987) 9
Loughlin, Lori 129
Lovecraft, H.P. 91, 93, 107, 153, 154, 155
The Lovely Bones (2009) 32
Lowe, Rob 143
Lowry, Lynn 149, 178
Lugosi, Bela 198
Lupino, Ida 83, 85
Lynch, David 40, 65, 189
Lynch, Jennifer 37-40
M (1931) 10
Mad Love (1935) 43
Mad Max Beyond Thunderdome (1985) 56
Magee, Patrick 13
Making Contact (1985) 98
Mamoulian, Rouben 69, 75
The Man Who Laughs (1928) 60

The Man with the X-Ray Eyes (1963) 107-111
Maniac (1980) 68
Maniac (2012) 76
Map of The Human Heart (1992) 33
Markes, Tony 98
Martin (1977) 6, 112-116
Marvel Comics 43
Marvin, Lee 127
Mary Shelley's Frankenstein (1994) 117-121
Mason, Marsha 16
The Masque of the Red Death (1964) 88, 107
Massacre at Central High (1976) 129
Masters of Horror (TV series) 42
Matheson, Richard 54, 104, 105, 106, 133
A Matter of Life and Death (1946) 99
The Matrix (film franchise) 192
The Matrix Reloaded (2003) 192
Merhige, E. Elias 70
McCarthy era 43, 100, 102
McCarthy, Joseph 100, 102
McCarthy, Kevin 100
McDowell, Malcolm 182
McDowall, Roddy 139, 140
McMaster, Niles 8
Meet the Feebles (1990) 32, 34, 35
MGM 77, 79, 143
Men in Black (1997) 39
Meshes of the Afternoon (1943) 76
Midnight Vampire (1936) 124
Milland, Ray 107, 109
Miller, Dick 165
Miller, Jason 9
Miller, Linda 9
Minority Report (2002) 193
Mirror (1975) 98
Miyazaki, Hayao 95, 96

Mona Lisa and the Blood Moon (2021) 37
Monkey Shines (1988) 112, 195
Monster on the Campus (1958) 49
Montgomery, Robert 75, 76
Monty Python (TV show) 32, 36
Moody, Elizabeth 35
Morrow, Vic 127
Morse, Barry 14
Mr. Nobody (2001) 187
Mr. Sardonicus (1961) 110
Mr Vampire (1985) 122-126
Much Ado About Nothing (1993) 120, 121
Mulheron, Danny 34
Müller, Aldine 84
The Mummy (1932) 17, 118
The Mummy (1959) 17
Murakami, Jimmy T. 96
Murder à la Mod (1967) 135
Murder by Numbers (2002) 30
Murnau, F.W. 74, 75
Murphy, Geoff 33
Myrick, Daniel 20, 23, 24, 25
National Lampoon's Animal House (1978) 167
Nausicaä of the Valley of the Wind [Warriors of the Wind] (1984) 95, 96
The Navigator (1988) 33
Neal, Tom 83
Nebo Zovyot (1959) 95
Neill, Sam 85
Neilsen, Leslie 46
Nero, Franco 85
The Nesting (1981) 162
The New Kids (1985) 127-131
New World Pictures 27, 95, 96, 98, 99, 108, 114, 165, 166, 168, 182, 183
Nicholson, James 108, 165
Nifas Diabólicas [Diabolical Nymphs] (1978) 84

A Night in The Woods (2012) 21
Nightmares in a Damaged Brain (1981) 68
Night of The Demon [Aka *Curse Of The Demon*] (1957) 64
Night of the Living Dead (1968) 5, 54, 80, 112, 132-134, 148, 177, 197, 201
Night of the Juggler (1980) 9
Night of the Zombies (1981) 9
A Nightmare on Elm Street (1984) 20, 34
The Nightwalker (1964) 12, 91
No Time to Die (1956) 128
Noé, Gaspar 72-76
North, Ted 83
Noyce, Phillip 85
Nóz w wodzie [*Knife in The Water*] (1962) 85
O'Dea, Judith 132
Los Olvidados (1950) 185
The Omen (1976) 10, 16, 17, 18, 19, 158, 159, 164
On a Clear Day You Can See Forever (1970) 17
On the Beach (1959) 132
Once Upon A Time in America (1984) 189
Only You (1983) 97
Ormond, Julia 38
Orphan (2009) 10
Osamu, Tezuka 96
Oshii, Mamoru 95, 97-99
Otomo, Katsuhiro 96
The Outer Limits (TV series) 42
Paranormal Activity franchise 20, 21, 23
Parkins, Barbara 13
Pate, Michael 48, 49, 51
Patric, Jason 9
Pandemonium (1982) 6
Pasolini, Pier Paolo 72
Peel (1986) 189

Peeping Tom (1960) 21, 23, 174
Peli, Oren 20
Peñalver, Diana 35
Petit, Chris 10, 11, 171
Perkins, Anthony 70
Perrier, Mireille 190
Pertwee, Jon 94
Phantom of the Opera (1925) 91
Phantom of the Paradise (1974) 135-138
Phantom Town (1998) 49
Ping, Yiu 124
Pirates of the Caribbean (2003) 197
The Plague of the Zombies (1966) 133
Planet of the Apes (1968) 139-141
Plummer, Amanda 171
Polanski, Roman 17, 85, 88, 132
Porter, Edwin S. 72
Portraits of Women (1970) 175
Potter, Dennis 189
Powell, Michael 21, 174
Powell, Robert 12
Predator (1987) 142
The Premature Burial (1962) 107, 108, 110
Presby, Shannon 129
Pressman, Ed 135
Pretty Baby (1978) 6
Price, Dennis 89
Price, Vincent 132, 155
Progeny (1998) 155
Psyche-Out (1968) 128
Psycho (1960) 12, 14, 15, 51, 70, 91, 92, 132
Psycho II (1983) 70
Psycho III (1986) 70
The Psychopath (1966) 12, 59, 92
The Public Enemy (1931) 127
Pump Up the Volume (1990) 130
Pumpkinhead (1988) 142-146
Pumpkinhead II: Blood Wings (1994) 142

Pumpkinhead: Ashes to Ashes (2006) 142
Pumpkinhead: Blood Feud (2007) 142
Quart, Barbara Koenig 27, 29, 183
The Quick and the Dead (1995) 63
The Quick and the Undead (2006) 48
Quigley, Linnea 129
Quinlan, Kathleen 84
Rabid (1977) 147-152
Rabid (2019) 19, 147
Race with the Devil (1975) 144, 145
Radio On (1979) 171
The Ramones 80, 167, 168
Rampling, Charlotte 14
Raimi, Ivan 64
Raimi, Sam 32, 35, 63-66
The Raven (1935) 43
Ravenous (1999) 48
Raver, Lorna 63
Raw (2016) 37
Rayns, Tony 18
Re-Animator (1985) 32, 153-156
Reed, Joel M. 9
Reed, Oliver 119
Red, Eric 82
The Redeemer: Son of Satan (1978) 17, 157-164
Redgrave, Michael 60
Reeves, Michael 90, 174
Reeves, Saskia 171
The Reincarnation of Peter Proud (1970) 17
Reitman, Ivan 150
Remson, Kerry 145
Repulsion (1965) 15, 132
Reservoir Dogs (1992) 182
The Resurrection of Eve (1973) 152
Return of The Living Dead 3 (1993) 153, 155, 156
Revenge of the Zombies (1943) 198

Revolt of the Zombies (1936) 133
Rigg, Diana 105
Ritvo, Rosemary 217
River's Edge (1987) 128
Rochant, Éric 190
Rock All Night (1957) 165
Rock Around the Clock (1956) 165, 167
Rock 'n' Roll High School (1979) 165-169
The Rocky Horror Picture Show (1975) 135
Roe, Poppy 170
Roeg, Nicolas 8, 10, 188
Roller Blade (1986) 98
Rollin, Jean 199
Romero, George A. 6, 32, 42-46, 53-58, 112- 116, 132, 133, 149, 150, 174, 195, 197, 201
Rope (1948) 30
Rose, Joe AKA Willard Butz 8
Rosher, Charles 75
Rosemary's Baby (1968) 17, 145
Ross, Gaylen 46
Rothman, Stephanie 37
Rouge (1987) 123, 124
Rubinstein, Richard P. 15, 42, 54, 55
Ruby (1977) 157
Rumble Fish (1983) 75
The Running Man (1987) 98
Running Wild (1955) 127
Russell, David O. 65
Russell, Jamie 197, 198, 199, 200
Russell, Ken 70, 119, 174
Russell, Kurt 84
Russell, Ray 110
Russo, John 55
Ryshpan, Howard 149
Salò, or the 120 Days of Sodom (1975) 72
Sanchez, Eduardo 20, 21, 23, 24, 25

Santa Sangre (1989) 67
Sarrazin, Michael 119
Satan's Triangle (1975) 85
Saturday Night Fever (1977) 165
Savage, Ann 83
Savage Streets (1984) 129
Savini, Tom 33, 53
Saw (2004) 192
Saw (film franchise) 192
Scalvi, Patrícia 84
Schober, Adrian 16
Schwarzbaum, Lisa 26
Schweitzer, Darrell 13, 92, 93
Scanners (1981) 151
Scarface (1932) 127
Scorsese, Martin 214
Scott, Ridley 33
Scream (franchise) 65
Scream and Scream Again (1970) 86
Scum of the Earth (1974) 144, 146
The Search for Bridey Murphy (1956) 17
Secretary (2002) 130
Secrets of Sex (1970) 88
See-Luk, Chow 124
A Serial Killer's Guide to Life (2019) 170-173
Seven (1995) 158
Seven Guns to Mesa (1958) 49
Sex, Lies and Videotape (1989) 130
Shadow of the Vampire (2000) 70
Shaw Brothers 124, 125
Shaw, Vanessa 86
Sheen, Charlie 28, 30
She-Freak (1967) 80
Sheppard, Paula 6, 9
Shields, Brooke 6, 7, 9
The Shining (1980) 23, 42
Shivers (1975) 148, 149, 150, 151, 152, 174-181
Shock Suspense (comic) 43
Shock Waves (1976) 199

A Short Vision (1956) 96
Shutter Island (2010) 143
Siegel, Don 100, 102 103
Sightseers (2012) 170
Silence of the Lambs (1991) 68, 176
A Simple Plan (1998) 63
The Simpsons 80
Sin City (2005) 43
Sinbad and the Eye of the Tiger (1977) 89
Sinclair, Stephen 34
The Singing Detective (1986) 189
Sisters (1972) 135, 137
Skip, Martin 86, 88
The Skull (1965) 12, 62, 92
Slater, Christian 130
Sleeper (1973) 136
Society (1989) 153, 155
Solaris (1972) 98
Sole, Alfred 6, 7, 8, 9, 10
Soles, PJ 167, 168
Son of Dracula (1974) 88
Son of Frankenstein (1939) 67
The Sorcerers (1967) 90
Soska, Jen and Sylvia 37, 147
The Sound of Music (1965) 17
Spacek Sissy 137, 52
Spader, James 127, 130
Spheeris, Penelope 27-31, 182-186
Spiderman (franchise) 64, 65
Spielberg, Steven 17, 23, 29, 32, 42, 83, 185
Spratling, Tony 70
Stalker (1979) 98
Stargensky, Joseph 10
Star Wars (film franchise) 58
Steele, Barbara 176
Stereo (1968) 176
Stevenson, Robert Louis 68, 69, 70
Straight-Jacket (1964) 12, 91
Stoker, Bram 25, 50, 117

Stone, Oliver 62
The Strange Case of Dr Jekyll and Mr Hyde (novella) 68, 69
Struss, Karl 75
Stuck (2007) 153
Subotsky, Milton 12, 59, 61, 91, 92, 93
Suburbia (1984) 27, 29, 30, 182-186
SubUrbia (1996) 185
Sunrise (1927) 75
Supernatural Activity (2012) 21
Supervixens (1975) 88
Surveillance (2008) 37
Survival of the Dead (2009) 57
Suspiria (1977) 70
Syms, Sylvia 13, 14
Swanberg, Joe 23
Swift, Susan 16
Swoon (1992) 30
Tales from the Crypt (1972) 59, 93
Tales from the Darkside (TV series) 42
Tanya's Island (1980) 6
Tape 407 (2012) 20, 21
Tarantula (1955) 200
Tarkovsky, Andrei 98
Teenage Doll (1957) 165, 168
Teenagers and Teenpics: The Juvenilization of American Movies in the 1950s (book) 127
Teenage Crime Wave (1955) 127
Tenshi No Tamago (*Angel's Egg*, 1985) 95-99
The Terminator (1984) 142, 194
Terminator 2: Judgement Day (1991) 98, 192, 194
The Terror (1963) 107
The Terrornauts (1967) 59
The Texas Chain Saw Massacre (1974) 24, 43, 67, 133, 144, 177
They Came from Beyond Space (1967) 59
They Shall Not Grow Old (2018) 32

Thalberg, Irving 77, 78, 79
Thank God It's Friday (1978) 215
Thelma and Louise (1991) 170, 171
This Way Out (2013) 170
The Three-Thousand-Year Old Vampire (*Sanqian Nina Didi Jiangshi*) (1939) 124
This Film is Not Yet Rated (2006) 40
Tierney, Lawrence 83
Titane (2021) 37
Todd, Richard 13, 14
Tokuma Shoten studio 96
Top Gun (1986) 53
Torture Garden (1967) 12, 59, 92
Toto the Hero (1991) 187-191
Touch of Evil (1958) 102
Tower of Evil (1970) 87
Towers Open Fire (1963) 87
Transfer (1968) 176
Treasure Island (1972) 105
Tromberg, Sheldon 158, 159, 160, 161
The Trip (1967) 109, 110, 165
Truck Stop Women (1974) 88
Truffaut, François 27, 76, 189
Tuff Turf (1985) 130
Turner, Ann 189
Turner, Peter 24
The Twilight Zone (TV show) 42
Twins of Evil (1971) 105
Two Thousand Maniacs (1964) 144, 145
Ulmer, Edgar G. 83
Underground (1958) 132
The Unknown (1927) 161
Upgrade (2018) 192-196
Upworld (1990) 142
Vampire Circus (1972) 88
Vampire Woman [*Xi xue fu*] (1962) 124
Les Vampires (1915-16) 75

Vampires of the Haunted Mansion (Gui wu jiang shi) (1939) 124
Van Dormael, Jaco 187-191
Vaughan, Robert 128
Vault of Horror (1973) 59, 93
Veidt, Conrad 60, 70
Vengeance of the Vampire [Jiang shi fu chou] (1959) 124
Vernick, William 159, 161
V/H/S (2012) 23
The Violent Years (1956) 128
Villiers, James 14
von Trier, Lars 74
Walker, Paul 84
Walker, Pete 87, 90
Walsh, Fran 34
Walsh, JT 84
Wang, Tian-Lin 124
Ward, Vincent 33
Warner Brothers 42, 80
Watkin, Ian 35
Waxworks (1924) 59, 60
Wayne's World (1992) 27, 30, 182
We Sold Our Souls for Rock 'n' Roll (2001) 182
Weaver, Dennis 84
Weber, Jake 38
The Wedding Party (1966) 135
Welfare (1975) 185
Welles, Orson 10, 105, 120
Wenders, Wim 171
West, Ti 23
Whale, James 78, 117, 118, 119
Whannell, Leigh 192-196
What Dreams May Come (1998) 33
When the Wind Blows (1986) 96
The Wild Angels (1966) 128, 165
Wiseman, Frederick 185
Willeman, Paul 109, 110, 111
Winston, Stan 142, 143
Winterbottom, Michael 171, 172
Witchfinder General (1968) 90, 174
White Buffalo (1977) 48

White Zombie (1932) 133, 198
The Wicker Man (1973) 86
The Wild One (1953) 127
Williams, Michael 24
Williams, Paul 135, 138
Wilson, Colin 29, 104
Wilson, Lisle 137
Wise, Robert 6, 16, 17, 19, 104
Wolfpack (1988) 130
Women in Love (1969) 119
Wood, Christopher A. 6
Wood, Robin 53, 58, 112, 115, 118, 179
Wood Jnr, Edward D. 128
The World, The Flesh and The Devil (1959) 132
A World without Pity [Un Monde Sans Pitiè] (1989) 190
Woronov, Mary 165, 168
Wrong Move (1975) 171
Young and Wild (1958) 127
The Young Captives (1959) 128
Young Frankenstein (1974) 156
Young Guns 2 (1990) 33
Yuzna, Brian 32, 153-156
Zahn, Steve 84
Zane, Billy 85
Zombi 2 [Zombie Flesh Eaters] (1980) 199
Zombie (1979)
Zombie Flesh Eaters [Zombi 2] (1980) 199
Zombie Lake [Le lac des morts vivants] (1980) 199
Zombies of Mora Tau (1957) 5, 133, 197-201
The Zombies That Ate Pittsburgh (book) 53
Zotz! (1962) 110

Printed in Great Britain
by Amazon

9868bb92-ab8a-4f09-bccf-fe70164796c6R01